TOTAL BLACK EMPOWERMENT

A GUIDE TO CRITICAL THINKING IN THE AGE OF TRUMP

DR. JOHNNIE CORDERO
B.A., J.D.

BES PUBLISHING COMPANY, LLC
COLUMBIA, SOUTH CAROLINA
USA

TOTAL BLACK EMPOWERMENT
A GUIDE TO CRITICAL THINKING IN THE AGE OF TRUMP

Copyright © 2017 by Dr. Johnnie Cordero

This is a revised edition of

Total Black Empowerment Through the Creation of Powerful Minds®
A *Mind Power Primer* for the Twenty-First Century and Beyond

Copyright © 2007 by Dr. Johnnie Cordero

All rights reserved. No part of this book may be used or reproduced by any means, graphic, electronic, or mechanical, including photocopying, recording, taping or by any information storage retrieval system without the written permission of the publisher except in the case of brief quotations embodied in critical articles and reviews. BES books may be ordered through booksellers or by contacting:

BES Publishing Company, LLC
4204 Mandel Drive
Columbia, SC 29210

www.bespublishing.com

1-803-873-0039

Because of the dynamic nature of the Internet, any Web addresses or links contained in this book may have changed since publication and may no longer be valid. The views expressed in this work are solely those of the author and do not necessarily reflect the views of the publisher, and the publisher hereby disclaims any responsibility for them.

Author photo by Shirley J. Dilbert

ISBN: 978-0-9985041-1-7 (pbk)

Printed in the United States of America

TOTAL BLACK EMPOWERMENT

TO MY BELOVED WIFE BELINDA:
YOUR LOVE AND UNDERSTANDING
HAVE TRANSFORMED MY LIFE AND MADE
THIS ENDEAVOR POSSIBLE.

WITH ALL MY LOVE.

TOTAL BLACK EMPOWERMENT

BES, EGYPTIAN GOD FIGURE (4TH CENTURY BC)

Bes is a Kemite (Egyptian) Neter (deity) of childbirth and war. He is originally from Nubia and his representations appear as early as the Old Kingdom (c. 2686 BCE). He is widely recognized as one of the oldest gods of the African people. Bes is above all the overt symbol of war for the purpose of protection and survival. Bes prosecutes war. His main responsibility, however, is the protection of children and mothers. He protects against malevolent forces whether mental, physical or spiritual and that would by whatever means, thwart, impede, undermine or destroy our children. His protection of mother's is linked to culture because mothers are not only pro-creators, they are the first teachers of our children. What the mother teaches the child is invariably the culture of the ancestors into whose bloodline the child is born. Bes is, therefore, also the protector and guarantor of the transmission of the Authentic Ancestral Culture. Children are our national immortality. Mothers are, therefore, the birth givers of our immortality. Bes is then the guardian of our future and our ability to have a future. When these facts are considered Bes becomes the divine composite symbol of survival, destiny, security and war.

TOTAL BLACK EMPOWERMENT

IN MEMORY OF MY GRANDMOTHER
JESSIE MCCRARY

IN MEMORY OF MY FATHER
ROBERT HENDY

"WE HAVE NEVER BEEN TAUGHT TO THINK ...
ONLY WHAT TO THINK."

DR. CARTER G. WOODSON, PH.D

"THE FUNCTION OF EDUCATION IS
TO TEACH ONE TO THINK
INTENSIVELY AND TO THINK CRITICALLY."

DR. MARTIN LUTHER KING, JR.

"WE HAVE TO TALK ABOUT LIBERATING MINDS
AS WELL AS LIBERATING SOCIETY."

DR. ANGELA DAVIS, PH.D

TOTAL BLACK EMPOWERMENT

"YOU DIDN'T LEAVE ANYTHING IN AFRICA?
.... WHY YOU LEFT YOUR MIND IN AFRICA."

MALCOLM X

CONTENTS

Preface

xii

Acknowledgements

xvi

Introduction

xviii

PART I
THINKING

CHAPTER 1
THE MECHANICS OF THINKING 32

CHAPTER 2
BELIEFS AND BELIEF SYSTEMS 44

CHAPTER 3
BELIEF SYSTEMS AND MENTAL DISORDER 59

CHAPTER 4
CRITICAL THINKING 78

CHAPTER 5
WHY CRITICAL THINKING IS ESSENTIAL 94

TOTAL BLACK EMPOWERMENT

CHAPTER 6
THE MECHANICS OF CRITICAL THINKING 101

CHAPTER 7
THE NINE THRESHOLD QUESTIONS 116

CHAPTER 8
THINKING AS PROBLEM SOLVING 124

PART II
THE MIND

CHAPTER 9
THE ANCIENT CONCEPT OF MIND 131

CHAPTER 10
THE CORPUS HERMETICUM 140

CHAPTER 11
THE CHARACTERISTICS OF OUR MENTAL IMAGE 148

CHAPTER 12
HOW THINKING BECOMES CREATIVE 157

PART III
POWER

CHAPTER 13
UNDERSTANDING POWER 162

CHAPTER 14
THE SPIRITUAL DIMENSION OF POWER 181

CHAPTER 15
WHO ARE OUR ANCESTORS? 205

CHAPTER 16
WHAT IS OUR AUTHENTIC ANCESTRAL CULTURE? 214

CHAPTER 17
THE MECHANICS OF SPIRITUAL POWER 221

PART IV
SACRED SCIENCE

CHAPTER 18
WHAT IS SACRED SCIENCE? 245

CHAPTER 19
THE SEVEN UNIVERSAL LAWS 272

CHAPTER 20
CRITICAL MASS: VANGUARD OF THE NEW AGE 282

PART V
FOOD FOR THOUGHT

PREFACE TO REVISED EDITION 289
INTRODUCTION: 293

CHAPTER 21
MASS INCARCERATION 295

CHAPTER 22
THE WAR ON DRUGS 308

CHAPTER 23
"WE THE PEOPLE" 316

CHAPTER 24
A LONG TRAIN OF ABUSES 327

CHAPTER 25
GUN! 337

CHAPTER 26
TIME TO TAKE OUR COUNTRY BACK 342

CHAPTER 27
CRITICAL THINKING IN THE AGE OF TRUMP 347

CHAPTER 28
CALL TO ACTION 357

CONCLUSION 359

NOTES 362

PREFACE

This book is intended to facilitate the development of a *New Mental Attitude* in African Americans. The *New Mental Attitude* will be fueled by powerful ideas that are elevated and transcendent. This book seeks to encourage the type of thinking that will produce fundamental change. Not in circumstances but in how we think about them and ultimately respond to them.

This book is a *mind power primer*. It is about perfected vision, mind-set reconstruction, cultural, l political transformation, and understanding of the power elements that make such reconstruction and transformation possible. This book is also about the attraction, utilization and distribution of temporal and spiritual power.

As a threshold matter this book presupposes that as a whole African Americans have failed to develop a mind-set that permits and encourages revolutionary, innovative, success-oriented thinking. More precisely, it posits that African Americans, by and large, lack clarity of vision and as a result simply do not think *logically* or *efficiently* when it comes to matters that affect our cultural, religious, political and economic development.

The premise of this book is succinctly stated in Dr. Carter G. Woodson's prescient, revolutionary treatise *The Mis-Education of the Negro*. Writing in the 1930's Dr. Woodson observed that "[t]he Negro has not yet learned to think and plan for himself as others do for themselves." He also observed that "[w]e have never been taught to think ⋯ only what to think." He left us with a suggestion and a final admonition; we "... *should learn to think before it is too late.*"[1]

In spite of the powerful formula contained in Dr. Woodson's words no one, to my knowledge, has attempted to address the problem in a formal manner. It was initially difficult for me to understand why if others recognized the problem no one had actually confronted it. It was then that I realized that it had to do with *change* and *obstinacy*, those devilishly subtle twins of complacency.

The notion of change is difficult for most people to consider and virtually impossible for them to accept. As a result, we become *obstinate*. That is, we "... perversely adhere to an opinion, purpose, or course in spite of reason, arguments, or persuasion." [2] When we add to this recalcitrant mix the fact that politics and religion are subjects that we have made taboo, it becomes apparent why no one has attempted what is likely to be a thankless task.

It has taken me much longer to write this book than I anticipated. The reason is because I too was reluctant to *confront* change. I knew that in order for this book to serve its intended purpose it had to deal with the subjects that we have been taught *not* to talk about. Of course, I am referring to religion and politics. Although it may be true that the political taboo is now honored mostly in the breach, the religious taboo is as strong, if not stronger, than ever.

Let me explain. During the course of my life I have been called everything from blasphemer to atheist. I am neither. I admit, without hesitation or shame, that my religious views are, to say the least, unconventional. This is mainly because I am, in the proud tradition of my ancient ancestors, a *pagan*. Therein lies the problem.

To be a pagan (neither Christian, Muslim nor Jew) is to curry the ample, often virulent disfavor of Christians, Muslims and Jews. It is to be branded an infidel, heathen or Goy— none of them complimentary names. I am a proud pagan nonetheless. I am so because my ancestors too were *proud* pagans.

I believe that our ancestral culture and beliefs should be preserved, respected and whenever possible adhered to. I am, admittedly, at a loss to understand why most African Americans are unaware of the fact that their ancient ancestors developed a belief system that is, in many respects, superior to and diametrically opposed to that of the European.

It seems that little, if any, consideration has been given to the fact that our most ancient ancestors were widely considered to be the *founders of civilization* and the most *spiritual people in the world before* they adopted the views of Jews, Christians and Muslims or that they have been in a cultural, political, economic, military, power deficient, downward spiral ever since.

Perhaps more astonishingly in our search for answers to our collective problems we have completely ignored the views of our ancient ancestors developed *before* our unfortunate encounter with the wily European. We have utterly failed to consider the possibility that the people who gave civilization to the world may have discovered and recorded information that may contain the answers to our present problems. The European, on the other hand, studies our ancient culture with obsessive ferocity.

Those of us in the African American community who have diligently researched the records of our ancestors have concluded that, in fact, the answers to our present day problems, including sound advice on the importance of the control of thought, were recorded millennia ago in their *Sacred Science*.

Sacred Science is a rich, living source of knowledge and sound, scientific advice that we have all but ignored in favor of the unsound, counterintuitive and counterproductive advice of those who have demonstrated historically their virulent malice and ill will toward us.

My paralysis of indecision ended when it occurred to me that if this mind power primer teaches anything it is that there are no *sacred cows*. I am not looking for a fight, but I am not going to run from one either. If this book has any value at all it will vindicate our ancestors and me by creating in our people the long overdue tendency to *question everything. There can be no sacred cows in the search for the an-*

swer to the problems that have held our progress and us captive to the whims and caprices of others.

As you will see this book advances a method by which what I view as the detrimental, counterproductive mind-set of African Americans can be changed for the better. In order for that change to occur we must root out that which prevents the elevation of our thinking to the heightened clarity of vision necessary to visualize the strategies and tactics that will insure our advancement from mere survival to abundant prosperity.

The method outlined here will not alter valid beliefs; in fact, it will serve to make valid beliefs stronger. It will, however, permanently remove from our thinking ideas that are invalid and therefore unworthy of belief. In any event, the conclusions that you reach, if any, will be the product of your own exhaustive analysis and not those foisted upon you by your erstwhile captors.

Make no mistake about it. This book is about change. But, we need not fear change. Change is the only constant in life. Everything changes over time. This is an inevitable and unavoidable fact of life. Change can be positive or negative. In either form we must adapt to it. To fight change solely for the purpose of preventing it is counterproductive. The old saying goes "if it is not broken don't fix it". I would only add that if it is broken you are absolutely required to fix it—the longer you delay the worse the problem becomes.

One thing is certain as Albert Einstein pointed out decades ago - *a problem cannot be solved with the same level of thinking that created it.* We must elevate our thinking in order to solve our problems. This book is my humble attempt to assist us in doing so.

Dated: Columbia, South Carolina JC 9 May 2007

ACKNOWLEDGEMENTS

My first acknowledgment is of my woeful inability to recall all of the people who have assisted me in one way or another to bring this work to fruition. To those who have provided support and encouragement please know that your contribution is no less important than those who will be acknowledged hereafter. I know that this work would not have been possible without you. I owe you more than I can say.

JENNIE CORDERO

There is no greater gift than life. I exist because of you. I am, because you are. I hope this book will make you proud. I love you.

FRANKLIN HAGINS, JR.

In the dark days of circular walks and elevated talks your feedback gave substance and direction to ideas yet untested. Without your wisdom and guidance this work would never have been. Thank you Hesy, my brother my friend.

ABDUL BROCKINGTON

At a time when I could not be certain what the future would hold for me. When it seemed that all the best was past and the future was bleak your youthful curios- ity and desire for answers motivated me to carry on if for no other reason than to answer your searching questions. You challenged me at every turn and by so doing made me stronger. Thank you my brother. You will always be my friend.

BRIAN "*STRONG WIND*" WILLIAMS

You have inspired me for more than two decades. At every turn, by your words, deeds and life you were the living proof that I was on the right track. This book is a testament to the profound effect you have had on my life. You have often said that I changed your life but the truth is that you have changed mine in immeasurable, indescribable ways. You are at once my son, my friend, my brother, my student and my teacher. In a very real sense your life has validated mine. Thank you.

DARLENE HENDY-GREEN

I love you. I never would have imagined that my little sister would grow up to be my big sister. I am so proud of you. I only hope this work will make you proud of me. You have been my biggest fan and supporter. Each time I doubted my ability to complete this work or questioned its worth you were there to reason, implore and command. The truth is I finished this work because I could not let you down. I love you.

INTRODUCTION

My life has been an intermittent, but consistent intellectual crossing of four streams of interest: power, mind, ancestral heritage and the search for solutions to the collective problems of the African American people.

This seemingly incongruous mix of intellectual pursuits is not, on careful analysis, as discordant as it seems. In fact, these provide the *matrix of ideas* that form the basis of my studies that have, in turn, culminated in the ideas set forth in the primer you are now reading.

I have had a life-long fascination with these subjects, but it was not until I *visualized the connections* between them that I began to perceive the seamless *fabric of thought* that they had woven. Of course, it took some time for me to recognize that the *golden thread* in all my research was *power* and the connections, some obvious others not, between it and everything else.

Some years ago one of my daughters and I were rearranging books on the shelves in my den. *Kyphi*, who was then about ten years old, said to me, "Daddy, the names of all your books have the word power in them." Her observation was only slightly exaggerated. Many of the books in my personal library did, in fact, include the word *power* in their titles. It had not occurred to me until that moment that my fascination with the concept of *power*, though not yet clear to me, was obvious to a ten year old.

My academic training is in political science, philosophy and law. My first love is ancient *Kemit* (Egypt in Greek), and as an ordained clergyman I have studied religion extensively as well.

In each of these disciplines I eventually came to realize that all one has to do is scratch the surface to reveal the underpinnings of *power*, not only in those subject areas, but in every aspect of life and human endeavor.

It is as if I knew, *intuitively*, that *power* was at the heart of everything important. Over time I began to see that *power* is, in fact, central to our existence when it is considered that *energy, force, strength, ability* and *spirit* are all synonyms for power. Since it is true that life cannot exist in the absence of power, I concluded that *life and power are interdependent and causally related.*

As an African American male, descendant of African slaves, I also concluded that if it is true that *power* is central to everything (it is) it must also be true that *power is at the core of the historic and deep-seated political and economic problems of African Americans* as well. If *power* is at the core of the problem, *it must also be at the core of the solution to our collective problems.*

A secondary motivation in my life has been the need, perhaps obsession is a better word, to find the underlying cause of the plight of African Americans and our consistent failure to develop effective strategies to ameliorate our seemingly intractable, collective, power deficient cultural, political, social and economic condition. I recognize that this motivation is not entirely altruistic because it derives from a personal interest, hopefully shared by all, to insure that my children and my children's children will not only fare better than I and my ancestors, but also that they might claim and receive the long overdue compensation, by way of reparations, that our ancestors labored for but never received.

What I did not fully understand was the connection that all of this had with *our ancestral heritage and the teachings of our ancient ancestors.* It all seems so logical now. After all, our ancient ancestors literally *invented* civilization. In order to do so they had to *find solutions to problems* similar, if not identical, to our own. As a result they formulated and mastered all of the plastic and useful arts upon which civilization is based.

Our ancestors *isolated the problems and implemented solutions.* The solutions were so effective that they led, over time, to the compilation of a *body of knowledge* that directly or indirectly bequeathed civilization to the world.

If this is true (it is) it follows that they may have found and recorded strategies and tactics that may be of service to us in the formulation of solutions to our collective, modern-day problems. The premise is not illogical if it is conceded (as it must be) that though the world has changed dramatically since ancient times, *fundamental human nature has not.*

Human beings are the same now as they were ten thousand years ago. Our thought processes have not changed. That which motivates us and drives us is no different and our responses to various stimuli are still as predictable, when discovered, as they have always been. In short, *the universal laws of yesterday remain universal laws today.*

I further concluded that we ignore our ancestral culture and its teachings at our own peril. I say this because the teachings that comprise our culture were created, as *defensive and offensive weapons,* intended by our ancient ancestors to be utilized, by their descendants (us), to insure our continued survival and prosperity–for all eternity. *We are, therefore, the intended recipients and rightful heirs of their knowledge, civilization and culture.*

In order to stand the test of time and be available to be utilized by generations yet unborn, these strategic, intellectual weapons were themselves based upon timeless principles of human nature.

With these seemingly disjointed, but apparently connected pieces of a larger puzzle whose full picture I could not then envision, I began an intellectual journey that has lasted more than a decade and whose findings represent the foundation of the principles that are contained in this primer.

I began with a simple question the answer to which I believed would lead, in stages, to the solution to our collective problem. The question, dictated by our history, asks why have we failed in more than 350 years to attain *power proportionality* in America?

The accurate statement of a question often reveals the answer. In this case, the question focuses on *power proportionality,* that is, the *power relationship* between African Americans and other Americans with respect to the comparative quantity and magnitude of their respective power. That as African Americans we have not acquired power proportionate to our numbers in the population is, at this late date, axiomatic.

Clearly, our problem is related to power. But, power, as we will see, is *neutral* and *expansive*. It will serve any master and will naturally grow in the hands of those who have it. It follows that our problem embraces more than just power deficiency. The problem is, at once, simpler and more pervasive than I had previously recognized. We must have a complete *understanding of* power: what it is, how it operates, where it can be found and how it can be acquired.

Subsumed in this notion is the fact that although all of our problems are related to power issues, our problems are also and perhaps more fundamentally, related to our ability to *solve* problems. I concluded from this that a more exact statement of the question is *why have we failed to develop effective strategies that would enable us to attain power proportionality?* The distinction is more than semantic.

The first question directed my attention to power. The second and more accurate question directed my attention to the *thinking process* itself. This shift of focus led me to a concept that is so simple yet profound that it has been overlooked by all but a few of our greatest minds and missed entirely by our so-called leaders. The concept is *Critical Thinking* (CT).

In short, our problems are more the result of our inability to *think critically* (which is itself a *power deficiency*), than any other single factor. The connection that others and I have overlooked is that between *power* and *mind*. Our ability to understand the central importance of power is, after all, an operation of the mind. If we concede, for the sake of argument, that this is true it follows logically that the accumulation of power proportionate to our numbers in the population begins with our ability to *think*.

The final and perhaps most important connection was made when I under- stood, intuitively at first, that if our ancient ancestors were able to build civilization out of savagery and were able to transcend and conquer problems more daunting than our own they could not have avoided the connection between the *concept of power* and the *power of the mind*.

I also knew, again intuitively, that such information must be contained in the corpus of accumulated knowledge, scientific in nature, steeped in spirituality and reduced to quantifiable, verifiable universal law and known to our enlightened ancestors as *Sacred Science*.

Almost immediately my extensive studies of ancient Kemit sprang to mind. I recalled that long before our ancestors built the greatest civilization in the history of the world, they did, in fact, realize and expound upon the connection between power and mind.

Our ancestors learned that whether it was the power of their enemies or the power of nature they were always confronted with power and power issues. They even concluded that God itself is power—undoubtedly the Supreme Power, but power nonetheless. They understood that everywhere we turn we are confronted with power and that everything that exists is full of power.

In their basic make-up all things are comprised of power. Power can neither be created nor destroyed. It follows that there can be no such thing as anyone or anything being *powerless*. We may have accumulated insufficient power to accomplish a particular task, but we are never *totally* without power. We are either power *sufficient* or power *deficient*.

Our ancestors, unlike their descendants, knew that their survival and the survival of their descendants was dependent on their ability to *gather, accumulate* and *focus* sufficient power to overcome the power of their enemies and nature and sufficient power to accomplish their own goals and objectives. Even in our distant and remote past our ancestors knew the importance of power and made its *acquisition, distribution* and *control* the center of their collective existence and the foundation of their teachings.

Our ancestors also knew that thinking was a function and operation of the mind. They incorporated the knowledge of that fact in the *Sacred Science* they preserved for us. They saw the universe and everything in it as *a thought in the mind of the Supreme Power that we now refer to as God.* They believed that *the mind is divine* in origin and that thoughts are *divine creations* that are themselves infused with *creative power.*

Our ancestors also knew that thinking is unavoidably driven by *cultural imperatives.* We think, by and large, as the dominant culture commands us to think.

The raw material of our thoughts is comprised of the beliefs and belief systems with which we have been indoctrinated. *We think, therefore, within the confines of a predetermined, highly structured, cultural universe of thought and idea.*

The cultural universe in which our thoughts are formed and informed, has been constructed from a fabric woven of the custom and traditions of those whose cultural perspective and world-view, on most subjects, is diametrically opposed to that of our ancestors. The reality is that *we think what we have been subliminally programmed to think.* In short, we see the world, think about the world, and develop strategies to overcome our problems in the world, from the cultural perspective with which our enemies have programmed us.

Our *Sacred Science* teaches us that the first of the *"Ten Virtues"* (those principles whose application releases us from the hold of the *"Ten Fetters"*) is the *control of thought.* First we control our thoughts, then and only then, can we control our actions (the second of the *"Ten Virtues"*) and/or the actions of others. The control of thought refers to an indispensable, individual inner function that necessarily requires us to be the *exclusive controller* of our own thoughts.

Our ancestors also knew that thinking is a process that is dependent on *perception.* The raw material of our thoughts is, and can only be, the information, data, stimuli received by us through our senses. In order to see the world accurately we must see it *clearly*. In order to take action to solve a problem we must be able to see the problem clearly. This all-important *clarity of vision* was known to our ancestors as *Oudja* and was considered prerequisite to all decision-making and problem solving.

We learned our first lessons about power, clarity of vision, mind and problem solving thousands of years ago, in our own *African Cultural Universe*, in resplendent temples, nestled along the banks of the River *Hapi* (Nile in Greek), where we were taught that *God is the Divine Power and Divine Mind* that resides in each of us and which endows us with *the latent ability to become gods in our own right*.

We control our thoughts by the process known as *Critical Thinking*. When we control our thoughts we simultaneously develop a *New Mental Attitude (NMA)* that re-minds, re-structures and thereby *transforms our minds* from weak minds steeped in gullible, subservient thought patterns, into *powerful minds* permeated with creative, reality-based thoughts and ideas

When I took the principles embodied in *Sacred Science* and compared them with the modern science of physics and other disciplines I found that the scientific genius of the modern age is no more than a grudgingly belated confirmation of the principles of our *Sacred Science*. The more I confirmed them the more I discovered. Each new discovery led to another until finally the answer was written everywhere I looked. *God is power* – God's power in humankind is in the mind – the untapped power of our minds is the greatest resource we have and it is more than sufficient to change, constructively, the course of our future.

When I related this revelation to the question of our failure to attain power proportionality the conclusion was unavoidable. We suffer a *power deficit*, but it is essentially illusory because the power *exists*. The failure is in our ability to harness it and use it to our collective advantage. More importantly, the failure derives from our *programmed inability* to see connections, reason accurately and develop our minds into *powerful weapons.*

Let us be real. Our severe power deficiency exists despite nearly five hundred years of continuous hard labor. It is abetted by the illogical assumption that we will be accepted as full-fledged American citizens if we only work hard enough and, apparently, long enough.

The assumption is illogical and insulting precisely because we have worked diligently for centuries without just compensation and at hard labor. The effort has availed us little.

Since it can hardly be disputed that African Americans have failed to achieve a level of power proportionate to our numbers in the population, despite our hard work, the need for in-depth discussions among African Americans about power is both obvious and long overdue.

There are those who will argue that our social, political and economic circum- stances have changed dramatically because we are no longer *physically* enslaved, can go to the same schools and use the same toilets as white folks.

When these so-called accomplishments are compared to the achievements of whites who have come to America after us and who have not been constrained by slavery, segregation, Jim Crow and other forms of government sponsored or condoned discrimination, we see that the accomplishments so lauded are no more than humiliating crumbs discarded from a sumptuously appointed table that our ancestors built but never feasted at. Even the crumbs provided us over the centuries and always under the table came only at times when extraordinary external pressure, borne of actual or potential unrest, was applied–never because we were sufficiently powerful to force change.

Our power deficiency exists. *Either we confront it or we ignore it.* We ignore it at our own peril. Of course, the easiest thing to do is to ignore it. Confrontation requires action–to ignore something requires us to do nothing. To confront something we must actually *do something*. Confrontation has an odd way of getting you involved. In this case the confrontational route immediately compels one of two conclusions. Either African Americans are in some way inferior to whites and are thereby incapable of competing with them, or we have, for some other reason, been unable to develop and accumulate *group power* in the social, political and economic arenas.

Group power means collective power proportionate to:

- our numbers in the population;

- the value of our labor and other contributions to the accumulated wealth and power of the United States, compounded with interest over the last three and one half centuries; and

- our historical position as co-founders and heirs, in perpetuity, of the American nation.

The first conclusion, that of our inferiority, is so preposterous as to only be worthy of rejection out-of-hand. We only need consider then the second conclusion.

The second conclusion posits that some other reason exists to explain the apparent power deficiency. Why, it asks, have we been unable to attain the goal of power proportionality in the nearly five hundred years since our arrival on these shores and the one hundred thirty five years since the abolition of slavery.

We must begin from the position that our goal of power proportionality is attainable, despite the fact that it has yet to be attained. This simply says that if we do not believe our goals are attainable they become, *ipso facto*, unattainable.

Second, if our goals are possible of attainment it follows that a set of strategies and tactics must exist and are discoverable and that will enable us to attain our collective goals. To believe otherwise is to believe that our future advancement can logically be left in the hands of those who have historically demonstrated their disinclination to assist us.

Third, if effective strategies do, in fact, exist all that is required is that we discover them and implement them. Discovery of the strategies is dependent on *Critical Thinking* and analysis–research and experimentation–and the use of *scientific method*.

The *scientific method* requires that the first thing we must do is state the problem accurately. We cannot overemphasize the importance of this initial step. We must state the problem accurately before we can determine the important facts. Of course, in order to state the problem absolutely requires the ability to see the problem, *i.e.*, to isolate the problem from problems in general.

Our ancient ancestors have instructed us that things are seldom exactly what they seem. The Sun appears to rise in the East and set in the West, but, in fact, does neither. The Earth seems to be a stationary globe at the center of the universe and around which everything revolves, but, in fact, it isn't. People smile at you and extend their hands in what appears to be a gesture of friendship when their real intent is to stab you in the back.

Our ancient ancestors taught us these and other important lessons so that we would constantly strive to develop *clarity of vision* that we might always, at very least, accurately see the things that are before us. They concluded that *clarity of vision* was absolutely essential if we are to survive and prosper. Always, they instructed us to see the world as it is, not as we want it to be. They knew that in order to survive we would have to make daily decisions of vital importance – decisions that would affect the lives and fortunes of our people. Without the ability to see clearly and accurately that which is both immediately before us and in the distance, we are incapable of seeing the real problems and thereby incapable of developing effective strategies and tactics to solve real problems. It seems obvious that if you do not recognize the existence of a problem the chance of your finding the solution is remote. It also seems obvious that merely seeing the problem is not enough to guarantee the finding of a solution to the problem.

Our ancient ancestors also taught that problem solving requires *elevated thought* because you cannot solve a problem at the same level of thinking that created it. *Thinking for the purpose of problem solving (literally all thinking) must be, therefore, thought that is transcendent, that rises above common thought and ideas.*

Our ancient ancestors understood the connection between *power, clarity of vision* and *Critical Thinking*. They also recognized that an understanding of power, in all its manifestations, is essential; that our vision must be clear, and our thinking sound, if we are to survive and prosper.

As long as we remained true to the teaching of our ancestral *Sacred Science* we were a formidable power, a force to be reckoned with. The world beat a path to our door to learn the principles of effective harmonious government, to observe civilization in operation, and to witness, first hand, the greatest political and economic system of the time.

Though thousands of years have passed since our ancient ancestors were a world power, the thinking process that they employed to gain such primacy remains one hundred percent applicable to our present circumstances.

It is true that computers now run the world, but they are mere imitations of the world's computer marvel, the human brain. The human brain has not changed over the last few millennia, nor has the mind. They continue to operate according to the same universal laws and by the same processes that they did in the distant past. The principles observed and recorded in our *Sacred Science* will continue to serve us well, regardless of the passage to time.

Part of our historical problem has been our lack of *clear vision*. It is as if we have been blinded to the reality of our circumstances and have, as a result, been unable to formulate effective *group* strategies because we did not see things clearly.

TOTAL BLACK EMPOWERMENT

This *mind power primer* has been created to guide you, step by step, on a journey that will *empower your mind, elevate your thought* and *transform the way you think*. It will provide you with the *clarity of vision* that is absolutely essential if we are to transform our power deficient condition and alter the future for our children.

As you read this *mind power primer* you will embark on an intellectual journey – one that will transport you from a basic level of understanding to increasingly higher levels until you achieve *Oudja – true clarity of vision*. On this intellectual journey *Oudja* is our *destination* and *Critical Thinking* is the *vehicle* that will get us there.

If you are willing to approach new ideas without prejudice or bias, this *mind power primer* will help make you a conduit for *transformative, change-provoking ideas* by radically improving the way you think and thereby creating in you a *powerful mind. Your powerful mind, linked with other powerful minds, will initiate a quantum leap in the level of consciousness of our people as well as in our collective ability to formulate effective strategies and tactics to eliminate our collective problems*. What this *mind power primer* seeks to do is *train a new generation of leaders*. Men and women who will take control of our collective destiny, and their own, and who *by the force of their powerful minds, driven by powerful ideas*, will assemble and organize the *Critical Mass* that will initiate a cultural/political chain reaction that will change the course of human history and insure our continued survival and abundant prosperity.

That is why this book is a *mind power primer*—a collection of ideas designed and presented, in introductory form, to help facilitate the *total empowerment* of African Americans, whose present and historic *power deficiency* has enabled others to *control* and *manipulate* us.

This *mind power primer* is designed to facilitate a *revolutionary way of thinking* that is formulated to help us understand the underlying reasons for our *power deficiency* and help us *systematically formulate strategies* to increase our individual and group power and secure the economic benefit of the uncompensated labor of our ancestors.

Let us be clear. This book does not advocate a return to our glorious past, which is, in any event, impossible. It does, however, strongly suggest that it is high time that we began to carefully consider the timeless teaching of our ancient ancestors, where and only where, such teachings prove applicable to our present circumstances. One such area is that of the *Control of thought*, which necessarily includes *analysis* and *problem solving techniques*.

A final warning: This book is not for those who think they know it all or for those who believe that they cannot be taught anything. Remember this book is a *primer*, in every sense of the word.

First, it is a brief treatise on a specific subject that is intended to be introductory and is created to supply the *foundation* for more expansive, in-depth study.

Second, it is *prime* in that it represents the earliest or beginning stage of a *cultural/political transformation*.

Third, it is also a *device* that will detonate an *explosive intellectual charge* that will initiate a long awaited chain reaction that will change the course of our history.

This book is a mind power primer on the subject of power, mind, Critical Thinking, problem solving and the effective utilization of Spiritual Power. It is a primer that will assist African Americans in their quest for Total Black Empowerment, by creating in us, powerful minds with revolutionary ideas that will, when diligently applied, change the world.

PART I
THINKING

1

THE MECHANICS OF THOUGHT

In this section we will examine the *mechanics* of thought, that is, *how the thinking process works*. The thought process is a logical starting point in our effort to deter- mine why we have been unable to attain power proportionality in the more than 135 years since the abolition of slavery because our ability to solve complex problems is inseparable from our ability to *think*.

In answering the question of why we have been unable to attain power proportionality in America, we concede, at the outset, that powerful forces have been aligned against us to retard our collective development and insure that we remain no more than marginal players in the game of social, political and economic achievement. We make this concession based on a historical pattern of overt as well as covert attempts by government and private interests to thwart, impede and undermine our collective ability to attain power proportionality in America. We must also concede that we have unwittingly aided and abetted such efforts by our failure to develop strategies to counteract them.

It is a premise of this *mind power primer* that our failure to develop strategies has been, at least partially, the result of our inability to think *logically*. In turn, our ability to think logically has been intentionally *underdeveloped* by those who we have permitted to control our education and thereby *what* and *how* we think. In short, we must begin by understanding how the thinking process works in order to see how it has been effectively manipulated without our knowing it. *Recognizing a problem is the initial step in mastering it.*

THOUGHT

In its most fundamental aspect thought is the process by which physical energy is converted into electrical impulses. This physical energy is the data collected by our information sensors. This conversion is required because much like the computer that cannot r e a d information until it is converted into zeros and ones, our brain, cannot read sensory messages until they are converted into electrical impulses. Thought is the *process that transforms information into intelligible electrical impulse.*

THINKING

Thinking *is carried out by recognition and manipulation of symbols that have been previously deposited in our memories.* We think *symbolically*. Much like the computer our brains utilize a form of programming language. Programming language is a language of symbols that is, a language constructed of *symbols*. Computers convert raw data (information) into *symbolic language*. Our brains too utilize symbols to convert sensory information into a language that it can understand.

SYMBOLS AND SYMBOLIC LANGUAGE

A symbol is defined as something that represents

something else by association, resemblance or convention. The word is said to derive from the Greek *sumbolon* meaning a *token for identification*. One author claims that the word is more accu- rately defined as a sign of recognition formed by the two halves of a broken object which are brought together."[1]

In the context of thinking a symbol should be understood as something that brings to mind the idea or concept of the thing of which it is a part. Put another way, *a symbol is the part of a thought that creates a whole thought by the act of thinking of the part.*

A symbol can also be understood as a picture that represents an idea. An example of this is the Nike swoosh or Wal-Mart's smiley face. When we see these simple symbols, that standing alone have nothing to do with the companies they represent, we automatically think, of the products or services of Nike or Wal-Mart. The symbol is a picture of an idea.

This is one of the reasons for the scientific conclusion that memory, itself a stage in the thinking process, is essentially *constructive*. Since thinking is, in part, the manipulation of symbols, what are deposited in our *Long Term Memory* are symbols (pictures of ideas) that are themselves only representative parts of the whole idea. When we recall (remember) we retrieve *symbols* and construct the rest.

This means that when we think we use these symbols to perform a *constructive operation*. Symbols only *represent* a part of the picture of the idea involved. As a result we are required to *fill in the blanks*. This helps explain why much of our thinking is a matter of *deduction* and *inference*, one way of making sense of the symbols and filling in the blanks. It follows that when we think we begin with symbols that are themselves only part of the picture and fill in the blanks to construct a whole picture. Not surprisingly, that picture may not be an accurate representation of fact.

Like the computer our brains do not automatically question the sensory messages they receive. These *symbolic sensory messages* received by our brains are routinely accepted as *accurate*.

For example, if a computer is programmed with a formula that indicates that two plus two is fifteen it will always calculate on the basis of that formula *it will never question the formula*. The result, of course, is that it will always give the wrong answer to a question that requires it to calculate the sum of two plus two. The human brain operates in much the same way.

We may add to this that our symbolic sensory messages are received via the *five senses*. The snippets of raw data received become, in time, the information upon which we base our decisions. As we are about to see the five senses are, at best, unreliable reporters of reality.

THE FIVE THIEVES

We all know *what* the five senses are. Few of us know *who* they are. The Chinese, a people with a culture more ancient than that of the European, refer to the five senses as *thieves* because they *rob* us of the *accurate perception of reality by deception*. They work their deception by presenting only a segment of reality. The information they provide is incomplete and therefore a *misrepresentation*. Misrepresentation is, of course, a form of *deception*. The problem is that we *believe* the snippets of reality presented to us by the five senses to be the whole of reality and rely upon them as such. The true perception of reality is stolen from us without our realizing it. Who said there is no such thing as a perfect crime?

It is a fact that on the personal level we never come into direct contact with the outside world. We do not see, hear, taste, touch or smell anything *directly*. Anything that comes to us *indirectly* is second-hand and subject to alteration or distortion and is, by that fact alone, *inherently unreliable*, and, therefore, *suspect*.

TOTAL BLACK EMPOWERMENT

Our *information sensors* (sight, hearing, taste, touch and smell) are naturally limited in what they register and are easily deceived as a result. We must accept the fact that they are, at their best, *unreliable reporters of reality*. A few examples of our sensory deficiencies will suffice to illustrate the point.

SIGHT

Sight is perhaps the least reliable of the senses. Magicians have made fortunes over the centuries by *deceiving the eyes* of their audiences. They say the hand is quicker than the eye" it is. But, the reason the eyes are so easily deceived is because of their limited capacity.

The function of the eye is to facilitate sight. This function depends on the eye's sensitivity to light energy. But, when we consider the light spectrum itself we learn that only a very small percentage of it is *visible* light. This means that not all of what there is to be seen can be detected by the human eye. And, of course, where there is no light at all, we cannot see at all. Moreover, only about half of what we believe we are seeing is actually the result of information recorded by our eyes. Fully half of what we think we see is created from our own *expectation* of what the reality *should* be. In short, what we think we see is conformed to our *personal* reality. Of course, our personal reality may not be accurate when compared to what really exists.

We should also note here that the eyes actually see the world upside down. Our brains somehow reverse the image so that we see things right side up. The eyes also have a *blind spot*. The place where the optic nerve passes through the eyeball is a place where the eye cannot see at all. We can also add that objects smaller than a certain size, cannot be seen by the unaided eye, and objects moving beyond a certain speed appear distorted or cannot be seen at all.

Optical illusions present another example of how easily the human eye can be tricked into "seeing" things that do not exist. An optical illusion is simply an image that has the tendency to deceive the eye. The existence of literally thousands of uncanny optical illusions developed over the years only attests to the numerous ways the eye can be deceived. In spite of these facts we still say I see" to mean I understand".

SMELL AND TASTE

The senses of smell and taste are also unreliable because they are, like sight, so easily deceived. The sense of smell is least developed in human beings and can be easily deceived. As we all know the common cold will significantly reduce or eliminate the sense of smell altogether.

The success of the scent industry is proof of how easily the sense of smell can be deceived. A wide variety of artificial scents have been created that simulate natural odors. They run the gamut from new car smell to citrus fruits. In these cases the nose will conclude that what it smells is an orange and will actually make your mouth water, when in reality what you smell is a mixture of laboratory produced chemical compounds.

Of the sense of taste we need only point out that fully 80% of what we think we taste, we actually smell.

HEARING

Hearing is perhaps the most direct and arguably the most reliable sense but even it is incapable of detecting all sound. Animals possess a far more acute sense of hearing than do human beings. Dogs, for example, detect sound that we are incapable of hearing. The sounds do *exist;* we just cannot hear them. The best that can be said for all of the senses is that they are inherently unreliable. That is, they do not gather complete data and can, therefore, be easily deceived. Because we are dependent on them for *all* our information regarding the outside world, that is the world outside of our bodies, they can be accurately described as thieves, at worst, and unreliable reporters of reality at best. Through their limited capacity they fail to provide us with the *full picture* of the reality that is the world around us.

When we consider that the symbolic sensory messages received by our brains are, at best, unreliable and that we have the innate tendency to construct or fill in the blanks in our thinking we cannot help but conclude that without additional measures to insure the accuracy of our thinking we will *naturally* reach inaccurate conclusions in our decision-making. Remember what we perceive as reality is what our five senses tell us reality is. Of course, we make decisions in response to our view of the reality of the situation.

We must also remember that the brain is a *sensory transformation matrix*—a system that mechanically processes information. Like any system it is comprised of a group of interacting elements. The elements of the *sensory transformation matrix* are: Sensory Element, Attention, Short Term Memory, Long Term Memory and Retrieval. The more we know about these elements and how they interact the more we are able to understand how to compensate for their deficiencies and thereby better control the thinking process.

Let us look at each of these elements individually. We will begin with the *Sensory Element*.

THE SENSORY ELEMENT

The *Sensory Element* is an internal process by which the *sensory messages* detected by our information sensors are transformed from physical energy to electrical impulse. Whether they detect light, heat or sound all of our senses detect *energy*. When sensory messages are received the sensory element is automatically *acti-vated*. It serves the purpose of *holding* information until processed by the brain. This holding period is brief, and seems to exist only for the length of time it takes to link one sensory message to the next.

ATTENTION

Attention is the process by which we *direct* and *focus* on incoming sensory messages. Attention permits us to pick and choose from among the millions of bits of information (data) received by our brains during the course of our lives. Attention focuses *mind energy* on vital tasks and supervises the expenditure of that energy.

Attention improves perception because it determines, based upon the previously set parameters, which sensory messages will be *attended* to and which will be ignored literally paid no attention. In this way an important, limited natural resource is conserved.

SHORT TERM MEMORY (STM)

Short Term Memory (STM) is the element of our sensory transformation matrix that holds sensory messages for short periods of time, presumably in the brain, in order to process them for appropriate action. It is often referred to as the *working memory* because it carries out the bulk of our *mind labor*. It is believed to be able to hold approximately seven bits of information for roughly eighteen seconds. As you can see its storage capacity and duration are extremely limited. Short Term Memory is utilized automatically and seems to require no conscious action on our parts.

LONG TERM MEMORY (LTM)

After sensory messages have been processed in the STM they are either forgotten, that is no longer registered, or they are transferred to *Long Term Memory*. This process is what we call *memorization*. To speak of memory is actually to refer to Long Term Memory. It seems that some types of information are automatically transferred to Long Term Memory while other types have to be stored by conscious effort.

The duration of information stored in the *Long Term Memory* seems only to be limited by the life span of the individual. The storage capacity of the Long Term Memory is apparently unlimited. In any event, there are no reported cases of persons whose Long Term Memory became so full that they could not store any new information.

RETRIEVAL: THE MEMORY MECHANISM

The ability to remember is the key to the physical process we call thinking. This is because for the purposes of thought, information that cannot be called up when needed is functionally *non-existent*. The implications of this fact are far reaching.

All of our conscious activities require us to remember previously stored information. Even the most routine, ordinary tasks that we so often take for granted require that we first *remember* how to perform them. Walking, talking, the names of people, places and events, the meaning of words and symbols, and even self-identification, are all impossible without the ability to remember, more precisely to *retrieve* stored information. Memory is a *mechanism* that is actually comprised of at least two processes these are *Storage and Recall*.

STORAGE

Storage is the process that enables sensory messages to be recorded and maintained in the Long Term Memory.

Precisely how this is done remains a mystery. It appears that at least two methods of information recordation are used.

The first is the simple act of repeating, to oneself, over and over, the information we wish to remember. This may be because the longer the information stays in the Short Term Memory the more fixed it becomes when deposited in the Long Term Memory. This technique is known as *maintenance rehearsal*.

The second requires us to think about the new information in terms of related overall *concepts*, to connect the new information to information already stored in the Long Term Memory. Perhaps this is because the information must be organized and filed according to previously established categories with which we are already familiar. This approach, known as *elaborative rehearsal*, links information and creates comparisons and contrasts that preserve it in a collective of information that may be accessed from different angles through multiple connected ideas and concepts.

RECALL

Recall is the process by which we are able to recollect information that has been stored in our memories. The effectiveness of our ability to retrieve information is partially due to the way in which it has been stored in memory in the first place.

ENCODING

Encoding is the process by which we, more or less efficiently, prepare information for storage so that it may be easily retrieved when needed. Encoding is, in some ways, similar to a *tickler* or *filing system*. It *codes* information and then *files* it according to the code. An efficient encoding system is one that *enhances* rather than *impedes* our ability to recall information. In the process of encoding we file information away in specific categories according to its code. Depending upon how information is coded we may have a vital piece of information stored away that will solve a problem but because it is not properly *cross-referenced* we may never realize that it can be applied to another set of facts. In other words, important information may be known by us but totally ignored because we are unable to connect it, by cross-reference, to other information.

This, then, is a necessarily brief description, a broad outline, of the *Mechanics of Thought*. We will return to some of these in greater detail later in our discussion. What we have described thus far is *thinking*. We have attempted to demonstrate that thinking is an *information processing system*. In this context the key word is *information*.

When we think we process symbolic sensory messages. We now know that these messages, received by the five senses, may or may not be accurate because of the inherent unreliability of the sensors. When it is further considered that our memories are partially constructed the importance of accurate information becomes pivotal to the thinking process.

It is believed that our memories are partially the result of our tendency to add bits of information to our perceptions. This tendency has the further effect of cre- ating a picture that comports with our personal reality, which, as we know may be completely dissimilar from universal reality. As a result what we remember may be fundamentally inaccurate. Moreover, our information filing system may prohibit us from finding information previously stored or may prevent us from making connections between seemingly unrelated bits of information previously stored.

Our ability to make connections is to a great extent dependent on our underlying belief systems and the extent to which they will permit connections in certain subject matter areas. As we shall see our *personal reality* is driven,

TOTAL BLACK EMPOWERMENT

almost exclusively, by our preexisting *beliefs* and *belief sysems*.

2

BELIEFS AND BELIEF SYSTEMS

Our attitudes, in the psychological sense, are nothing more than *beliefs,* developed over time, which cause us to react in a certain way when we are confronted with specific perceived facts. Attitude is the tendency, developed over time, to perceive, think, learn and recollect in ways that are consistent with our predetermined beliefs. Our *beliefs* determine for us whether a thing is *real* or *unreal, positive* or *negative.* They also dictate how we *react* in a given situation. We harbor thousands of beliefs. When these are viewed as a whole they represent a *belief system,* that is, the sum of what we believe about the world around us and everything and everyone in it.

A *belief system* is comprised of several categories of beliefs. Of these the most important and influential deal with our values, goals our standards for the deter- mining if information is accurate or reliable, the system of logic by which we make that determination, our foundational beliefs about important subjects and our overall world view.

A belief system, by its very nature, is *goal-oriented.* When a belief system is insufficiently defined and goal oriented it will be ineffective. In extreme cases it can serve to undermine, impair or impede the ability of its adherents to engage in logical, productive thinking because it amounts to a hodge-podge of contradictory information that leaves its adherents confused and perplexed by the information they receive, rather than enlightened by it. In most cases the believer is unaware of this or, at best, *confused* by the contradictory information. *To be confused is simply to be unclear in mind or purpose.*

Our individual and collective belief systems operate without regard to consistency, accuracy or fact. These systems provide our understanding of the world, and create for us the defenses that we ultimately rely on to protect ourselves in the world.

It follows that our ability/power to protect ourselves and those to whom we owe the duty of protection and care is, in large measure, governed by the content and nature of our attitudes, beliefs and belief systems.

In short, if these are well informed, productive and reality-based, our power to protect, including problem solving and strategy development, is enhanced. Ill- informed, illusory and fantasy-based beliefs and belief systems are, on the other hand, counter-productive and even detrimental to our individual and collective progress.

Beliefs are powerful thoughts. It is now indisputable that what we believe can and does affect our physical well-being. The *placebo affect* and so-called *miraculous cures* are examples of the power our thoughts to affect us physically.

The *placebo effect* tells us that in any test situation, the patients who are given a placebo (a substance containing no medication, administered for its psychological effect on the patient) 32% will show improvement solely based on their belief that they have received an effective medication.[1]

Miraculous cures are often no more than the result of a person's belief that they will be cured. People with HIV/AIDS and cancer who believe that they will be cured tend to live longer than those who believe they are doomed.

It is important that we recognize and understand that beliefs are *powerful*. Like any form of power our beliefs tend to take on a life of their own and must be *controlled* by us or we run the risk of having them controlled by others. Unfortunately, we are not born with the knowledge or how to control our beliefs. We must, therefore, be trained in the *technique of belief control*.

BELIEF CONTROL

The concept of belief control is, admittedly, a controversial one. This is because of its definitional similarity to the concept of mind control or brainwashing. Belief control is best understood in its similarity to damage control. Belief control, like damage control and unlike mind control, consists in having a set of strategies to be employed when a belief has the potential to damage or undermine our thinking and our ability to deal with the vicissitudes of life. It is additionally dissimilar in that the control and its parameters are determined and applied by the individual to his or her own thinking.

In order to control our beliefs we must begin by understanding belief and belief systems in the context of the process of thinking.

Beliefs are essentially of two kinds: those that are based on facts and those that are not. Beliefs based on fact are *theories*. Beliefs not based on facts are *opinions*. This distinction is an important one that cannot be overemphasized.

A theory is simply a set of statements or principles devised to explain a group of facts, and that has been repeatedly tested. An opinion, on the other hand, is a belief or conclusion held with confidence but not substantiated by fact.

The fundamental difference between theory and opinion is that theory is based on fact, while opinions are not. More importantly, a theory requires *repeated testing* to verify its accuracy/validity. Opinions are merely held with *confidence*. It is, in short, a belief based on *no facts*.

Although it is certainly true that knowledge can be defined as what we *know*, and we may question whether anything can be known with *absolute certainty*, we can safely say that knowledge, to be of any real value must, at least, be factual it cannot be *false*.

A belief system is an interconnected, and therefore, dependent set of beliefs. As such belief systems tend to be more powerful than singular beliefs because each belief supports and gives validity to the others so that they all stand or fall together. As a consequence we come to accept the belief system and all the beliefs it contains, in most cases without prior analysis. Over the course of time these beliefs become part and parcel of our personal reality. The level of acceptance grows, imperceptibly at first, until these unexamined beliefs become fixed.

Belief systems are also *defensive* and *self-reinforcing*. Defensively, belief systems operate to *protect* what we believe from the necessarily devastating assault of *reason, logic* and *contradictory fact*.

Whenever our beliefs are contradicted or questioned by others, or *by our own minds*, our bedrock belief in our power/ability to accurately assess reality is potentially undermined. Rather than accept even the possibility that we have been wrong in so crucial an assessment, we simply refuse to deal with what is presented.

In logic this is known as the *fallacy of invincible ignorance—we insist on the validity of our beliefs despite contradictory facts*. Belief systems are self-reinforcing in that they tend to reject, out of hand, ideas, thoughts, concepts that are at variance with the individual's personal reality which is nothing more than his perceptions filtered through his attitudes, beliefs and belief systems. The result is that existing beliefs are not challenged but are reinforced by virtue of the fact that only information deemed acceptable is recorded in the Long Term Memory. This is the inevitable result because your belief system controls your attention function. The result is a form of mental paralysis that makes it virtually impossible to think outside of the box constructed by our beliefs and belief systems.

CIRCULAR THINKING

A belief system's defense mechanism and associated self-reinforcement mechanism leads, almost invariably, to a form of mental paralysis known as circular thinking.

Thought progresses in a straight line from sensory input to problem identification, to problem resolution. This linear process is natural and generates a solution to most problems in the orderly course of its operation. *If this process is disrupted or interfered with in some way a secondary, unnatural and therefore abnormal thinking process, known as circular thinking supplants the linear thinking process.*

Circular thinking occurs when a disruption takes place between sensory input (perception) and problem resolution, causing a sensory loop.

A sensory loop operates like a magnetic tape joined end to end that forms a continuous strip of endless repetition. The loop runs from sensory input to identification to sensory input. It eliminates problem resolution because it does not recognize the sensory message as problematic. It eliminates altogether dissection of the problem and in-depth analysis. The loop is characteristic of circular thinking. Let us look at this aspect of the thinking process to see how our beliefs and belief systems operate to undermine our ability (power) to think efficiently.

First, there is *perception*, that is, the sensory input that becomes the symbolic sensory messages sent to our brains after they are converted into electrical energy/ impulse by the Five Thieves. Next the *attention function* determines whether the information/stimuli/data is important enough to pay attention to. This is itself a two-stage process consisting of identification and analysis.

The *identification stage* of the process requires you to be alert, that is, aware of what you are being confronted with. It is both a defensive and an offensive *alarm system*. *Defensively* it protects you from danger, attack or harm. *Offensively*, it instructs you to be aggressive, violent or to attack when necessary.

Analysis is also a two-stage process. When information has been received and identified we either take action or ignore it (i.e., pay it no attention). In either case the decision is made, in the span of seconds, on the basis of whether the information (symbolic sensory messages) is important or unimportant. In each case the determination of importance is based on our pre-existing beliefs and belief systems.

In order for us to take action we must first recognize the information received as important. Only then do we conclude that some type of action, whether defensive or offensive, is required. When action is required it means that you must do something or suffer the consequences of inaction. In the overwhelming majority of cases the information received is ignored.

This is simply because most of it is, in fact, unimportant. This should not be surprising when we consider that thousands upon thousands of bits of irrelevant information are received and processed by our brains each day.

When our analysis concludes that the information is not to be ignored our *sensory alarm system* alerts us that some action is required. Functionally, the determination of importance is a *wake-up call* that alerts us to the need for action. Circular thinking disrupts this natural process by ignoring, as unimportant, wake up calls that do not conform to pre-determined beliefs and belief systems. This is precisely where the problem we are discussing arises. It is known as decision-making. This is where the real thinking, the genuine thought processing, takes place. Its negative counterpart is indecision.

DECISION MAKING

The object of decision-making is, of course, to decide. To decide is to put an end to *vacillation*. When we are dealing with a serious problem we are confronted with a *dilemma*.

A dilemma is defined as a choice between two equally unfavorable alternatives. Decision-making, or deciding, therefore, amounts to both a choice between alternatives and an end to vacillation. In any given situation the facts may vary but the options (alternatives) are always the same to do or not to do yes or no. This may seem unremarkable at first glance, but let us look at it more closely.

We have sensory input. The attention function tells us that the sensory input is important and that some sort of action is required. But, for some reason we are indecisive or reluctant to act—we are confronted with a dilemma.

The dilemma may cause *procrastination* and in extreme cases outright mental paralysis. But, why and how does this occur? The short answer is as a result of the unique human ability to make comparisons.

COMPARISON

When we compare, we mentally put things side by side and note the differences or resemblances between them. In short, we begin thinking through or by *comparison*. We compare the new information with information that has been previously stored in our Long Term Memory. It is this ability to *dichotomize* that creates indecision.

We think and solve problems by comparing current situations to those we have previously experienced or learned about and stored in our memory banks. It follows that the accuracy and appropriateness of our decisions, the effectiveness of our strategies is, in a very real sense, dependent on our ability to compare things that is, in turn, dependent on what is deposited in our memory banks.

MEMORY BANKS AND MENTAL BANKRUPTCY

In one sense *memory bank* is a more accurate description of the Long Term Memory. Our memory is literally the depository in which is kept the mental capital through which our ideas will be rich or poor.

Rich ideas are enlightened ideas that lead to effective, successful decisions, plans and strategies. *Poor Ideas*, on the other hand, are not only unenlightened and lead to ill-conceived and often disastrous decisions, plans and strategies, but are also the result of what may be accurately described as *mental bankruptcy.*

The deposits made in our memory banks are fashioned by and gleaned from our perceptions, experiences and Interpretations that have, in turn, been filtered through our beliefs and our education. No decision can be made, no thought can occur, without the use of our mental capital.

When comparison tells us that we are confronted with a dilemma that is sufficiently objectionable, linear reasoning may be supplanted by circular reasoning without our being aware of the change in our mode of thinking.

One of the primary reasons this occurs subconsciously in most cases) is as a result of the beliefs and belief systems that we have adopted over the course of our lives and which control, to a greater or lesser degree, our ability to reason.

Reason, is the capacity for logical, rational and analytic thinking. *Reason is the ability to* think logically. Reason is also, in large part, dependent on *meaning.*

MEANING
COMPREHENSION
UNDERSTANDING

We are unavoidably controlled in our thinking and reasoning by the meaning that we have given to the terms with which we reason.

Meaning is the key to understanding. Understanding is another word for comprehension. That is, when we comprehend we understand the meanings of things. Without an understanding of the meanings of the terms we use comprehension is virtually impossible.

Meaning is constructed. It is formed, built if you will, from and with the raw material provided by our belief system. Our belief system literally controls our under- standing/comprehension of the world around us by controlling the meanings of words we use to think, reason and communicate.

Unfortunately, even the meanings of the words that we use to communicate are controlled and determined by those who benefit from our confusion, diminished comprehension and understanding.

Clearly, our ability to reason is affected by our belief system. It is either positively affected, in which case it is improved, or it is impeded by the negative effects of an ill-conceived belief system. If the underlying belief system itself is ill-constructed (deformed), that is, based on an inaccurate or illogical set of fundamental beliefs, our understanding will also be inaccurate and illogical, to a greater or lesser degree in all subjects. It is virtually impossible to reason effectively when our overall understanding is inaccurate.

Viewing the world through our belief system, as we must, is much like wearing tinted contact lenses. If the lenses are green everything we view will be colored green. If we view a yellow object, for example, we will see it as blue.

TOTAL BLACK EMPOWERMENT

It is important to understand here that the object viewed does not change its color. It will only appear blue to the observer who wears green contact lenses. It is also true that to the observer the objects viewed actually appear to be blue, while at the same time an observer without green contact lenses will view the same object as yellow. Our beliefs systems, like the green contact lenses, color (distort) our comprehension of what we see.

Remember too that our belief system, which may be accurate or inaccurate, insures that what we see is accepted by us whether it is accurate or not. The implications of this are truly profound.

It can be persuasively argued that we have our being in two worlds simultaneously. On the one hand, we reside in the world that is described for us by our perceptions. This is best described as mental, because it is the world that exists within the four corners of our minds. This world, the mental one, may or may not conform to the reality of the *physical world in which we live and is assisted in that conformity or nonconformity by the color of our belief system.*

The physical world, on the other hand, may be substantially different from our mental picture of it. To the extent that our mental picture conforms to the physical world of reality we are able to deal more effectively with the situations that arise and that require us to make decisions. If, however, our mental picture does not conform to the reality of the physical world, we are more likely to make decisions that are inappropriate or counterproductive.

These two worlds are linked, and the differences between them are reconciled, by our ability to reason, which is, in turn, dependent on meaning. Since meaning, comprehension and understanding are, in large measure, the product of our belief system, we cannot separate what we see from what we believe. In fact, it is accurate to say that *we see what we believe rather that believe what we see.*

The connection between the mental and physical worlds is scientifically verifiable. We know that what we think and believe can and does affect us physically. This indicates that the power of our beliefs cannot be taken lightly. Among African Americans certain beliefs and belief systems are so wide spread that they can be viewed as *collective belief systems*.

COLLECTIVE BELIEF SYSTEMS

Our beliefs are more or less permanent and form a set of related, interconnected ideas. Moreover, we learn these related ideas from others, and we, in turn, transmit these ideas to others. In effect, our beliefs form not only an individual belief system, but can also form a *collective belief system* when they are linked with the beliefs of others who, having been influenced by contact with our beliefs, or who have been influenced by the same belief source, believe as we do. When it is further considered that our individual beliefs are self-reinforcing the Law of Power Units (discussed in section on Power) tells us that when these beliefs become collective belief systems their ability to reinforce each other is multiplied exponentially. It should be noted here that although collective belief systems can be beneficial they have the tendency to develop, over time, into what is known as groupthink a phenomenon that has potentially dangerous implications.

GROUPTHINK

Groupthink is defined as a pattern of thinking that, overtime, renders group members unable to evaluate realistically the wisdom of various options and decisions."[2]

This phenomenon is said to develop when groups are isolated from outside influences and when the leader is not impartial. When this happens the group "... tends to become close-minded and to rationalize their decision as the only reasonable one. They dismiss other options and quickly suppress dissenting voices. As a result, the group becomes more and more certain that its decision cannot be wrong. Such groups have been known to make amazingly *bad decisions."* Id.

Groupthink can be avoided by the simply encouraging the use of techniques that teach individual group members to independently examine the information they receive before accepting it as fact. A group member who employs such techniques will enhance the mind power process at every level of its operation. This is why such techniques are an effective form of collective belief control. *Critical Thinking* and *belief deconstruction* are effective techniques that we will discuss at length later on in our discussion.

BELIEFS DEVELOPED EARLY IN LIFE

When our beliefs are developed early in life, are derived from a source that we believe to be reliable, or are the result of intense indoctrination, they may become so deeply ingrained as to be virtually impossible to dislodge. Eighty percent of what we learn in life is learned during the first four years of our existence. What we learn during that period is so deeply ingrained as to be virtually impossible to unlearn. One of the reasons for this is the source of our early learning.

Clearly, our parents (or grandparents as the case may be) are our first sources of information. In fact, they are, during this formative period, our exclusive source of information. This is as it should be. Our parents are our protectors, our guardians, our link to the past and our guides to the future. They are our first gods. We do not easily forget or lightly challenge what our parents have taught us. Some of us will never challenge anything they taught. There are those of us who believe things that they agree are potentially detrimental to them solely because their parents believed it. This too is perhaps as it should be.

We must recognize, however, that our parents were not always logical or right. Our parents view the world through the eyes of their parents. For the most part they taught us what their parents taught them. They gave to us the best that they had to offer. But, they were not privy to the wealth of information that we are. We are not obligated to accept what they taught when we know it is false. We are certainly not obligated to perpetuate a known falsehood by teaching it to our children. What our parents taught was valuable for the purpose that it was intended. Their purpose was, almost invariably, to insure our survival. Without them we would not have survived. We must be forever grateful for their gift of the technology of survival. But, as you will see, in the 21st century survival is not enough. Another reason for the deep-seated nature of our beliefs is that many of them came to us as a result of intense indoctrination.

INDOCTRINATION

African Americans have been taught (actually indoctrinated) and have subsequently adopted a belief system that, like all belief systems, effectively governs our lives. The problem is that we have failed to subject our adopted (actually indoctrinated) belief system or its individual components to critical analysis. This is apparent in light of the fact that our belief system has proven consistently *detrimental* to our collective interests.

Though the word indoctrination is an emotionally charged one, I use it intentionally. I use it because we do not like to be told that we are indoctrinated. The word indoctrinate has a decidedly negative connotation. We instinctively resist the notion because of what it necessarily implies. To be *indoctrinated* or *brain- washed* is to be men-

tally, psychologically, controlled. The implication is clear and unavoidable. Our thoughts—our most personal, intimate possessions—are under the control of others—the operation of our minds is *not* under our control.

The thought that we are, or can be, indoctrinated is to many a thought that contradicts our fundamental belief system. Of course, we understand now that contradictory thoughts will always give rise to our *innate defensive mechanism,* precisely because they go against the grain of our *belief system. Contradictory thoughts* will always be *attacked* by our minds rather than critically examined.

It bears repeating here that a belief system is a set of interconnected beliefs. Each supports and gives internal validity to the others so that they all stand or fall together. Whenever our beliefs are questioned, even subconsciously by our own minds, we become automatically and often unconsciously defensive—in effect the belief system reinforces itself by preventing the introduction of facts or information that it deems contradictory to our present belief system.

None of us want to believe that we have been indoctrinated. We all want and even need to believe that we are independent, free thinkers because that belief is also part and parcel of the underlying belief system. However, our reluctance to *accept* the fact that we have been indoctrinated does not change the fact that we have, albeit in sometimes subtle and imperceptible ways. Add to this scenario an *emotion factor* and we have a set of beliefs that can easily undermine our most earnest attempts to change our collective circumstances.

THE EMOTION FACTOR

The *emotion factor* is best defined as a *multiplier.* It serves the purpose of *multiplying* the *intensity* and *concreteness* of our belief and gives rise to the *Fallacy of Invin-*

cible Ignorance mentioned previously.

Emotions are powerful feelings *that can develop into a state of mental agitation or disturbance.* When our most cherished, most deeply held beliefs, such as our religion or politics, are challenged or contradicted by anyone, including our own minds, our alarm system goes off, our defenses go up, and our emotions take control. We see ourselves as under attack. And, in fact, we are under attack. The attack is aimed at the very core of our being. *As a man thinks so is he.* Because the attack is *belief threatening*, we close our ears and lock our minds against the horrific assault of a different point of view.

You can always tell when the emotion factor is in play. Invariably the person who feels himself under attack will say something like, "I don't care what you say, you are not going to change my mind!" Translation: I will maintain my point of view no matter how many contradictory facts you raise.

What happens if in addition to the powerful influence of our beliefs and belief systems we are also victims of other forms of mental disorder that further inhibit our ability to think effectively?

3

BELIEF SYSTEMS AND MENTAL DISORDER

I tread very lightly here. I am well aware that the idea of a group mental disorder is one that people are not likely to easily accept. I only ask the reader to bear with me for a moment while I define the terms and make my case.

A mental disorder is defined as "... any of various conditions characterized by impairment of an individual's normal cognitive, emotional, or behavioral functioning, and caused by social, psychological, biochemical, genetic or other factors...."

By the above definition a mental disorder can be an impairment of awareness and thinking caused by social factors. The term mental disorder is used here to mean an abnormal mental condition that is the result of disturbance of the natural order of thinking. Remember we are talking about impairment or diminishment, in some material respect, of awareness and thinking ability—not group insanity.

Mental disorder is, believe it or not, the most common cause of disability in the United States. Twenty six percent of American adults (over 18) suffer from one or more varieties of mental disorder.[1]

There are now 374 mental disorders listed in the Diagnostic and Statistical Manual of Mental Disorder, Fourth Edition (DSM-IV).[2] We will here look at a few of the mental disorders that seem to apply to the collective mental state of African Americans in the 21st century. We will begin with the broad category known as the Inferiority Complex.

THE INFERIORITY COMPLEX

The Inferiority Complex *is a neurotic condition characterized by feelings of inferiority that derive from real or imagined physical or social inadequacy.*

A neurotic condition is a mental, functional disorder characterized by anxiety, compulsions, phobias, and dissociation.

Anxiety *is an abnormal state characterized by a feeling of being powerless and unable to cope with threatening events.*

Compulsion *is an irresistible, repeated, irrational impulse to perform some act.*

Phobias *are irrational, excessive and persistent fears surrounding some particular thing or event.*

Dissociation *is a split in the conscious process.* When dissociation occurs a group of mental activities break away from the mainstream of consciousness and function as a separate unit as if belonging to another person. It is also characterized by *abnormal separation of related ideas, thoughts and emotions.*

What the inferiority complex describes is a *seriously conflicted person*. Persons who suffer the symptoms of the inferiority complex are those who feel socially inadequate and powerless. Such persons will also have irrational and persistent fears. And, will become different persons as a result of the irrational separation of thoughts, ideas and emotions from which they suffer.

If it is true that groups of people can exhibit the symptoms of neuroses we have also described a *conflicted group*. Several noted African American psychologists have independently concluded that as a people we suffer from a wide range of mental disorders resulting from the conditions of oppression, and/or Post Traumatic Slave Syndrome as well as from the social stress and confusion of the attempt to assimilate. Clearly, the notion of a conflicted group is not new or far-fetched.

Be that as it may, that African Americans collectively exhibit characteristics of the inferiority complex seems obvious. Anxiety, compulsions, phobias and dissociation have historically been, and unfortunately remain, our constant companions. Let us look briefly at each.

ANXIETY

We have felt powerless and unable to cope with threatening events since the days when we were abducted from our ancestral home, shackled and chained, buried in the holes of monstrous merchant slave ships and brought to these shores, against our will, to be auctioned like cattle.

We were then dispersed to slave plantations where we remained for centuries under the watchful eye of vicious overseers, whips and guns at the ready, who inflicted mortal wounds for the slightest infraction of the barbarous slave codes. We survived in abject poverty and constant humiliation. The lingering message of that dark period was that we were powerless to change our circumstances. *Think about it.*

- We were powerless to rise up against our sadistic captors;

- We were powerless to protect our women and children;

- We were powerless to keep our families intact;

TOTAL BLACK EMPOWERMENT

- We were powerless to publicly speak our ancestral tongues;

- We were powerless to maintain our ancestral culture;

- We were powerless to invoke the Gods of our ancestors aloud;

- We were powerless to fight and powerless to run;

- We were powerless to hold property and powerless to make plans or exercise our intellects.

And, after so-called emancipation we remained powerless.

- We were powerless to do anything that we could not do when we were legally slaves;

- We were powerless to travel;

- We were powerless to participate in the so-called democratic process;

- We were powerless to prevent the Ku Klux Klan from terrorizing our communities;

- We were powerless against the infamous Black Codes and Jumpin' Jim Crow;

- we were powerless to force the United States Government to come to our aid.

- Today we remain powerless to prevent the mass incarceration of our men, women and children;

- We are still powerless to prevent the raging, virulent hostility of the judicial and legislative branches of the government toward any policy, program or philosophy that would do anything to level the playing field;

- We are still powerless to travel the highways and by ways of this land without being profiled at every stop sign and intersection;

- We are still powerless to prevent our communities from being redlined and designated crime and drug-infested areas;

- We are still powerless to stop the agents of law enforcement from ignoring the Constitution to enter our homes, businesses, houses of worship and schools without legal cause or justification and without warrants;

- And, we remain powerless to appoint judges who will not countenance such abuse and powerless to remove those who do.

Under these circumstances is it any wonder that we suffer from anxiety? Can anyone logically argue that we do not?

COMPULSION

Compulsion is an irresistible, repeated, irrational impulse to perform some act. Irresistible means you just cannot resist and irrational means even though it makes no damn sense. When you do it over and over again, it is a compulsion.

By the foregoing definition African Americans have at least one compulsion that we cannot logically deny. That is, the irresistible, repeated, irrational impulse to seek the solution to our problems from those who have repeatedly demonstrated their unwillingness to help. It seems that we just cannot resist the impulse to value the advice, guidance and leadership of our erstwhile captors and slave masters over the lessons of history and common sense.

That such an impulse is irrational and that we repeat it over and over again seems undeniable. Even a dog will stop coming when called if he keeps getting kicked in the teeth. Even a mouse in a maze will learn, after a few unsuccessful attempts, that turning right leads to a dead end and will go left from then on.

PHOBIAS

A phobia is an irrational, excessive, persistent fear about something or event. Fear is a paralysis; a mental and physical disruption of vital processes that causes a person to be helpless, inactive, ineffective and powerless.

Fear binds action. It literally disrupts your ability to move and on the intellectual and psychological level, your ability to think. The deer that crosses the road in the dead of night and finds himself caught in the headlights of an oncoming vehicle is unable to escape because it is paralyzed by fear. Fear locks his brain and the paralysis of his brain binds his action so that he cannot move to avoid the oncoming vehicle. *His brain locks up. He cannot act—even to save his own life.*

Fear is specialized. Fear is always directed toward something. African Americans have an abundance of interconnected fears that all derive from one basic fear. These interconnected fears are numerous. We need only name a few to make the point.

We fear authority. African Americans who do not become visibly shaken by an encounter with the police, the courts, social service agencies and their ilk are few and far between. This deep-seated apprehension has little or nothing to do with guilt. It results from the fact that since before the founding of this republic the law, its makers, interpreters and enforcers have ignored our rights and our basic humanity. They have used the law as an effective tool to insure that we remain at the level of subsistence.

Our fear of authority stems from our collective experiences over the centuries of our unfortunate sojourn in America. It stems from our dealings with a system that has been used to humiliate us and keep us in the place deemed suitable by others.

We fear speaking out. In a land that sanctimoniously prides itself on its protection of the so-called inalienable right of free speech, we are afraid to speak our minds. Few of us will admit it but it is, nonetheless, true. This phenomenon stems from the fact that we have learned that survival requires us to keep our thoughts to ourselves. We have become programmed over the centuries to hide our feelings and never let anyone know what we are thinking.

We fear success. Too often success has meant publicity and publicity makes one a target. Over the centuries those who have excelled have fallen prey to the jealousy of those who had a vested interest in our individual and collective failure and continued subservience. All over the land night riders of various stripes brought carnage and unspeakable violence to bear on those of us who dared to be successful.

Here we need only recall *Black Wall Street*, Tulsa and the hundreds of thousands of acres of land taken from our ancestors by those who could not allow them to be successful because *success leads to power.*

There is one fear, however, to which all the others are connected and from which they derive. More than anything else *we fear death*. This is truly a curious phenomenon. It is one that has its roots in the slavery experience. It is curious because most of us believe (due mainly to our religious upbringing) in life after death. Everybody wants to go to heaven, everybody believes in heaven, but nobody wants to die to get there. Curious indeed. *Think about it.*

The fear of death is perhaps the most effective method of social control ever devised. It is diametrically opposed to, and effectively undermines, the powerful notion that to live is to have something to die for. It is no mere coincidence that the most dangerous person is one who feels he/she has nothing to live for. It is no coincidence that in any contest it is the most committed who wins. This is because the most committed person is the one who is committed unto death.

The slavery experience informed us that the slightest infraction of the rules was to be met with swift, brutal punishment. And, the ultimate punishment, death, could be inflicted for any reason, but, was most often exacted for acts that indicated the spark of *revolutionary thinking.* Self-confidence was totally unacceptable.

We were severely punished (up to and including the death penalty) for sassing a white person, for failing to get off the sidewalk when a white person approached, for raising our voices to a white person, looking them in the eye, for raising a hand to them or for learning to read.

The purpose was to instill in us the *fear of death.* The fear of death, like all fears, served to *bind our action. It served to paralyze our minds.* It served to make us accept virtually any indignity, any injustice, so long as we believed the alternative to acceptance was death. It is said that human beings are born with only two fears—the fear of falling and of loud noises—all other fears are learned.

Julius Caesar is said to have been so deeply impressed by the courage and tenacity of a group of warriors against whom he had occasion to do battle that he sought them out to determine the reason for such unprecedented valor. The reason was surprisingly simple. The warriors had been raised to believe in an ancient African belief that holds that upon death the soul immediately reincarnates in another body. The valiant warriors had never been taught the fear of death.

Another example is being played out every day in the Middle East. Arabs/Muslims are blowing themselves up and raising their children to die for the cause. They do not fear death. America for all her military prowess and sophisticated weapons of war cannot stop them because these people do not fear death. How many African Americans are willing to die for any cause?

DISSOCIATION

Dissociation *is a psychological* process *that is characterized by a* split in consciousness. Those who suffer from dissociation become, in effect, two persons. More accurately, they become *one person in whom two different minds are active simultaneously*. Dissociation causes the separation of related ideas, thoughts and the emotions that flow from them. The word means to disunite, to estrange. To disunite is to alienate or to destroy the unity of something. To estrange is to remove something from its usual surroundings or associates. Estrange also implies the development of hostility toward that from which we are estranged.

Dissociation is also characterized by the development of a genuine, deep-seated hostility between the two minds. If we consider that the root of the word hostility means enemy, *the dissociative person is psychologically his own enemy—he is hostile to himself*.

Dissociation begins when a specific group of mental activities *separate*, that is, break away from the mainstream of the person's consciousness. Mental activity is, of course, essentially thought, or more properly, thinking. Consciousness, on the other hand, is the state of awareness of the things and conditions in our environment as well as our awareness of our thoughts, feelings and emotions.

TOTAL BLACK EMPOWERMENT

When thinking (mental activity) separates from our awareness of our environment, our feelings and emotions, we become another or different person. Since this separation is mental and since the two minds exist at the same time, we are engrossed in a constant state of mental conflict, dilemma and ultimately, confusion. *It cannot be overemphasized that we are talking about two minds living in one body.*

Dissociation is a defense mechanism. It occurs in persons who are suffering from an emotional conflict. The conflict is a result of impulses that are unacceptable to the conscious mind. An impulse can be an incitement to action arising from a state of mind. The conflict is between something that we instinctively know is right (or required) and is, nonetheless, rejected by the conscious mind.

Dissociation is a defense mechanism in that it is a process of reasoning that protects us from the psychological effects of the conflict. Why would something that is right (or required) be rejected by the conscious mind?

Let us imagine that a person who is responsible for the care and protection of another individual is confronted with the following scenario: The person (let us call him/her the Protector) witnesses the physical abuse of the person (let us call him/her the Protected) to whom the Protector owes the duty of protection.

The Protector's first instinct is to spring to the defense of the Protected by taking affirmative action to stop the physical abuse, violently, aggressively and immediately. But, despite his/her first instinct he/she does nothing. He fails to act as if his very ability to act has been paralyzed. Perhaps more importantly, he does not find his failure to act unjustified.

On the other and instinctive level, however, her failure to act is irrational and counterproductive. It is as if he has two minds counseling diametrically opposed actions simultaneously. The conflict lies in the fact that instinct informs the Protector that he/she must take immediate action to insure the survival of the *Protected*. *This is* instinct—*this is survival technology at its life-sustaining best. This is survival technology operating to insure protection* defensively, and collectively.

The conscious mind, however, is heavily influenced by the belief system upon which it must necessarily rely to make decisions, to plan and counsel. The belief system includes beliefs about life and death. The conscious mind may have concluded that the aggressor in the scenario is too big, too strong, or that he has a gun, or that there are too many of them—the Protector could suffer bodily injury or worse, he could get killed.

To the conscious mind what is right, what is required is to do nothing because to act may mean death. The right thing to do is to avoid even the possibility of death by doing nothing.

At the instinctive level, however, the Protector has only one concern—survival. At all costs, and to the exclusion of all things, protect and defend so the genus survives. Of course, this is also why the fear of death is not instinctive. The fear of death is learned and incorporated in our belief system. If the fear of death were instinctive it would defeat or neutralize the innate tendency to survival.

We should also note here, in passing, that this is precisely why self-preservation cannot be the first law of nature. *It is the genus, the group, the race that must be preserved, not the individual.* It is of course true that the genus cannot survive unless the individuals who comprise it survive. But, *self-preservation cannot possibly be* the main focus of survival. *The survival of the individual means nothing in the wider context of the continuation of life.*

Let us say that an individual adopts the self-preservation rule. Let us also say that he/she adheres to the rule religiously. What is the result? We have a person who, no matter what, will insure his/her own survival. This necessarily means that he/she will be forced to choose between his preservation and that of his family, clan, tribe or nation. His/her only concern is his or herself. In the worse case scenario the survival of *me* insures that *I* live, but I cannot reproduce *alone*. What I have accomplished then is that I will have the dubious distinction of being the last one of my line. *I have lived to become extinct.*

The dissociative mental disorder that we have described above causes a disturbance in the normal integrative functions of our consciousness and affects our personality. If we consider that personality is an enduring pattern of perceiving, relating to, and thinking about the environment and ourselves that is exhibited in a wide range of important social and personal contexts, we may easily understand how our individual and collective personalities may also be affected by dissociation.

The thrust of all of this is that a connection between the ability to control things and abnormal psychological functioning exists. In short, there is a direct correlation between the lack of power and self-confidence, between the lack of power and clear thinking. All of these things contribute to the highly detrimental mind-set and thinking incapacity that was first foisted upon us and that we have now unwittingly adopted in the centuries since our initial imprisonment *in America*.

It should be apparent to you how potentially volatile the mix between imprecise thinking and mental disorder can be. But, these are the facts that we must deal with.

Before we move on let us take a close look at one aspect of our adopted (forced may be a better word) belief system that has been instrumental in distracting us from what should be our true goal of prosperity through power sufficiency. You know it as the *American Dream*, I call it the *America Deception*.

TOTAL BLACK EMPOWERMENT

THE AMERICAN DREAM/DECEPTION

The overall belief system that we have so uncritically accepted is euphemistically referred to as the *American Dream*.

The *American Dream* teaches two interrelated beliefs. The first holds that everyone can make it in America if they just work long and hard enough. It conjures the notion of a Horatio Alger hero, and a multitude of other rags to riches tales.

The second interrelated belief implies that in America social equality is a reality and that those who do not succeed are not victims of a conspiratorial system, but are the victims of their own laziness and utter lack of initiative.

The fact that any Americans, least of all African Americans, have accepted the American Dream and all that it implies is further evidence of our failure to think clearly. I say this because if we had critically analyzed the concepts embodied in the American Dream we would have concluded that it is the purest form of *deception*.

To deceive a person is to make him or her believe what is not true. The root of the word means to *ensnare or to catch in a trap*. This means that without even examining the underlying claims of the American Dream we find that *on its face*, the term really means the *American deception* and implies a *trap for the unwary*. Had we applied critical analysis in this case we would also have been required to examine the underlying claims of the American Dream.

Can African Americans *logically* claim that we can make it, *collectively*, if we simply work hard enough when the reality is that we are, and have always been, the hardest working people in this country? Can African Americans *logically*, conclude that social equality (or any other equality for that matter) is or has ever been a reality, *for us*, in the United States? It seems obvious that the answer should be a resounding no! Unfortunately, and too often, it is not.

The reason for this enigma is to be found in (1) the ability of the American Media Establishment (AME) and the American Educational System (AES) to sell the American Dream; and (2) the willingness (gullibility) of African Americans to buy it. It goes without saying that *a product cannot be sold if no one is willing to buy.*

THE AMERICAN MEDIA ESTABLISHMENT

The first prong of this two-part enigma arises from the fact that the *American Media Establishment* (print, electronic and advertising) is the most sophisticated, pervasive and effective *persuasion device* ever invented. Its tentacles reach into all areas of modern life and there is almost no field of endeavor, from government to garden hoses, where its influence is not felt. All people, including African Americans, are prey to that powerful, virtually uncontrolled influence. In 2017 we may add to this the internet, Facebook, Twitter, Snapchat and other modern mass communications variations.

The *American Media Establishment* is comprised of the *print* media, that is everything from the stately *New York Times* ("All the News that's *fit* to Print") to the *National Enquirer* and *Hustler Magazine*. It also includes the *electronic* media, that is, the major networks *ABC, CBS* and *NBC* as well as *CNN, MTV, BET* and radio. We also include the advertising industry and behavioral psychologists in this group. From the slick Madison Avenue advertising agencies to the *behavioral psychologists* in the ivy covered halls of academia, together they comprise the *American Media Establishment. They all serve the same purpose, that is, they all package, propagate, sell and reinforce the American*

Dream for domestic and international consumption. No matter how you look at it they are all complicit in the grand deception that is the American Dream. Now the internet allows others who do not own their own print, television, radio or cable networks to disseminate alternative facts. Although the internet has the potential of democratizing the spread of information in real time it can still be used to propagate the American Dream for a new generation of believers.

THE AMERICAN EDUCATIONAL SYSTEM

The American Educational System, on the other hand, is the *indoctrinator extraordinaire,* whose purpose is to take young, impressionable minds and socialize them into the uncritical acceptance of this dream.

The educational system operates for the purpose of socializing the young into the current system and culture and to train them to prevent radical change in the system of government—in short, to maintain the status quo. No educational sys- tem teaches its students to seize power nor can any educational system be realistically expected to do so.

The educational system's prescription for change in the system of government is always the same. The only acceptable change is slow and incremental. It must be non-violent. It always employs passive hard work to convince the majority that you are worthy of inclusion. The implication is that if you cannot convince them by this one and only *legitimate* method, there must be something wrong with your view. Teachers tell you that the "majority rules". The *democratic* way must prevail because it *serves the greatest number.* You might want to ask yourself who in America is the greatest number? Given this background of deception and indoctrination it is not surprising to learn

TOTAL BLACK EMPOWERMENT

that many African Americans can be psychologically and deeply *conflicted*. To be conflicted is to *suffer emotional disturbance as a result of a clash of opposing ideas*. Let us look at how this clash of opposing ideas comes about.

As children, at least in modern times, our first and nearly exclusive teacher is television. It cannot be logically disputed that television exists by virtue of, and for the purpose of *advertising*. Advertising is defined as the act of *informing*. But clearly, it is much more. Advertising seeks not merely to *inform. The number one objective of advertising is to persuade you to take action, to do something—to buy—to believe—to trust—to rely*. If this were not so advertising would not be so intimately related to and dependent on *behavioral psychology*. In short, advertising may properly be referred to as a science—it is the *science of persuasion*.

Persuasion is the act of causing a person to believe one thing rather than another. It is the act of influencing the mind. It follows logically that there can be no functional or substantive difference between advertising and mind control. And, it makes no difference whether you call it persuasion, brainwashing, education or indoctrination.

When it is considered that children learn at least 80% of what they know in a lifetime by the time they are four years old the importance and impact of their educational fare during the formative stages of their lives becomes predictive of what they will *think* as adults.

During the first eight years of life African American children spend the overwhelming majority of their waking hours watching television. No matter how poor the household, we all have televisions. Most of us have more than one. Even before our children can sit up we prop them up in front of the television for their young minds to consume an intellectual diet of Sesame Street and cartoons. We do this out of necessity. Of course, we excuse this lack of attention to our children and their early development by proclaiming Sesame Street *educational* television, but the fact of the matter is that we do it because we are so busy pursu-

TOTAL BLACK EMPOWERMENT

ing the American Dream that we do not have time for anything else. It should be noted here that the vast majority of us who pursue the American Dream never really advance beyond the pursuit of food, clothing and shelter. In spite of what we believe most of us never rise above the level of subsistence no matter how hard we try.

After the initial eight years of *educational* television, cartoon fantasy and repetitious, gratuitous violence, we send our children off to school. We send them off to school, whether we want to or not, because we are compelled to so. Education is now *compulsory*. Those of us with longer historical memories will recall when it was *non-education* that was compulsory for African Americans. Little more than a century ago it was a crime, punishable by death, to teach us to read or write. Now we are compelled to be "educated".

When our children are delivered, by us their natural protectors, into the hands of those who have demonstrated historically their intention to prevent, at all costs, our advancement toward, and accomplishment of, the goal of freedom and equality, one of the first things they are taught is that their ancestors were slaves to white people in America. They are taught, among other things, that Abraham Lincoln freed the slaves (he did not); that God-fearing Abolitionists led the fight for our freedom and that one day America woke up and realized that slavery was evil. One may wonder why this bit of historical tripe is earmarked as so important as to be among the first subjects our children are taught as they embark on an educational journey that will last all of their lives.

This subtle message is insidious. Our children are taught that, yes, white folks *enslaved* their ancestors but white folks also *saved* them. Our children are taught that the slavery *experience* was *unfortunate*, maybe even traumatic, but now they should be grateful that they are now free in the land of liberty and equality.

TOTAL BLACK EMPOWERMENT

COLLECTIVE MENTAL DISORDER AND THE AMERICAN DREAM

We have already noted the possibility of collective or group mental disorder. Now let us look at this in the context of a specific belief system, i.e., the American Dream.

The American Dream *concept* stands for the proposition that anybody can make it in America. Of course, hard work is the key, but if you are not afraid to work you too can become an Oprah Winfrey or Bill Cosby. (Editor's Note: Only consider where Mr. Cosby was in 2007 and where he is now).

In the specific case of African Americans, however, there is an implicit added dimension. It says that sure what has happened to you was wrong (we refuse to apologize) and of course, you were never compensated for the work or the wrong (you slept on your rights) but everything is going to be all right (may take about four more centuries) just keep on working hard. Unfortunately, many of us actually believe this popular tripe. So did Booker T. Washington.

To think that the people who enslaved us will save us; or that the system that encouraged, permitted and endorsed our slavery will provide redress for that which it made legal in the name of the inalienable right to property, is a clear distortion of the logical relation between ideas. To continue, in the 21st century, to promulgate plans and advocate strategies that enlist your former slave masters, or the political or judicial system that permitted them to be your masters, as a way to secure social, economic or political equality in America is to take actions that are unquestionably inappropriate to our life situation.

There is an ancient African maxim that proclaims that the leopard does not change his spots. It is as true now as when it was first spoken. *The person who thinks that the leopard does change his spots or will do so in the future, is clearly a person who suffers from a distortion of the logical relation between ideas.*

    We have taken a brief look at the mechanics of thinking, the elements of which it is composed, and the beliefs and belief systems that inform our thinking in order to establish the fundamental idea that our thinking is at the heart of our problems. We have attempted to demonstrate that although impaired thinking is partially the result of how the thinking process works this fact should be accepted as notice to African Americans that the information upon which they rely to make decisions and formulate strategies must be carefully, rigorously, exhaustively analyzed and examined before it is accepted as fact.

    We have also seen that African Americans are, to some degree, conflicted, because of the combined effect that the media and the educational system have upon our intellectual development. What has been demonstrated thus far is perhaps an unfortunate reality, but it is one that can be changed.

    Change will require Critical Thinking. Let us now look at Critical Thinking and how this ancient approach to the acquisition of reality based knowledge can provide the answer to problems that only seem intractable because of our inability to think effectively.

4

CRITICAL THINKING

AN ANCIENT PHILOSOPHY FOR A NEW AGE

The concept of *Critical Thinking* is not new. European historians and Egyptologists have done a masterful job of concealing the origins of the *ideas* that they admit form the foundation of Western civilization. The concept of *Critical Thinking* is no exception. The reasons for this centuries-long concealment will become apparent to you as our intellectual journey continues. Let us begin at the beginning.

Modern observers assert that the roots of *Critical Thinking* are to be found in the teachings of the ancient Greek philosopher Socrates (469–399 BCE). Wrong. Socrates was undeniably a *critical thinker*. However, his *ideas, philosophy* and *method of examination* were millennia old when he *discovered* them and they certainly did not *originate* with him. It should not be surprising then that his ideas and methods were considered *foreign* to Greek culture and perhaps *new* to Greek Athenians.

If we look closely we will see that the concept of critical thinking, that is, the approach to thinking that entails careful analysis of all information before it is accepted as valid, is deeply rooted in our ancient African traditions. We will also see that the source of Greek wisdom was an indigenous black African nation. This important fact has been a closely guarded secret for centuries. The reason for its concealment has more to do with control than racism.

A people who recognize that their ancestors possessed skills that enabled them to master their environment and prevent their conquest by enemies foreign and domestic cannot be convinced of their inferiority or forced to accept an inferior status in society. This simple fact is important not to give us bragging rights but to teach us that the level of sophistication and power attained by the European is, in large part, the result of critical thinking techniques learned from our ancestors. The European knows and we must learn that no matter what the subject, all roads lead to Kemit—epitome of black African culture.

Let us begin with our ancient ancestral concept of *Oudja*. Then we will return to Socrates and his mentors.

OUDJA: CLARITY OF VISION

The word *Oudja* comes from the *Kemitic* word *oudjat* and refers to the *Eye of Heru* (< Greek, Horus). Although many African Americans are familiar with the symbol of the *Oudjat* eye few are aware of its profound meaning.

In order to understand and appreciate the full implications of this ancient symbol and to see how it relates to *Total Black Empowerment* we must familiarize ourselves with the *Legend of the battle between Heru and Set* (< Greek, Seth).

THE LEGEND OF HERU AND SET: ALL ROADS LEAD TO KEMIT

The *Kemitic* legend of the battle of *Heru* and *Set* is one of the oldest legends in the world. It is found related, in advanced form, in the pyramid texts (the oldest books in the world) as well as countless ancient documents the world over. The legend is of purely African origin as were the original *Kemites*. In this sense the legend is of ancient African ancestral origin.

Heru was the son of Asar (Greek Osiris) the legendary, historical first King of Kemit (Greek Egypt). One of his epithets was the *Good King*. Set was the brother of Asar and the uncle of Heru. Set, jealous of his brother's power, plotted against him in league with Aso, Queen of Ethiopia, to assassinate the Good King. After they had succeeded Asar visited his son (in a dream) and commanded that he avenge his death so that on the day of his victory Asar would return to rule the world through his son and rightful heir Heru. In order to avenge his father's death Heru was required to do battle with his uncle.

On the fateful day of the legendary battle Heru sustained an injury to his eye and was partially blinded. *Heru's inability to see fully and clearly* gave Set the upper hand and seemed to doom Heru to defeat. Just when it seemed that all was lost Tehuti (the Kemitic God of *divine intelligence*) appeared and repaired Heru's eye making it *whole* again. Armed with a whole eye (i.e., clarity of vision) Heru was victorious. But, he was nearly defeated because of his temporary *loss of clear vision. Victory alluded him until his ability to see was restored.*

The Kemitic word *oudjat* literally means whole or sound eye and refers to the reconstructed Eye of Heru. By extension *Oudja* means the power of the restored ability to see clearly. The whole eye is, in a word, the eye that has attained clairvoyance. Clairvoyance is the power of vision so clear that one who has it can see things that are not visible to the senses.

The moral of the legend is simple, straightforward and instructive. In order to win our battles in life we must see clearly. Put another way, Impaired vision is the bane of our success in life.

The legend of the battle of Heru and Set is instructive on many levels. This is the beauty of method our ancestors used to convey truth. They were masters at conveying information by myth and analogy so artfully that the breadth and depth of the information conveyed is only limited by the level of sophistication of the reader. In this way profound truths could be recorded without fear of them falling into the hands of shallow minds.

The legend of Heru and Set conveys many lessons. For example, Set was the blood brother of the good king. Yet, he was jealous not because his brother was a bad king, but because he was not king. Set wanted to be king himself. He was willing to go to any length to achieve his goal. He enlisted the aid of outsiders and conceived a plot to lead his brother into a trap. The good king fell into the trap because he could not believe that his brother would plot against him.

After the deed was done and in the course of appropriate time, Set's nephew reached the age of maturity and came to avenge his father's death and claim his birthright as heir to the throne. Set, whose name has been immortalized in the Judeo-Christian myths as Satan, author of confusion and deceit, nearly succeeded in defeating his nephew by injuring his eye (some accounts hold that he ripped it from the socket) so that his vision was impaired—by undermining his ability to see clearly. It was only through the intervention of Tehuti (Divine intelligence) who restored Heru's ability to see that he was able to be victorious in his quest to avenge his father's death and regain his birthright.

In the quest for *Total Black Empowerment*, our first step must be attainment of the ability to see the world with absolute clarity—with whole eyes. The importance of this fundamental step cannot be overemphasized. We must see the whole picture and that clearly before we can succeed at solving our problems. Heru could not succeed until he did so, nor can we.

Oudja necessarily implies clarity of vision for the purpose of accurate, informed decision-making. This is why

TOTAL BLACK EMPOWERMENT

Oudja is the first destination of an intellectual journey that will lead, in stages, to the level of mind at which true vision is encountered.

True vision is only attainable when our thinking is elevated to its next level of power. When this happens thought becomes *visual*. Interestingly the word idea comes from the Greek word *idieu* meaning *to see*. Ideas are, therefore, literally *visible* forms. It follows that *in order to have an idea you must be able to see it*. Thoughts must take visible shape and form before they can properly be said to be ideas.

Elevated thought becomes vision. Elevated thought is the vision without which the people will perish. Put another way the vision that the people will perish without is not hallucination, it is elevated thought. This means that without elevated thought to guide us, to inform our decisions and structure our lives we will not survive and certainly will not prosper.

Vision is elevated thought because when you raise the level of your vantage point you can see farther. Compare what you can see from the ground with what you can see from the rooftop and you will see the point vividly.

A caveat is necessary here. We must remember that although elevated thinking leads to vision it is not useful if it is *illusory*. Vision that is not clear is *illusion*. *An illusion is an erroneous perception of reality, concept or belief*. When something is *erroneous* it is simply mistaken or incorrect.

It seems too obvious to state that once we have achieved *Oudja* we must cultivate the ability to make sense of what we have seen clearly. Let us remember that a clear vision of a blurred picture is still a blurred picture. This is why clarity of vision alone will not solve our problem. The answer is clarity of vision plus *improved or elevated thinking*.

Now let us return to Socrates. We will examine where and from whom he received the ideas that enabled him to be recognized, by Europeans, as the first critical thinker. *All Roads lead to Kemit.*

THE AFRICAN (KEMITIC) ORIGIN OF CRITICAL THINKING

Critical Thinking did not start with Socrates or in ancient Greece for that matter. Like most of the European's claims to ancient knowledge their assertion that the ancient Greeks were the first critical thinkers is inaccurate. Many of the so-called original ideas attributed to the ancient Greeks were, in fact, learned from others.

To their credit it was not the ancient Greeks but the Europeans who came after them who attempted to conceal the origin of their alleged intellectual prowess. In fact, the ancient Greeks for the most part recognized their indebtedness to Kemit without shame. Herodotus, the so-called father of history not only recorded the fact but also recorded that the Kemites were black and had woolly hair.[1] Let us start with the modern view that critical thinking began with Socrates.

SOCRATES: WORLD'S FIRST CRITICAL THINKER?

We should begin by noting that Socrates was indicted, tried and sentenced to death for exposing his *ideas* to the public mind. His death sentence, carried out by his own hand, resulted from his absolute refusal to apologize for his actions, to retract his words, or desist from his prior actions in the future.

Socrates was adamant that he would not be deterred from his mission, even upon the threat of death. But, what had he done that was so heinous as to require the imposition of the death sentence?

Socrates is said to have developed a *new approach*

to knowledge (i.e., new to the Greeks) that included the notion that the *soul was the seat of consciousness*, that the universe was *mind-ordered*, and that *the quality of knowledge is dependent on knowing the essence of things as they really are.* He also taught that there is a *real world different from the world of sense* and that in order to perceive this world of true essence we must first be taught to think.

Socrates is *also credited with* developing the so-called *Socratic method* as a way of substituting inaccurate ideas for accurate ones. He believed that the best way to accomplish that goal was by what I refer to as *thought deconstruction*. That is, to take a *thought construct* (something constructed by the mind) an idea, especially a popular one, and follow it to its logical conclusion, by connecting the ideas inherent in it or implied by it, and *deconstructing* them until you arrive at the *essence of the idea* and then, determine if the *essential* idea is *valid*. We will consider thought deconstruction in detail later in our discussion.

Socrates taught his students to develop *the power of individual, self-driven thinking*. He taught that *political power* and the *power of thought* (he referred to it as philosophy) must be combined for the human race to survive and prosper.

Apparently, Anaxagoras assisted Socrates in the development of his *mind-centered* theories. One chronicler of Socrates records the following as Socrates actual words.

"[t]hen one day I heard a man reading from a book, as he said, by Anaxagoras, that *it is the mind that arranges and causes all things*. I was pleased with this theory of cause, and it seemed to me to be somehow right that the *mind should be the cause of all things* and I thought, 'If this is so, the mind in arranging things arranges everything and establishes each thing as it is best for it to be.... They were *ordered by intelligence*."[2]

I have added the emphasis in the above passage to draw the reader's attention to concepts that we will discuss later that are derived directly from the *Sacred Science* of our ancient ancestors.

It bears repeating here that Socrates was tried and sentenced to death for among other charges, *corrupting the youth of Athens*. Essentially the charge was that he taught them to *use their minds, to question, examine and evaluate everything*. And, that he taught a *foreign doctrine*. It seems, however, that his *real offense* was that he was a *critical thinker, a radical thinker*, if you will, who dared not only to challenge *accepted* belief but who also dared to encourage and train the youth of Athens to think critically and for themselves.

In the indictment of Socrates he was also accused of *atheism* and *introducing new divinities*. It is difficult to understand how he could be both an atheist and an advocate of divinities foreign or domestic. If however, we look to our *ancestral Sacred Science* (as we will later in our discussion) we learn that the *Divine Mind* was the *Neter Neteru* (God of Gods), a divinity, *manifested in thought* that could easily be believed in by one who does not otherwise believe in the existence of god.

When we look at the teachings attributed to Socrates and the words placed in his mouth by Plato and others we cannot help but notice that they sound suspiciously like the teachings contained in our Kemitic *Sacred Science*. But this is as it should be.

Our ancient ancestors gave civilization to the world. They provided humanity with the tools and the example of the heights that human beings could attain when they exercised *control of thought*. Moreover, they accomplished this grand feat while the rest of the world was mired in savagery and brutishness.

This *Sacred Science* was transmitted to the Greeks. Unfortunately, the Greeks only partially understood what they were given. After a time this sacred, powerful and transformative knowledge was permitted to become dormant.

It was not until the Arabs came along and resurrected these sacred teachings and transmitted them to the European world mired in the *Dark Ages*, that the greatness of our ancestral philosophy became known and appreciated anew. It is not insignificant that the resurrection of our sacred teachings precisely coincided with the end of the *European Dark Ages* and the beginning of the so-called *Renaissance*.

Nearly all of Socrates teachers and the persons who are said to have influenced his thinking were students of the priests of ancient Kemit. These include his primary teacher *Anaxagoras*, and other noted Greek philosophers such as *Zeno of Elea*, *Parmenides* and *Heraclitus*. We should also note that both Parmenides and Heraclitus were said to be *Pythagoreans* who learned their doctrines from Pythagoras a student of the priests of Kemit.

The chroniclers of Socrates' life and teachings and from whom we owe the bulk of our knowledge of him (Socrates left no writings of his own) are *Xenophon*, and Socrates' most famous disciple, *Plato*. Oddly, Socrates seems to be the only one of this illustrious group of ancient Greek philosophers who did not study in Kemit. Curious indeed.

We need only look at the alleged teachings of Socrates mentors to discern the profound influence of the *Sacred Science* of our ancestors on the thoughts and ideas that gave rise to Western civilization. Let us begin with the pre-Socratic philosophers—those who taught or influenced Socrates. Most notable among these are *Anaxagoras*, Socrates' teacher, *Zeno of Elea*, *Parmenides* and *Heraclitus*, and the *Pythagoreans*.

ANAXAGORAS

Anaxagoras (c.500–428 BCE) is perhaps the most revealing of Socrates mentors. First, he was Socrates' *teacher* while the others merely *influenced* his thinking. Second, he not only studied in Kemit, but also, with the exception perhaps of Pythagoras, remained truest to the teachings of the *Sacred Science* that he learned there.

Anaxagoras has received the moniker "mind" because of one of the seminal components of his philosophy. He taught that the universe is an *eternal, unchanging dynamic mind* and that all processes in the universe are *expressions* of that mind. He taught that *mind is the force that makes change possible*. He described this mind (Greek, *nous*) as *a vast, infinite, indescribable, rational, universal force* that pervades all things. Although indescribable the operation of this universal mind, according to Anaxagoras, could be seen in natural law because law is the *intelligent activity of mind* and mind is, in turn, a *rational principle of change through natural law*. Anaxagoras was convinced that *universal mind is intelligent, eternal, incorporeal, insubstantial, and responsible for all change*. The universal mind, according to Anaxagoras, perceives and knows everything and since nothing is hidden from it, it can be said to be *intelligent*.

The Pre-Socratic Anaxagoras also opined that the universal mind was at the heart of creation. According to him, prior to the *activity of the mind* nothing existed but *chaos*. Nor did perception exist. In an unknown and unknowable way *mind moved matter* and creation was under way. In so doing the *universal, intelligent, rational mind refined matter* into the world that we know.

Anaxagoras also taught that the universe was comprised of *seeds of varying qualities*. These creative seeds (I call them *seed/ideas*) were, in effect, used by the universal mind to form or create all things.

Finally, Anaxagoras taught the value of *true skepticism* and that *elevated, precise, rational inquiry leads to knowledge*. We should also mention here that Anaxagoras was also a Pythagorean.

ZENO OF ELEA

Zeno of Elea, (490–430 BCE) was associated with the *Eleatic School* founded by *Xenophanes* and was famous for arguing that by *logical thinking* one could show that the popular notions of time and space are erroneous. He went so far as to argue that motion is *logically* impossible. Zeno is also attributed with introducing the *dialectic method* by which truth could be arrived at by *examining the implications of statements* under the rubric that true statements could not lead to false conclusions. Socrates is said to have *refined* this method of examination. He is also said to have met with *Zeno* and later talked with him about his presentation. *Zeno of Elea* studied in Kemit and only after having done so arrived at his ideas on *logical thinking* and the *dialectical method*.

PARMENIDES

Parmenides (b. c. 515 BCE) was another Greek philosopher associated with the Eleatic School who is said to have introduced the method of *reasoned proof for assertions*. He argued that changed motions are *illusions of the senses*. He also used the *dialectic method*. Socrates met and discoursed with Parmenides. Parmenides studied in Kemit and only after having done so arrived at the now famous ideas attributed to him. He was also said to be a Pythagorean.

HERACLITUS

Heraclitus (c. 535–475 BCE) was a Greek philosopher of Ephesus, who taught the *illusory nature of the senses* and the *law of opposites* Heraclitus also proclaimed that the unity underlying all things was the *Word* (Greek *logos*).

He is also recognized as perhaps the most important philosopher before Plato. He too was a *Pythagorean*.

PYTHAGORAS

Only brief mention of Pythagoras will be made here and that only because *Anaxagoras, Parmenides* and *Heraclitus* are all alleged to have been members of the group known as the *Pythagoreans* who were, in turn, the followers or disciples of *Pythagoras*.

We are told that as a young man of eighteen Pythagoras was advised by *Thales of Miletus* (who was known as the greatest pre-socratic philosopher) to go to Kemit to be instructed by the wise men (priests) that instructed him.

Upon his arrival in Kemit Pythagoras studied with the same priests that had instructed Thales. He spent *twenty-two years* there and was eventually initiated into the mysteries of Kemitic *Sacred Science*. During his twenty-two year sojourn in Kemit Pythagoras studied mathematics, astronomy and music. Upon his return to Crotona, Italy, the Crotonian senators were so impressed with his newly acquired wisdom that they built him an institute from which to instruct the youth of Crotona. *As an acknowledgment of the source of his wisdom Pythagoras had a statue of Tehuti, Kemitic God of Divine Intelligence erected at the door to the school.*

This then represents a brief review of the educational backgrounds of the philosophers who taught and/or influenced Socrates.

We have taken this, extended but necessary, tangential journey to emphasize the fact that the concept of *Critical Thinking* is not new and that its conceptual, if not its nominal roots, can be found in the *Sacred Science* of our ancient ancestors.

In short, the ancient Greek's *new approach to thinking* predated them by millennia and, in fact, as they readily admitted, came to them from our ancestors. We hasten to add, however, that this information is necessary to establish *anteriority* not *superiority*. It is also necessary because the very goal of *Critical Thinking* demands it.

THE GOAL OF CRITICAL THINKING

The goal of Critical Thinking is the accurate discernment of reality, or what may closely approximate it, in the process of our thinking, in an effort to insure that our decisions, both mundane and sublime, may be reality-based and the very best they can be. Subsumed in this goal is the knowledge that when critical thinking is achieved as a routine universally accepted and applied approach to thinking we will then be equipped to attain the goal of power proportionality in the United States and the world.

It only seems fitting then that we begin with the truth of the origin of the concept itself. Having done that the next logical question is what is *Critical Thinking* and how does it fit in with our stated overall goal of *Total Black Empowerment through the Creation of Powerful Minds®?*

Critical Thinking (CT) is a process—a series of changes and actions that bring about an intended result. In this case the result is a mental transformation. We will be transformed from a people who routinely and uncritically accept what we are told into people who examine statements and information carefully, critically, before we reach conclusions and take action.

Critical Thinking is a systematic, analytical approach to the discovery of reality. It stimulates, in African Americans, the desire and intention to remove the long- standing obstacles to the acquisition, distribution and control of individual and collective power.

Critical Thinking is also a methodology that serves to focus and systematically direct our attention to what is real, discoverable and verifiable. It is a way to insure that the information we receive and thereafter rely upon to make decisions that affect our lives and fortunes is accurate and reality-based.

Critical Thinking is designed and intended to challenge old patterns of thought for the purpose of generating new ideas, insights and points of view.

Critical Thinking increases the *level of accuracy of our thinking* and increases our *ability to organize our thoughts*, to discern between that which is important and that which may, upon careful analysis, be only apparently so.

Critical Thinking is philosophic in nature and involves the development of *systematic doubt and questioning* as the best way of eliciting a *clear expression of truths* known *implicitly* by all rational beings.

Critical Thinking then, is a positive, constructive method of problem identification, problem analysis and problem solving that leads to new perspectives, ideas, insights, knowledge and creative, innovative ways to approach problems and solutions.

Critical Thinking is the method prescribed by our ancient ancestors and embodied in their and our *Sacred Science* that will enable us to create effective strategies that will insure our attainment of power proportionality, compensation for past labors, and guarantee our survival and prosperity.

When properly understood *Critical Thinking* will be recognized as a *birthright* designed by our ancestors and bequeathed to us with the intention that by it we would survive and prosper and never perish from the earth.

CRITICAL THINKING IS NOT BLACK MILITANCY

"The Negro needs to become radical, and the race will never amount to anything until it becomes so, but this

TOTAL BLACK EMPOWERMENT

radicalism *must come from within."* Dr. Carter G. Woodson

No word in the English language strikes more fear in the hearts of African Americans than the word *radical*. This is a legacy of our centuries old indoctrination at the hands of the European. The European's historical concern with what we *think* is based more on his desire to prevent our discovery of *revolutionary ideas* than our prosecution of an *actual revolution*. He is not afraid of our thinking as much as our thinking *radically*.

I anticipate that critics will make one or more criticisms of the suggestion that African Americans adopt *Critical Thinking techniques*. They will likely conclude that it is *Black radicalism* by another name, or that it is flawed in one or more of the following ways.

First, as to *Critical Thinking* being Black radicalism by another name, I agree with Dr. Woodson, we will never amount to anything unless and until we become *radical from within*.

Let me further state, at the outset, that *Critical Thinking* requires you to critically analyze everything from the root up. *Critical Thinking* will not, however, transform you into a *Black radical* (radical simply means *root*, to be a radical is to get to the root of things). When people refer to *Black radicals* they usually mean *Black militants*. The reader should have no fear on that score either. *Critical Thinking* will not turn you into a militant. It will, however, *transform* you into a *critical thinker* who sees the forest, the trees, *and* the subsoil roots.

Critical Thinking does *not* require you to adopt *radical or militant* ideas. It will, however, cause you to analyze all information critically, and yes, *radically*. The ideas that you ultimately adopt will be the fruit of your own analysis.

A second criticism of *Critical Thinking* will likely be that it only finds *fault*. Although it is certainly true that a critical thinker will find mistakes and errors, if they exist, in the natural course of her analysis, faultfinding is not the *primary* goal of *Critical Thinking*.

A teacher who grades a student's spelling test is not doing so solely for the purpose of finding mistakes in spelling; he does so for the greater purpose of *teaching* the student to spell correctly. The same can be said for the primary purpose of *Critical Thinking*.

The third criticism of *Critical Thinking* will likely be that it creates or in some way fosters vacillation or indecisiveness. We can only respond that if critical thinkers *appear* indecisive to the uninformed it is because they only reach important conclusions when all the evidence is in, or because they will modify, or change completely, a prior conclusion if new evidence warrants it. *Think about it.* Should a person cling tenaciously to a conclusion or decision that he or she knows to be erroneous? Or does wisdom dictate that he or she modify or alter prior decisions accordingly? Anything less would be intellectually dishonest. The so-called indecisiveness of critical thinkers is, on careful analysis, a positive and valuable aspect of *Critical Thinking* that is, nonetheless, frequently misunderstood.

5

WHY CRITICAL THINKING IS ESSENTIAL

The necessity for *Critical Thinking* among African Americans seems axiomatic. It is premised on the assertion that the historic and present state of our individual and collective *power deficiency* is partially the result of two interconnected factors: *impaired information sensors* and *impaired analysis and evaluation techniques.*

IMPAIRED INFORMATION SYSTEMS

All of the information that we receive and rely upon to make daily decisions comes to us, *exclusively*, through our *organic information sensors*. These sensors, commonly known as the five senses (taste, touch, sight, hearing, smell) are, at best, *unreliable* reporters of reality. Although they provide us with vital information, without which we could not function, the information they provide is woefully incomplete.

In fact, this often unrecognized impairment undermines our ability to understand that what we perceive may be and often is, diametrically opposed to what really exists. The salient point here is that *we enter this world equipped with a faulty sensory apparatus.*

Those who are aware of this natural impairment have historically used this knowledge to control and manipulate those who are unaware of it. As a result *we are on notice, from birth, that we can be easily deceived when we rely only on our senses.* Put another way, our ability to detect what is real is naturally impaired and as a result *we must employ additional safeguards to insure that the information that we receive is, in fact, accurate.*

IMPAIRED ANALYSIS AND EVALUATION

The existence of the first factor places us on notice that something is terribly amiss. Clearly, if we are to survive and prosper we must have access to accurate information with which to make the everyday decisions that determine whether we live or die. Surely, we must compensate for our natural, congenital impairment in some way.

Frankly, it is our failure to recognize the first factor that has directly or indirectly contributed to our inability to attain *power proportionality* over the period of nearly four hundred years. This is unavoidably true because knowledge of the first factor leads, logically, to the second. If the information that we routinely receive is known to us to be unreliable, we are simultaneously informed that all information is *potentially impaired* and must, therefore, be analyzed and evaluated for accuracy *before* we rely on it.

We all know at least one person who is an invariably unreliable reporter of facts. As a result of that person's reputation we take everything he or she says with a grain of salt, that is, we do not believe a damn thing they say until it is corroborated or verified in some way. This is common sense. Yet when it comes to the information we rely upon to make vital decisions that can determine our lives and fortunes we *uncritically* accept things on face value.

TOTAL BLACK EMPOWERMENT

An incident that happened to me when I was a child will illustrate the point. In the early 1960's there was a product known as *Diet Rite* bread. This product was advertised as having half the calories of regular bread and, of course, as great for dieters. It turned out that the bread did indeed have half the calories of regular bread but only because the slices of Diet Rite were half the size of regular bread. I heard the expose' on the evening news and promptly relayed the information to my grandmother. I should pause to mention here that my grandmother was the most intelligent person I have ever met. I still rely upon her observations about human nature and how to survive until this day. And it was the example of her uncanny ability to see things clearly that has inspired me during the course of my life. Yet, when I relayed the Diet Rite information to her (she had been using the product) she refused to believe it because—her words—"*they can't lie on television.*" Remember this observation came from the most intelligent person who I have ever met. Yet, she believed that everything on television, or at least in advertisements, had to be true. I dare say that my grandmother's belief was probably not unique among African Americans of the time.

Our naturally Impaired analysis and evaluation skills are exacerbated by the fact that much of our information comes from sources that have demonstrated beyond doubt that they will go to great lengths to mislead and deceive us.

Clearly, these two factors instruct us that *nothing can be accepted on face value* and this rule must apply whether the source of our information is our own senses, our elected leaders, the local pastor or the *New York Times*.

The first factor, that of *impaired information sensors*, is a fact of human existence that can be recognized and understood but cannot be altered, it is, for all intents and purposes, effectively beyond our control. The second factor is controllable and can be effectively remedied by *Critical*

Thinking and the clarity of vision and thought that it inspires.

Critical Thinking then, is a positive, constructive method of problem identification, problem analysis and problem solving that leads to new perspectives, ideas, insights, knowledge and creative, innovative ways to approach problems and solutions.

Critical Thinking necessarily involves three important factors the qualities of which are outcome determinative. These are: *perception, judgment* and *analysis*.

PERCEPTION AND THE FIVE THIEVES

Perception is the doorkeeper of knowledge. Perception controls what we know just as a doorkeeper controls what enters a building. It follows that what we perceive, after analysis, is and can only be, what we *know*.

We gather information/knowledge/data about the world around us by *perception*. In turn, the knowledge that we gather becomes the *storehouse of information* upon which we rely to make vital decisions that affect the lives and circumstances of ourselves, and those for whose care and protection we are responsible.

The word, perceive derives from the Latin *percipere* which means to take something *through* something else. In the act of perceiving we take knowledge/information/data through the *five senses*. To perceive then, is to become aware of something, including reality, through the *senses*.

The word, perceive also means to achieve awareness or understanding, again, through the senses. It follows that perception is the act and the result of perceiving and, simultaneously the awareness of and understanding of reality.

The quality of our thought is determined by the accuracy of our perception. Quality perception is, in turn, determined, at least in part, by the accuracy of our vision. Vision is thought elevated to the next level of its power.

It is inescapable that the validity of our perception is proportionate to: the *accuracy* of the knowledge/information/data perceived; and the *quality* of the analysis to which it is subjected.

The first factor is wholly within the realm of the five senses; our thought processes govern the second. It bears repeating here that all of our knowledge/information/data about reality reaches us, exclusively, through the five senses.

Defined by its simplest reality our knowledge of the world is what our five senses tell us it is. From this we can conclude that reality is of two varieties.

The first variety is the image of reality given to us by our brains by use of the *symbolic sensory messages* delivered to it by our information sensors (the five senses). The second is what is actually out there. The first is our *personal reality;* the second is, theoretically, a *universal reality*.

Our decisions are, more often than not, made on the basis of our *personal* reality and seldom on universal reality. In short, our personal reality, which may be entirely different than universal reality, is dictated by the efficiency of our senses. The point of all this is that our awareness of, and understanding of, reality is based on our ability to *perceive* the world and everything in it *accurately*. Our ability to perceive is, in turn, based on the five senses. To the extent that our senses deliver distorted or inaccurate information, our view of reality will be distorted and inaccurate. When we consider the facts it is apparent that *quality* decision-making is vital to our survival and prosperity. It goes without saying that *a decision is only as good as the accuracy of the information upon which it is based*. As a result we are forced to conclude that we are on *natural notice*, that we must analyze all information that we receive because it comes from an *inherently unreliable source*. When we decide we make *judgments*.

JUDGMENT

Judgment is the *mental power* to form an opinion, to distinguish relationships, or to draw sound conclusions. In order to accomplish the act of judgment one must base that judgment on sound information. The number of judgments we make on a daily basis is astronomical. Without giving it much thought we judge the veracity of everyone that we interact with. Are our children telling us the truth? Does the boss have the right to assign a particular project to me? Is the person requesting my license and registration really a police officer? Is the amount of money requested by the light company accurate? If it is not what can I do about it? Will I need an umbrella today? Is the television meteorologist reliable? When we answer questions like these we necessarily make judgments. Judgment necessarily and unavoidably involves the ability to think. The act of judging then is a part of the thinking process.

Perception provides us the information or data. We reach a more or less sound conclusion about the data and thereby render *judgment*. We render judgment after *analysis*. The linchpin between perception and judgment is analysis.

ANALYSIS

As we have seen perception is the function of the five senses and the brain. Analysis is a form of thinking and is, therefore, a function of the *mind* since the mind functions by and through the process we call thinking.

Analysis means a dissolving, a separation of the whole into its constituent parts for the purpose of study. This form of thinking allows us to separate the whole into smaller parts that each may be more easily understood in their relationships to other units and to the whole. When the information derived through this process is *organized* and *categorized and compared*, analysis has occurred.

Critical Thinking is the *corrective mechanism* without which our perceptions, judgments and analyses are hopelessly doomed to constant, potentially fatal error.

Critical Thinking is a *structured, self-correcting form of thinking*, but it is, at base, *thinking*. In order to fully appreciate the value of *Critical Thinking* we must understand the thinking process itself.

6

THE MECHANICS OF CRITICAL THINKING

In this chapter we will examine the *mechanics* of *Critical Thinking*. I define mechanics here as the functional and technical aspects of an activity. *Critical Thinking* is, among other things, a *mechanism*. It is machine-like in that it is a system of parts that work together like those of a machine. Like a machine *Critical thinking* employs a set of interrelated concepts that together form the complement of techniques that insure that the information that we rely upon to make individual and collective life decisions are reality based. When appropriately applied they allow us to elevate our thinking to the level at which true vision is possible. Among these techniques are *belief deconstruction, logic, scientific method* and the *Nine Essential Questions*.

BELIEF DECONSTRUCTION

Critical Thinking is an effective method of collective belief control. We have previously discussed the fact that belief control is necessary because our beliefs form a set of related, interconnected ideas that we learn from others and transmit to others. As a result our beliefs form not only an individual belief system but a collective belief system as well.

TOTAL BLACK EMPOWERMENT

Belief deconstruction is a short method of analysis that relies on principles utilized in building demolition. In the construction trade deconstruction refers to the method used to demolish a structure while preserving and, if possible, salvaging what may be reused.

The idea of belief deconstruction occurred to me some years ago while working at a construction project. I was assigned the job of moving a large wooden sign to a dumpster. The sign was too heavy for me to lift alone. I decided to break it into smaller pieces that would be easier to carry to the dumpster. The sign was made of oak and try as I might I could not break it. Being unwilling to ask for help (one of my many character flaws) I happened on the idea that since the sign was made of a number of parts nailed together if I first identified the weakest parts and concentrated on those perhaps the whole sign would fall apart. It did. So quickly that I am still amazed.

The key to deconstructing the sign was attacking the weakest point of its construction. In the case of the sign it turned out to be the places where the boards were joined together. The boards were joined with nails. While the oak itself was far too strong for me to break, a deftly placed rap with a hammer at the point where the boards were joined and *voila* the nails would loosen and the boards would fall apart by their own weight. Belief deconstruction applies the same concepts to beliefs and ideas.

Generally speaking ideas are connected. In most cases our beliefs and belief systems are mental constructions just as buildings are physical constructions. Like physical buildings they are constructed from component parts. The individual parts give strength to the overall construction. Just as a chain is only as strong as its weakest link, beliefs are only as valid as their weakest component idea.

Belief deconstruction works by attacking the weakest component idea, that is the point where the ideas are joined together. I should note here that this idea is intended for use when critically thinking about our own personal beliefs. It is a tool of *Critical Thinking*. I do not recommend it as a tool for debate. If a thought/idea/belief does not survive thought deconstruction it is not worthy of belief. An example seems appropriate here.

How often have you heard someone remark, "It's the law—it must be obeyed or society would fall apart." This belief is hard to understand in the case of the average American. It is incredible that many African Americans also hold this belief. It comprises the following beliefs: (1) the law, for some unexplained reason, must be obeyed; and (2) that it is the law that holds society together.

Let us apply the concept of belief deconstruction to this oft-repeated maxim—*the law must be obeyed*. The law is simply an edict passed by a group of legislators and backed by the state's law enforcement power apparatus. The question is why must it be obeyed? Is it because the law is always right or just? Or perhaps it is because the law is the product of exceptional wisdom, divine intervention or inspiration? Or is it because the legislators are themselves so wise, holy or righteous? Of course, the answer is a resounding no in each case. Then why must the law always be obeyed? Who said so? Since we have already ruled out God it must be a human being. Clearly, human beings make mistakes. Are we then to believe that even mistakes are to be obeyed?

Let us use an example from history that will sufficiently illustrate the insanity of the stated position.

For more than 200 years it was lawful to enslave Africans in the American colonies. After the colonies became states and well into the 19th Century slavery remained lawful. Slave holding was codified in the laws of many states. Without exception these laws presumed all Negroes to be slaves. The burden of proving free status was on the Negro. Is it logical to assume that Negroes obeyed these laws simply because they were laws? Or were the laws obeyed

TOTAL BLACK EMPOWERMENT

because of the massive enforcement power of the state?

Let us assume that the Congress of the United States passed a bill making slavery lawful once again (disregard for the moment the fact that slavery is still *legal* in the United States). Let us further assume that the President of the United States signed the bill into law and the United States Supreme Court upheld its constitutionality? Would African Americans feel obliged to obey the law? Would you? Would you immediately give up freedom and resign yourself to a life of slavery simply because *the law must be obeyed?* Would you care that society would fall apart if you chose not to obey the law? *Think about it.*

The popular justification for the idea that the law must be obeyed is that without laws society would fall apart. This argument is so weak as to be insulting. Its popularity arises from the fact that it is so often repeated. People are generally fearful of chaos. Make them believe that chaos ensues in a society without laws and they will fear society without government.

On this score we need only mention that the concept of government is abhorred by anarchists the world over. Anarchists believe that government is completely unnecessary. The anarchist view has always been anathema in this country. The anarchist has been viewed as a criminal in his *thinking.* His ideas were to be rooted out for fear that they would inflame the nation and bring about a reign of terror and chaos.

What are the *anarchist opinions* that are so vile as to make one an *enemy of all mankind* for merely holding them? You be the judge. Simply put, anarchists believe among other things that government is the enemy of the people and is itself unnecessary.

Curiously, anarchists hold views similar to those of our most ancient ancestors the *Twa* people of equatorial Africa who when asked by Europeans to take them to their leader only laughed. They found the question amusing because they never had a leader or government and never saw the reason for either.

The point here is that there are multiple sides to every issue. When we uncritically accept the view given as if it were the *only* view we do a great disservice to the power of our *divine intelligence* and its ability to find answers when given all of the information. Those who would have us remain mentally shackled to misinformation for the purpose of controlling and manipulating us are well served by our failure to be critical thinkers.

LOGIC

Critical Thinking also employs the principles of logic to evaluate new information. *Logic*, as an academic discipline, is defined as the study of the *principles of reasoning*. *Logic* also instructs us that there are *rules of correct argument* that allow us to eliminate *invalid* arguments at the outset. Let us briefly review a few of the rules of logic pertinent to our present discussion.

We are often persuaded to accept or reject information, whether written or verbal, by arguments that we find *persuasive*. Often persuasive arguments appeal to emotion or rely on some form of "proof" that is not, on careful analysis, proof at all. Let us begin by defining our terms. The key words are *argument, assertion, persuasion* and *validity*.

To persuade is to induce to undertake a course of action or embrace a point of view by means of argument, reasoning, or entreaty. The word comes from the Latin *persuadere* and means to urge. When someone is persuaded he is caused to take a particular action or believe a certain point of view by argument.

An argument is a course of reasoning aimed at demonstrating truth or falsehood. Put another way, an argument is a group of propositions one of which is said to follow from the others. Arguments consist of premises and conclusions. A premise is an assertion upon which a conclusion is based. A conclusion is the product of reason that validates the premise.

According to the rules of logic an assertion or argument may be fallacious. Assertions and arguments that may seem accurate but are, in reality, false are called *fallacies*. We will look at some popular fallacies that the critical thinker will be wise to question whenever they appear. These are fallacies of *ambiguity*, and fallacies of *relevance*.

Fallacies of Ambiguity are those that are attributable to intentional or unintentional inaccurate use of language. This brand of fallacy confuses the separate meanings of the key words or phrases, shifts the emphasis of key words, attributes the characteristics of the parts to the whole, or attributes to the parts the characteristics of the whole.

Fallacies of Relevance are those whose premises are logically irrelevant to their conclusions. This brand of fallacy attacks the person rather than the argument, or ridicules the argument, appeals to emotion, attempts to justify what is wrong by citing other examples of the wrong, or justifies the wrong because it is widely accepted, or alters the argument to make it easier to attack than the original argument, or insists on the legitimacy of the argument despite contradictory facts.

As an academic discipline logic teaches us that we must, in the first instance, critically analyze the form in which the argument is presented. This is significant because an argument may sometimes be summarily disposed of simply because the *form* in which it is presented is *invalid*. Anytime the premise of the argument does not comport with its stated conclusion the argument is invalid. This may seem like quibbling but it is a key component in the quest for truth. Because it is a colossal waste of time and energy there is no logical reason why we should be required to perform an exercise in futility by the pursuit of an argument that is improperly presented. We will now briefly discuss the method of investigation known as the *scientific method*.

SCIENTIFIC METHOD

The *scientific method* is a method of investigation that involves the *gathering, evaluation* and *interpretation* of information for the purpose of ascertaining its validity and to arrive at a reasonable explanation. This technique is important because it assembles a framework with which we are able to approach all information in a scientific manner. In the context of *Critical Thinking* the scientific method refers to *problem solving*, and *strategic planning*.

Scientific Method entails five discrete, interconnected steps. These are:
- *isolation* of the problem to be solved;

- *gathering* of known facts about the problem;

- *formulation* of an hypothesis regarding the problem;

- making logical *inferences* about the problem; and

- *verification* of the inferences (from hypothesis to theory)

PROBLEM ISOLATION

It is not a coincidence that the first step in our version of the scientific method requires that we *isolate* the problem. It seems obvious that before we can state a problem accurately and concisely, we must know what the problem is. In order to determine what the problem is we must set it apart, separate it, isolate it from problems that may be tangentially related but are not the *necessary cause*.

The importance of this seemingly minor distinction is illustrated when we consider that causes may be categorized as *necessary or sufficient, necessary and sufficient, or contributory*. A *necessary* cause is one that must be present for the problem to exist. The *sufficient* cause is one that is, by itself, enough for the problem to exist. The *necessary and sufficient* cause is one that must be present and will, by itself, cause the existence of the problem. A *contributory* cause is one that helps to create the problem but does not rise to the level of necessary or sufficient causation.

When we seek to isolate a problem so that we may state it accurately and concisely for the purpose of applying scientific method, we are really attempting to determine the necessary or necessary and sufficient cause. By way of example, imagine that you are confronted with the following set of facts:

You awaken one morning to find your basement flooded with water. You immediately realize that the flow of water can be stopped by turning off the water at the main. You do so and proceed to bail the unwanted water from the basement. Have you solved the problem? Depends on what the problem is. If the problem is to get the unwanted water out of the basement you have succeeded. If, however, the problem is to stop the basement from being flooded again, you have utterly failed. What have you done wrong? You have failed to isolate the problem before you attempted to solve it. You failed to determine the necessary cause, the one that must exist for the problem to exist.

You determined that you could stop the flow of water by turning off the flow of water at the main. Although that strategy solved the immediate problem, of continued water flow, it did not solve the *real* problem. Why? Because the water flow was contributory to the problem of the flooded basement, it was even sufficient, but it was not necessary. Clearly, the water is always turned on at the main. So why is it that on this particular occasion the basement is flooded?

Critical Thinking and the application of the *Scientific Method* require you to search further. When you continue your analysis you find that the real cause, the necessary cause, the cause without which the problem would not exist and by which the problem may be solved, the *necessary and sufficient cause* is a *broken water pipe*.

Let us carry this brief analysis to its logical conclusion. Having failed to find the necessary and sufficient cause you have solved the immediate problem, that is, stopped the flow of water and bailed out the basement, but you have not solved the *real* problem. Sooner or later you realize that by turning off the water at the main you have cut off the supply of water to the entire house. No bathing, drinking or cooking water is available. As a result of your failure to *isolate the real problem,* you have created another, separate and distinct set of problems to solve. Now you have to get water from another source because if you turn the water back on the basement will be flooded again. No matter how many times you turn off the water and bail out the basement the *real* problem will remain. Of course, had you established, at the outset, what the necessary and sufficient cause of the problem was, you would have simply replaced the busted water pipe and *voila!* The problem would have been solved, once and for all.

GATHERING FACTS

Gathering known facts about the problem is nothing more than *research*. It is the necessary task of finding information about the problem in order to carry out the overall function of problem solving. Problem solving requires information in the form of relevant facts.

The gathering of relevant information is indispensable. We should never be in the position of reinventing the wheel. Trite as it may sound, this is, indeed, the *information age*. Information about virtually every topic imaginable is assembled daily. The amount of information available doubles every three years.

There was a time when information was hidden from us. When we literally took our lives into our hands by letting it be known that we could even read. For the first time in our history in America we have access to facts and information on a par with others. Our access to information is unprecedented. We can now compete in the information big leagues. There is no excuse for our not being able to gather the relevant facts and information sufficient to solve any of the problems with which we are confronted. Let us remember though that quality research absolutely requires *Critical Thinking*.

HYPOTHESIS FORMULATION

Once we have *isolated* the problem, stated it *accurately* and *concisely*, once we have *gathered* the information (facts) that permit us to know all that we can about the problem we confront, we are ready to *formulate* a hypothesis.

A hypothesis is an *interim explanation that accounts for the facts and that can be tested or verified*. Put another way, the hypothesis sets forth a *plausible* explanation of the facts that have been gathered, and explains the problem in terms of the facts. We seek a *plausible* explanation at this point because an explanation that is *implausible* is not likely to be worth the time necessary to investigate it. We also look for *plausibility* rather than possibility because virtually anything in *possible*. If we establish a possibility standard we cannot exclude anything. The plausibility standard, on the other hand, allows us to exclude ideas that do not appear to be worthy of belief.

To say that the hypothesis is *interim* means that it is subject to verification and may be modified as we go along. The hypothesis is our *working explanation*. It provides the *framework* for our thinking and subsequent investigation. In problem solving half the battle is won when we have formulated an accurate hypothesis.

HYPOTHESIS AND THEORY CONTRASTED

A hypothesis is defined as "... a tentative explanation that accounts for a set of facts and can be tested by further investigation." A theory is a "... set of statements or principles devised to explain a group of facts or phenomena, esp; one that has been repeatedly tested or is widely accepted." It follows that hypothesis precedes theory and only becomes theory when it has been repeatedly tested and widely accepted.

INFERENCE/REASONING

Having established a working hypothesis we must now draw *inferences* from the facts we have uncovered as the result of our investigation. An inference is an *extrapolation*. It is the act of deriving unknown information from known information. When we infer, we reach conclusions based upon information that we believe to exist, but that is not explicitly stated.

Reasoning is simply *logical thinking*. As obvious as this may appear many people do not think *logically*. *Thinking is a process*. As such it requires a series of steps. Logic is simply a *technique* by which the steps may be carried out. Logic is a set of rules that facilitate correct reasoning. Logical thinking then, is reasoning that is in accord with the rules of correct reasoning. There are two types of logical reasoning, *formal* and *informal*.

FORMAL/INFORMAL REASONING

Formal reasoning is based on procedures developed in applied logic that are used to reach valid conclusions. *Informal reasoning*, on the other hand, involves the determination of the validity of a conclusion based on available supportive evidence.

While formal reasoning utilizes standardized rules, informal reasoning has no such structural formula. Most of our everyday reasoning is done *informally*. As a result, in most cases, we use only the evidence available to us (known by us) at the time to determine the validity of our conclusions. Of course, the evidence available to us at any given time may be insufficient, misleading, partially or even completely inaccurate. That we use informal reasoning to make the vast majority of our decisions only underscores the urgent need for the adoption of *Critical Thinking*.

Reasoning is also a process by which we *systematically gather and connect* at least two bits of information: that which is presented (new information) and that which we compare it with (previously stored information), to reach valid conclusions.

It bears repeating here that the purpose of thinking is at base, *problem solving*. It allows us to answer questions and develop strategies. In fact, all thinking is the act of problem solving. Even when our thinking is abstract, theoretical or philosophical we seek answers to conceptual problems regarding the existence of god or the problem of evil or the origins of the universe, the purpose or our thinking is *problem solving*.

Thinking is *problem solving* because the thought process requires us to *sense* information/data/stimuli and then solve the *generic* problem of what to do with it. In each instance we are required to *identify* the information (what is it—what does it mean?); *compare* it with previously stored information (have I encountered it before?); *decide* what action to take (how shall I deal with it?); and *carry out* the action decided on (make it happen!).

It can be seen from this that the thought process is also *naturally organizational and innovative*. It is *organizational* in that it naturally arranges information in coherent form. It is *naturally innovative* in that it combines newly received information with previously stored information *to create ideas* and *thoughts*, often *transcendent in nature*, which may or may not have previously existed.

VERIFICATION

Verification is simply the process that we employ to determine if our working hypothesis is, in fact, *plausible*. It entails not only the systematic examination of sources but also exacting scrutiny of the conclusions these sources have reached. Note that at this point in our analysis we are not attempting to determine if we are right, but whether we are on the *right track*. In this way we are able to discard hypotheses that are invalid early on and move on to those that are more promising. When our hypothesis has been verified we are able to test it, as theory, by the same exacting standards that we employed in the verification process.

We can see from this that in order to be *effective* thinking must be *systematic*. For the vast majority of us, however, thinking is anything but systematic. Our thinking is most often *random, disjointed, unfocused* and *non-directional*. This is primarily because we have, in Dr. Woodson's words, been "... taught facts ... but have never been taught to think." *Critical Thinking* teaches us *how to think* by employing a *systematic approach* to problem solving.

The thinking process, as we have seen, begins when our senses provide us with raw data (information) about the outside world. The information received is compared with previously stored information then organized, categorized and stored to form the *information base* upon which we rely to make future plans and decisions. A brief digression is required here to insure that the reader understands the fundamental difference between *fact, opinion* and *inference.*

FACT — OPINION — INFERENCE

The thinking process also involves the important ability to distinguish between *fact, opinion* and *inference.*

A *fact* is something that has real, demonstrable existence. *Opinion* is defined as a belief or conclusion held with confidence but not substantiated by proof. Put another way, an opinion is a belief without facts to support it.

An *inference* is a conclusion deduced from facts not explicitly stated. An example will illustrate the importance of recognizing the distinction between fact, opinion and inference in our reasoning.

Two identical jars are presented. Each is labeled as grape jam; one contains a purple substance, the other is empty. We smell and taste the substance in the first jar and conclude, *by examination*, that it is, *in fact*, grape jam. We can then state that it is a *fact* that the first jar contains grape jam and is, therefore, correctly labeled.

The second jar is empty, clean and bone dry. It contains no residue, smell or taste. We cannot state, as *fact*, that the jar has ever contained grape jam. We may logically *infer*, however, from our experience with the first jar that the second *may have* contained grape jam at one time. This inference is not, however, a *fact*. The jar may have contained grape jam, but it may also be a jar that never contained anything but air. *Inference is not necessarily factual.*

If we are asked to determine if the jam in the first jar is good, or tasty, all we can offer by way of answer is an *opin-*

ion that is a necessarily subjective evaluation not based on objective fact. We could also conclude that there had to be jam in the jar at one time because the label says so. That too, is an *opinion*, not a *fact*.

Facts are the raw material of the thinking process. Facts enable us to reach valid conclusions more or less free from prejudice and bias. Logical thinking requires that we clearly distinguish between fact, opinion and inference.

Critical Thinking makes logical thinking mandatory, because it requires us to examine *all information* critically.

Of course, the importance of the distinction is best understood when we consider that the information that we store in our Long Term Memory will invariably be accepted and recorded as *fact*. We can reach conclusions that are factual because they are based on fact, but, we can also reach conclusions that we *register* as fact, but that are actually based on opinion or inference. As a result every time such information is recalled it will be recalled as *fact*.

Critical Thinking serves to separate fact from opinion and inference, and also organizes and categorizes facts as important or trivial. Although Critical Thinking serves to train our minds to evaluate/examine all information, without regard to its source, it is most effective in its application to problem solving.

Critical Thinking requires that when we receive new information, we must ask and answer satisfactorily a series of *Nine Threshold Questions* before the information is deposited in our *Long Term Memory*.

7

THE NINE THRESHOLD QUESTIONS

That these are referred to as *threshold Questions* is itself instructive. The word threshold is of Middle English origin and the original meaning was *to thresh*. Threshing is an agricultural process by which the seed is separated from the harvested plant.

Threshold has the additional meanings of the point of entering or beginning; the point at which a psychological effect begins to be produced; and the point above which something is true and below which it is not. All of the definitions are appropriate here. Our threshold questions serve to separate the seed from the stalk, produce a psychological effect and set the bar for the finding of reality.

THE NINE THRESHOLD QUESTIONS ARE:

- WHAT IS IT?
- CAN IT BE BELIEVED?
- WHAT IS THE EVIDENCE THAT IS CLAIMED TO SUPPORT IT?
- CAN THE SUPPORTING EVIDENCE BE VIEWED IN ANOTHER WAY?
- WHAT, IF ANYTHING, IS MISSING?
- IS THERE OTHER RELIABLE, INDEPENDENT SUP-

TOTAL BLACK EMPOWERMENT
PORT FOR THE CLAIM?
- HOW AM I EXPECTED TO RESPOND TO THE INFORMATION?
- WHAT IS THE SOURCE OF THE INFORMATION?
- HOW IS THE INFORMATION PRESENTED?

These threshold questions represent the core of the mechanism by which *Critical Thinking* operates. They are important questions because they provide a *critical standard* by which all information should be judged. Let us briefly examine the principles underlying each one of these questions that we may attain a full understanding of the reason for their use in *Critical Thinking*.

WHAT IS IT?

This is the *identification* question. We live our lives under the *constant bombardment of ideas*. Ideas come to us through television, radio, newspapers, from preachers, teachers, politicians, friends, spouses. Virtually everyone and everything we come in contact with is the bearer, carrier or transmitter of ideas that we are, directly or indirectly, encouraged to accept. So, we must begin by asking what is it? What is this idea that I am being asked to believe or accept? When we receive symbolic sensory messages the first thing that our innate information processing system does is *identify* the message. It asks *what is it? Is it new or has it been experienced before?* Likewise, *Critical Thinking* requires us to determine, as a threshold matter, exactly what it is we are dealing with.

In most cases, we are required to identify the idea that we are being asked or encouraged to believe or accept. From books to commercials, to the blandishments of TV evangelists we are asked to believe or merely accept an *idea*. Because the belief in, or acceptance of, the *primary idea* leads to the development of *secondary, connected ideas*, the importance of scrutinizing the *primary idea* cannot be overemphasized.

The primary idea is the *foundational* idea that if accepted will lead over time to the acceptance of other, often more controversial ideas that you might not accept if they were presented first or in a vacuum. In this sense the primary idea may not always be the first idea presented, but it is always the *most important*. Example: all of the slick advertising in the world will not sell you a product unless you first believe that you have a need for it. The primary idea is the *need*. First they convince you that you have halitosis then they sell you the product designed to cure it.

CAN IT BE BELIEVED?

When we are confronted with a new idea, we are simultaneously confronted with the question of whether, on its face, it is likely or unlikely to be true. Oftentimes, ideas are, on their face, so incredible that they cannot possibly be true. Surprisingly, we routinely accept such ideas, claims and other information, without examination. The pitfalls of such an approach to thinking seem too obvious to require comment. If it does not *seem* right, chances are it is not right. If it appears too good to be true, chances are it is not true. Our initial determination of whether an idea is believable or even plausible is *critical*. This is not because it is in some way guaranteed to be accurate, but because it can be a tremendous time and energy saver. If I am told that a woman had a baby without having had intercourse with *someone (invitro fertilization excepted)* I do not have to be a rocket scientist to reject that idea out of hand. It is unbelievable on its face.

WHAT EVIDENCE SUPPORTS THE IDEA?

Sometimes claims that appear, on their face, to be *unbelievable* are, in fact, true. Because of this fact *Critical*

Thinking will not permit the analysis to end here.

When we are presented with information or ideas that we conclude are unbelievable, *on their face*, we must demand and receive supportive evidence or the idea must be rejected.

Supportive evidence is information that when taken as a whole, tends to support or verify a claim. It is evidence that must be considered even when an idea is unbelievable on its face.

We should also note here that the more incredible the claim the more exacting the supportive evidence must be. Just remember here that it is always the responsibility of the person making the claim or presenting the idea to provide the supportive evidence. We are never required to *disprove* a claim. Nor is the fact that a particular claim is not *disprovable* make it true or worthy of acceptance or belief.

CAN THE EVIDENCE BE VIEWED ANOTHER WAY?

Sometimes evidence may be presented as supportive that is *ambiguous*. Evidence that is *ambiguous* is evidence that may be viewed in at least two senses. Ambiguous supporting evidence requires us to ask what else we need to know before it can be accepted as proof of the validity of the claim. The importance of this step is that it alerts us to the fact that evidence in support of the claim or idea does not *necessarily* prove the claim.

WHAT IS MISSING?

Another reason we may initially find a claim *unbelievable* is because we have the distinct impression that something is *missing*. The feeling is like a computer prompt that tells you that more information needed. It directs and focuses our attention on the search for the specific information needed in order to verify the claim. In many cases a computer will not proceed with the program unless and until the information is provided. *Critical Thinking* serves the same purpose.

This step requires us to focus on what we are *not* being told. Oftentimes what we are not told is as important as what we are told. When information is intentionally hidden or downplayed the presentation amounts to *deception*.

WHO ELSE ACCEPTS THE IDEA AS TRUE?

We are not here asking whether your Aunt Sarah believes it. What is meant here is that normally if a claim has validity some other *reliable, independent source* has verified and accepted it. We may, therefore, need to determine if other verification exists. We are really asking if there is another reliable, independent source of evidence or proof.

We have all heard of individuals whose ideas have been so original, so elevated, so far and above other thinkers of their time, that initially there was no general acceptance of their ideas. We also know that such persons are so few an far between as to not present a problem for our analytical process. We also know that historically the reason for the refusal to accept new ideas has often been the fact that the new idea in some way undermines, contradicts or disproves accepted beliefs. What we are talking about here is a *general* acceptance of the underlying premises upon which the claim or idea is based and not necessarily on the conclusion reached.

HOW AM I EXPECTED TO RESPOND?

Most *directed* information, that is information that has been directed to a particular audience, has a *purpose*. The purpose is seldom to provide knowledge for knowledge sake. More often than not directed information is intended to cause the receiver to respond in some way. It could be a request for you to purchase some product, or to influence you to take a position on some issue.

In order to properly evaluate such information it is helpful to know why it has been created and how we are expected to respond to it. If you know that a particular item of information was created to deceive you or to obscure other information that might benefit you, or to influence you to adopt a position that you would not otherwise adopt, you would not be likely to rely upon it or would seek other less biased sources.

WHAT IS THE SOURCE?

Some observers have concluded that the critical analysis process requires you to determine the source of the information *first*. Here we take the opposite approach simply because although the source is an important factor it is not of *primary* importance. We must be guided here by the fact that the source of the information is *irrelevant* to an analysis of the value and validity of the information itself. If the grand dragon of the Ku Klux Klan provides information to me that is timely, accurate and useful am I expected to disregard it because the source is a white supremacist? Of course not! Just as it is counterproductive to reject information solely because of the source, it is also counterproductive to focus our analysis on the source before we evaluate what the information is and whether or not it is believable on its face. That being said let us look more closely at sources in general.

Obviously, all information that we receive *originates* somewhere. It is the *point of origin* of the information that our source question seeks to uncover. A source may refer to primary, secondary or tertiary sources. A source can also be a *person* who provides information.

Primary sources are first-hand observers—those who actually witnessed the event and in some way recorded their observations. Secondary sources are those who have recorded what someone else claims to have witnessed first-hand. Tertiary sources are everything else.

Primary sources represent the best information. But, it must be remembered that even the primary source may be inaccurate in his or her observation, or biased in recording it. At best the observer *interprets* what he or she has observed.

Secondary sources are, at best, *interpretations of interpretations*. We should also note here that observers do not record *everything* they observe, rather they record what they think is *important*. What they think is important is, in large part, determined by what they want to prove to disprove.

Source questions also seek to *identify* the person or organization that originates the information. If you know that a source has a reputation for shading the truth or for being unreliable in reporting facts, or for biased reporting, his or her word will be suspect. A person who is widely known for veracity will likely be considered a more reliable and credible source. This is not to say, however, that either source is accurate as to a given set of facts. Again, *Critical Thinking* requires that *all* sources be scrutinized, *critically*.

HOW IS THE INFORMATION PRESENTED?

We have saved this question for last because it directs our attention to the fact that the presentation of the argument or assertion may itself indicate, without further analysis that it is *invalid*. When this scenario presents itself we need not investigate further. According to the *rules of logic* certain arguments and assertions are simply unworthy of further consideration because of the form in which they are presented.

Critical Thinking represents an *elevated* or higher level of thinking. It shifts into high gear, or is at its greatest level of effectiveness, when we are confronted with a situation or set of facts that we perceive as *problematical*. The key word here is *perceive*. If we fail to perceive the situation as problematical our attention function will simply ignore it or assign it to the automatic/habitual response category.

As we have seen perception is a function of our five senses. But, perception is multi-dimensional as well. Perception has both *sensory* and *interpretative* dimensions. That which our senses perceive must be *interpreted*. When we interpret we explain or clarify the meaning of something. When we explain something we define it, we *make it comprehensible*, in modern parlance we *make it plain*. Interpretation necessarily involves our attitudes, beliefs and belief systems at every stage of the process. When we *interpret* we give *meaning* to the symbols from which we construct our thoughts.

8

THINKING AS PROBLEM SOLVING

The core function of thinking is *problem solving*. When a problem is entirely new, that is it has never been encountered before, and no solution, *known to us* exists, the thinking process develops *innovation, recombination* and *creativity*.

INNOVATION

Innovation is the process of taking the information (data/knowledge) stored in the Long Term Memory (after re-evaluation, if necessary) and then recombining it with *new information* to formulate *new ideas* and strategies that did not previously exist. Innovation is a *creative tool* whose primary function is the *recombination of information*.

RECOMBINATION

Recombination, like innovation, is a natural process that operates with or without our being consciously aware of it. Recombination is the *soul of creativity* and the *heart of invention*. Our definition of recombination is analogous to the definition given it in the science of genetics.

In genetics recombination is defined as *a new combi-*

nation of genes that appears in offspring that were not present in either of its parents. This phenomenon may also be understood as a *mutation*. Why and how these processes occur is still unknown.

Understood in the context of the thinking process, recombination is marked by the appearance of entirely new ideas (thought mutations) that did not exist in the Long Term Memory or the new information presented. Of course, the information contained in the Long Term Memory and the new information is equivalent to the parents of the new idea.

It should be remembered here that not all mutations are successful. Some mutations prove to be ill adapted for survival and simply die out. Thought mutations, like their genetic counterparts manage to coexist with superior ideas for significant periods of time but they too, eventually, die out.

The seemingly inexplicable durability of illogical, ill-conceived thought mutations has been referred to as a *thought vortex* that continues to maintain its powerful hold over the minds of otherwise intelligent, logical individuals and groups in spite of the existence of other, more logical, more persuasive and contradictory ideas. We will look more closely at *thought vortices* in the section on mind.

In the thinking process innovation and recombination are natural, but even positive thought mutations will only be effective in the marketplace of ideas and survive to influence the thinking of the present and future generations when the information upon which they are based is accurate, timely and useful.

CREATIVITY

Creativity is the *power* to create. It is the ability to bring original, new ideas into existence. The new idea is really nothing more than the *recombination* of preexisting ideas. Recombination is a natural process. Creativity is learned. Creativity develops from the ability to "see" connections. Often things that are connected do not, at first glance, reveal their underlying connections. It is often the appar- ently unrelated ideas that will bear the greatest fruit when they are examined for connections.

The quest to find underlying connections and thereby develop creative ideas is best understood as a search for *synergy*.

SYNERGY

The word synergy comes from the Greek *synergos* meaning working together, and implies, for the purposes of our discussion, the working together (relationship), of seemingly unrelated ideas, in a way that results in the development of other ideas that are greater (more productive, forceful, innovative) than the individual ideas from which they emerged. Synergy is a form of creativity.

Synergy is also a *power*. It is the energy created when things, in this case ideas, work together. Synergies may be discovered by investigation; the techniques of investigation may be taught, hence, *creativity may be taught*. Innovation, Recombination and Creativity operate effectively, if and only if: (1) the thinker is *not* a victim of circular reasoning; and (2) the information contained in the Long Term Memory is *accurate, timely* and *useful* for the purpose for which it is intended.

Thinking is the act of *processing* information. The thinking process enables us to receive (actually *sense*) information and then asks us to *solve the problem* of what to do with it. Each bit of information we receive presents the same question and it is the accuracy of our responses that determines success or failure.

In order to *solve* the problem we are required to *identify* the information (what is it?); *compare* it with previous memory/experience (have I seen it before?); *decide* what action to take in response to it (how shall I deal with it?); and *execute* the action decided to be necessary (make it happen!). This is normal, *linear* thinking. It should not surprise us that thinking is a *linear* in operation. We know that the shortest distance between two points is a straight line. Nor should it surprise us that In its most *efficient* functioning *thought progresses in a straight* line from sensory input to problem identification, to dissection of the problem into constituent parts, and finally to problem resolution.

The effectiveness of the thinking process is inextricably linked to the accuracy or quality of the information stored in our *Long Term Memory*. When new information is received each of the questions that we are required to ask in order to solve the problem rely on *previously stored information*. In other words, the *quality* of the answers to questions is directly linked to the *accuracy* of the information we have stored in our *Long Term Memories*. It is this information that determines the quality and accuracy of our decisions.

Critical Thinking serves the purpose of insuring, to the greatest extent possible, that information contained in our *Long Term Memory*, and upon which we rely to make decisions, is as accurate as humanly possible. It does so by *disciplining our minds* to ask the appropriate questions *before* the information is stored. *Critical Thinking* is absolutely essential because once the information is stored it will, invariably, be accepted and *retrieved* as accurate.

Critical Thinking trains our minds. It forces us to seek concrete verification of claims presented to us and finds worthy for storage only that which has been verified by more or less exhaustive analysis.

Critical Thinking tests incoming information. It tests claims, hypotheses, theories and strategies whether they are the product of our own thinking, or presented to us by other sources. It does so by use of *scientific method* and rejects that which does not stand up under rigorous examination.

Critical Thinking guards our mental survival arsenal. The information contained in our long-term memory is, in effect, the *ammunition* that we use in our daily battle to prevent inaccurate information and ineffective, ill-conceived strategies from finding their way into our *mental survival arsenal.* Just as perception is the doorkeeper of knowledge, *Critical Thinking* is the guardian of the *sacred vault* that is our memory.

Critical Thinking develops the innate human ability to compare. It does so by use of methodical questions that focus our attention on what is important regarding ultimate decisions and, perhaps more importantly, regarding the information necessary to make those decisions.

Critical Thinking enhances and elevates our Thought Power. It does so by demonstrating that thinking is a *power.* It is a two-step method of *systematic inquiry.* Through this two-step process we are able to develop our innate *thought power,* to unimaginable levels.

RECAPITULATION

We have now come full circle. *Critical Thinking* alerts us to the fact that our perceptions must be as accurate as humanly possible and provides us with a methodology for insuring that they are. This, in turn, assures that the content of our *Long Term Memory* is accurate so that the vital decisions and strategies we make and employ are the very best that they can be.

Critical Thinking is important to the *Black Empowerment process* because when we understand the thinking *process,* we are forced to conclude that our perceptions are, and have always been, inherently unreliable. Being aware of this fact, we are compelled to take action to compensate for that deficiency.

When we are *unaware* of this fact we necessarily fail to subject this inherently unreliable information (data, knowledge) to careful and intense scrutiny. The result is that we have developed a wide range of strategies and tactics that have, for the most part failed precisely because they have been based, in large part, on inaccurate and therefore unreliable information.

If we remember that individually and collectively, the decisions that we make, the strategies and tactics that we employ in the quest for empowerment will only be as effective, reliable, and useful as the information (data, knowledge) upon which they are based, we will understand that *Critical Thinking* is the foundation, the bedrock, the analytical underpinning of our quest, and the first step on the journey toward *Total Black Empowerment*.

What the mind power primer you are now reading is intended to do is lay the foundation that is prerequisite to our understanding of the concept of *Total Black Empowerment*. We are creating a *new and revolutionary thinking process* that promises to take us from subservience to success (individually and collectively) in our social, political and economic affairs.

The process is *radical*. But is it only so because we will require *radical thinking* and *radical ideas* if we sincerely wish to extricate ourselves and our people from the morass of impotence that has robbed us and our children of their share of the wealth of a nation that our ancestors did as much and more to build than any of the others who now sanctimoniously proclaim themselves to be Americans.

We must think critically, logically and yes, radically. We believe that once the foundation is securely in place our understanding will soar and our overall objective will be accomplished quickly, and methodically.

PART II

THE MIND

9

THE ANCIENT CONCEPT OF MIND

INTRODUCTION

Critical Thinking is a method of thinking that, of course, operates in the *mind*. It only seems logical that our analysis of thinking demands a discussion of the mind to insure that our understanding is as complete as possible as we continue the intellectual journey in our quest for *Total Black Empowerment through the Creation of Powerful Minds®*.

It is a sad fact that modern science knows so little about the mind. This apparent dearth of information is not because information does not exist. It results from the fact that modern scientists, departing from ancient practice, have adopted the view that what cannot be quantified does not exist. Mind falls squarely into that category. It is important that the reader understand that this science/spirituality separation is relatively new. Having recently divorced itself from spirituality, science now refuses to pursue the intangible, metaphysical aspects of existence. Our ancestors were not of so narrow a frame of mind. Their researches make the mind central to our understanding of the world and our development in it. Let us then turn to the pertinent beliefs or our ancestors that our study may be complete.

I must caution the reader, in advance, that the beliefs and belief systems of our ancestors are, in many ways, diametrically opposed to the beliefs and belief systems that we have adopted from our erstwhile captors.

To prevent what may accurately be referred to as *culture shock* we will first discuss the necessity for an *open mind* in our quest for *Total Black Empowerment Through The Creation of Powerful Minds®.*

THE OPEN MIND

Our ancestors believed that wisdom only speaks to an open mind. An open mind is, therefore, absolutely essential to the creation of a powerful mind. *An open mind is one that is not closed against new ideas and is free from prejudgment and bias.*

To *prejudge* is simply to judge *prematurely*, that is, before all the evidence has been analyzed. *Bias* is simply mental leaning or partiality.

We have noted that a belief system is an interconnected set of beliefs and that each belief supports and gives validity to the others so that they all stand or fall together. We also noted that when our beliefs are questioned or contradicted we become defensive so that the belief system, in effect, reinforces itself.

This belief system is a *defense mechanism* that is operative at all times, whether we are aware of it or not. This is true of belief systems and the many *subsystems* of which they are comprised.

A *belief subsystem* is one that operates within, and as a part of, a larger belief system. Belief subsystems include *ideology* and *values*, among other concepts.

Ideology may be accurately defined as a set of religious, cultural or political beliefs characteristic of a group as well as the manner of thinking of the group. It helps form the method of thinking used by the group as well as the content of their thinking.

Values, on the other hand, are *beliefs, social, political, religious or economic in nature, which inform a person's conduct and life goals.* Like ideology values become authoritative within the group and Influences the method and content of *group thinking.*

As you can see, religious beliefs help form both our ideological views and values and thereby form a significant, if not predominant, part of our belief subsystems that, in turn, make up our overall belief systems.

Among African Americans religious beliefs tend to be the most deeply held of all our beliefs and are, for that precise reason, the ones that we tend, as a group to be most defensive about when they are questioned or contradicted. Over time these beliefs create in us a *supersensitive zone of the psyche* that is easily *offended* and always vigorously *defended.* Unfortunately, this defense mechanism also tends, by natural operation, to create a *closed mind.*

Perhaps it is logical to conclude that if you know everything there is to know about a subject there is nothing that anyone can tell you and there can be no reason to listen to other views. More often than not, however, what we mean is "I have made up my mind and I will not listen to anything that might change my mind." The sad thing about this approach is that it is a tacit admission that you are afraid to be wrong. Afraid that your deepest beliefs accumulated over a life time are in error.

When we recall that *an open mind is absolutely essential to the creation of a powerful mind* it becomes apparent that a closed mind is counterproductive because it *inhibits* our ability to *accurately assess reality* and therefore contributes to our overall, centuries-long dilemma.

Let us now, with *minds open to new ideas* and free from prejudgment and bias, *focus* our heightened attention on our ancestral beliefs regarding the mind.

It should certainly be clear by now that one of the premises of this *mind power primer* is that the longevity and seeming intractability of the collective problems of African Americans, at least during the time of our sojourn here in

America, stems from our failure to *think* and *plan effectively*.

It is also posited here that since thinking is clearly an operation of the mind, it is all but impossible to determine if we are, in fact, deficient in our thinking, without examining the concept of mind.

Let us begin by noting that for all our professed genius a scientific definition of mind remains elusive. Of course, dictionaries inform us of the accepted nomenclature used by psychologists and others to facilitate discussion of the thinking process but no one has yet defined the mind. This is perhaps as it should be.

The problem is, however, that it is difficult to see how one can be *expert* in the study of a subject that one cannot define. Remember psychology is technically the *study of the mind*. It seems obvious that the study of the mind presupposes, at very least, knowledge of *what* the mind is. As surprising as it may seem modern psychologists claim not to know *what* or *where* the mind is.

Modern psychologists, for their part, have managed to solve this problem by *dismissing* the notion of mind entirely. They now conveniently refer to *behavior* rather than mind. In fact, psychology is now popularly defined as "... *the science* [sic] *that deals with mental processes and behavior.*" Psychology has become, at least for modern psychologists, the study of human *behavior*.

Lexicographers, on the other hand, have deceptively concluded that the mind is the "... human consciousness that originates in the brain and is manifested esp. in thought, perception, emotion, will, memory, and imagination." The definition obscures more than it elucidates.

The word *consciousness*, which is substituted for the word *mind*, means "... a *sense* of one's personal or collective *identity*." If, as the dictionary tells us, sense is "... *intuitive or acquired perception* ..." and *identity* refers to "... *the set of characteristics by which an individual is recog-*

nizable.", then, it follows, the mind must be understood as an *awareness or consciousness.* Or, to put it another way, the mind is *the faculty of being aware of the things by which you are recognized.*

The dictionary definition of mind also holds that the mind *originates in the brain.* We need only reiterate here that the origin of the mind remains, at least scientifically, unknown. That is not to say, however, that there are no extant *ideas* about what and where the mind is. For those ideas we must look to people other than modern (essentially European) psychologists.

The *American Heritage Dictionary* tells us that the word *psyche,* from which the word psychology is derived (Latin *psych,* meaning *mind* and *ology* to study), comes from the Greek *psukhe,* which means *spirit or soul.*

Curiously, the ancient meaning of the term is actually related to *life substances,* i.e., *blood and breath.*[1] The author does not indicate where the Greeks may have gotten the word, or how or why a word meaning *spirit* or *soul* came to mean the mind.

The ancient Greeks are relative new comers to the world of civilized culture having reached that stage of human development not earlier than the Sixth Century B.C.E. The astonishingly rapid *flowering* of Greek culture in the Sixth Cen- tury was suspiciously contemporaneous with the contact of their leading *wise men* with the wisdom of ancient Kemit.

The story has been frequently told, but bears retelling here, that Solon, the Greek Lawgiver, "morning star of Greek intellect," and one of the *Seven Wise Men of Greece,* visited Kemit where he was upbraided by the priests there because his people, they said, were *cultural and intellectual infants* compared to Kemit. Solon, apparently in agreement, did not protest this clear insult.

It is now accepted, albeit begrudgingly in some academic quarters, that the *ancient Kemites were the educa-*

tors *of the ancient Greeks* and that many, if not most, of the important ideas now attributed to the Greeks find their true origin in Kemit.

It should not be surprising then that Gerald Massey, the noted 19th Century Egyptologist, concluded that the Greek word *psyche* is of Kemitic origin.

In his *Book of Beginnings* Massey notes that the word psyche is derived from a combination of the Kemitic words *Su* meaning *she* and *Khe* meaning *soul—she soul*. Of course, *Psyche* is also the name of the ancient Greek *goddess* of the soul.

Now let us look more closely at the pertinent Kemitic ideas. First we can state categorically that the Kemites were the first to proclaim the *existence of the soul* and its *immortality*. The *transmigration* of the soul is also a concept originated in Kemit.

The Kemites believed that there are *seven souls* or *life forces* in nature. Six of these are pre-human elemental powers. The seventh is human. The human soul was known as the *soul of blood*. The *female* blood, as separate and distinct from the male blood, was considered to be the *soul of life*. In ancient Kemitic texts the soul is referred to as the *breath of the gods and the anima [Latin < spirit]* or *breath of life* was one of the six elemental powers.

Several neters (gods) of Kemit were also associated with air or breath. For example, Shu, was known as the soul of air, breath, and the breathing force. Atum, was said to have breathed the breath of life into the nostrils of the first living being and by so doing humanity received its immortal soul. Sound familiar?

The Kemitic language is also replete with words that provide an explanation for the unexplained connection between spirit and blood or breath. The word *Sakhu* mentioned by Gerald Massey has the additional meaning of *that which inspires*.

Interestingly, the word inspire, is derived from the Latin

spirare meaning to *breathe*. Another definition of inspire is to *inhale*—one of the two-fold actions of *breathing*. We may also add that the word *spirit* comes from the Latin *spiritus* meaning *breath*.

Finally, in the language of Kemit *snf* means to *breathe* while *snf-w* means *blood*. Here again we find a more than coincidental connection between breath and blood in the ancient Kemitic tongue.

We can also cite numerous examples of the connection between breath and spirit or soul in the religious lore of many cultures around the world both ancient and modern. All such examples speak of the soul (breath of life) being breathed into the first human beings. The most familiar, of course, is the biblical tale of the creation of Adam. Of course, the origin of all such tales is to be found recorded in extant Kemitic texts.

We can also add here that in the Christian Bible the heart is where the spirit and conscience reside and where all spiritual activity takes place. We also find that in it the words *heart* and *soul* are used interchangeably. Unlike Kemitic teachings, however, the Christian Bible teaches that the heart is naturally evil and a thing that pollutes our lives and bodies. The cure for this natural *evilness of heart*, according to the Christian Bible, is for the heart to be regenerated. As you might expect, believing in their doctrine (an operation of the mind) is the only way to regenerate the otherwise evil heart.

ANCIENT IDEAS ON THE LOCATION OF THE MIND

A brief digression is in order here. The dictionary definition quoted above tells us that the mind originates in the brain. In ancient times, however, both the Greeks and their Kemite educators believed the mind was located in the chest area and heart specifically.

TOTAL BLACK EMPOWERMENT

For the Greeks the concept of mind was embodied in the word *noos*, which later became *nous*. The word *noos* first appears in the *Iliad* (c. 850 B.C.) where it seems to represent a primitive notion of *perception* or *recognition* and later becomes, as *nous*, the conscious mind. Curiously, the *noos* was not located in the head but in the *chest area*. Once again the teachings of Kemit provide the explanation of a Greek anomaly.

The Kemites were of the belief that the locus of the mind was the heart, which is, of course, located in the chest area. The *ib (Kemitic for heart)* was recognized as the *seat of thoughts and emotions*. The word *ib* also means *mind, understanding, intelligence, mood, will, to think, and to suppose*. The connection between the heart and blood seems too obvious to require mention.

There is one other source that we must consult about the concept of mind. This source is recognized as a *rendering* or *distillation* of authentic Kemitic sacred teachings. Our ancient ancestors were notoriously skittish about reducing the *Sacred Science* to writing. They firmly believed that their sacred truths were best transmitted from *mouth to ear* and should only be written in the *mdw ntr*.

The mouth to ear tradition was carried out through the temple initiatory system where sacred information was made available to carefully selected initiates. The initiates, in turn, were forbidden from divulging the information they received to the uninitiated.

Our ancestors believed that sacred information was best reserved for those who would not abuse it. But, it would be a mistake to conclude that their intention was to keep such information to themselves. In fact, the Kemitic word *cheta* translated as *secret* by Egyptologists actually means *inaccessible*. The information was *difficult* to obtain not *impossible*.

The vehicle for the publication of this information was the hieroglyph (Kemitic *mdw ntr)*. These sacred writings were published in papyri, temples and monuments. Of course, initiates were taught to read the sacred writing. But, more importantly by the use of the *mdw ntr,* (symbols each of which had its own meaning) they were able to publish this powerful, transformative and potentially dangerous information in plain view. The information was readily accessible, even unavoidable, to those who could divine the sacred writing; *cheta not secret*.

The last source that we will examine, at length, is known as the *Corpus Hermeticum (Body of Knowledge of Hermes)*. If you have never heard of them you are not alone. Few people, other than scholars, know of them. Just remember that when you know their history and the influence (impact is a better word) that they have had on the ideas and thinking of the world you will wonder why you had not heard of them sooner.

That you may understand the importance of these ancient texts a bit of historical background is required here. But, before we begin our analysis of the *Hermetica* a caveat excerpted from it is an appropriate place to begin.

"My teachings," the writer of the Hermetica warns us, "will seem more obscure in times to come, when they are translated from our Egyptian tongue into that of the Greeks. Translation will distort much of their meaning. Expressed in our native language, the teachings are clear and simple, for the very sound of an Egyptian word resonates with the thing signified by it. All possible measures should be taken to prevent these holy secrets being corrupted by translation into Greek, which is an arrogant, feeble, showy language, unable to contain the cogent force of my words. The Greek language lacks the power to convince, and Greek philosophy is nothing but noisy chatter. Our Egyptian speech is more than talk. Its utterances are replete with power."[2] Of course, the English translation utilized here is from the Greek. Such is life.

10

THE CORPUS HERMETICUM

A GLIMPSE OF KEMITIC SACRED SCIENCE

The Hermeticum are written in Greek. They were compiled in Alexandria, Egypt. Although, the texts were apparently compiled around the second or third century C.E., it is now acknowledged that the *ideas* contained in it represent authentic Kemitic teachings millennia older than the date of their compilation.

Until the 17th century it was widely accepted that the *Hermetic texts had been written in the time of the Old Kingdom (c. 4,000 B.C.E.).* In 1614, King James I, then king of England, commissioned one Isaac Casaubon, a Frenchman to undertake an exhaustive analysis of the *Corpus Hermeticum*.

Casaubon was a French classical scholar. He joined the Church of England in 1610 after a visit to England at the invitation of the Archbishop of Canterbury. His benefactor was King James from whom he received a generous royal stipend. Casaubon's contemporaries believed that he had sold his conscience for English gold. Be that as it may, his work on the Corpus Hermeticum was dedicated to King James.

Casaubon concluded the texts could not have been

written earlier than the *second* to *third* centuries. Though Casaubon's analysis has proven correct as to the *dating* of the *Hermetica*, it does not alter the fact that the *contents* of the *Hermetica* represent authentic ancient Kemitic teachings recorded, by Casaubon's own admission, more than *fifteen hundred years before Jean Francois Champollion's partial* decipherment *of the hieroglyphs*. This is significant because prior to the publication of *Précis du systéme hiéroglyphique* in 1824, no one could read the papyri or temple, tomb and monument inscriptions.

The critical thinker will find it interesting that King James I employed Casaubon. King James was the ultra-orthodox Christian who commissioned the King James Version of the Christian Bible in 1611. James was obsessed with removing all vestiges of *pagan* influence from the realm. In so doing anything that would discredit the *Hermetica* would find favor with King James. It should also be observed that during the 17th Century the Hermetica still held sway over the minds of many influential scholars and philosophers of the time. Clearly, a religious and political motive underlay Casaubon's attack on the *Hermetica*.

This brief historical background and Hermes' caveat firmly in mind let us look at some of the information contained in the *Corpus Hermeticum* pertinent to our present discussion. In it we will find a wealth of information that indicates not only what our ancestors believed the mind to be, but also their belief in the importance of the *Divine Mind* and *Divine Utterance*.

TEHUTI:

LORD OF THOUGHT AND DIVINE INTELLIGENCE

The *Hermetica*, as it is popularly known, is attributed to Hermes. *Hermes Trismegistus (Hermes Thrice-Great)* was the Greek name for the Kemite sage and *Neter* of *Divine Intelligence*. We will refer to him by his Kemitic name *Tehuti*.

Tehuti's name appears in ancient Kemitic texts dating back to the Old Kingdom. (C. 3100 B.C.E.). Among the numerous references to him in ancient texts we find that he is variously described as the *Heart of Ra* (the Creative force); the "... *source of all law* ..."; the "... *founder of the social order.*"; the "... *author of the institutions of temple-worship.*"; the Lord of mdw ntr," (i.e., divine words). And, "... *the god of literature, ... science, ... theology, ... ritual, ... the fountain and source of all knowledge and wisdom....*"

Tehuti is also the "... All-Knowing One who dispenses every kind of strange and mysterious gnosis" (Greek < knowledge). He is "... the one who knows in every direction" and "... [i]n the end he comes to be looked on as Understanding (or Reason) itself, personified." And, perhaps most importantly he was recognized as the "... Lord of Thought."[1] In fact, the English word thought is derived from the Old English thoth which is, in turn, derived from the Greek thoth which is itself derived from the Kemitic thth. As it turns out then, we cannot even think of thought without calling on our ancient Lord of Thought and Divine Intelligence.

It is in his association with thought and thinking that Tehuti is most instructive for the purposes of our present discussion. It will profit us greatly to spend a few moments in contemplation of the *Lord of Thought*.

We have already discussed that to the ancient

Kemites the *heart*, not the *brain*, was the location of the mind. Now we see that Tehuti, the *Lord of Thought*, was revered as the *heart* of the Creator. In fact, it was said of him that "... [h]e is the source of all deep knowledge and acumen that men possess...."; that he gives to men knowledge itself and the faculties of mind."

Another important characteristic of *Tehuti* is that he is frequently identified with *Sia*. In Kemitic theology *Sia* is the personification of *Reason* or *Understanding*. In fact, *Tehuti's* identification with *Sia* in the ancient texts is so frequent that *Sia* became a second name for him.

Finally, it should be understood here that Tehuti is mentioned, with these and numerous similar epithets, in Kemitic texts and tomb inscriptions, as early as 3100 B.C., when it is believed that their sacred writing (hieroglyphs) was developed. The fact that the hieroglyphs appear fully developed at that time indicates that they were created long before 3100 B.C.E.

It seems obvious that the belief in this ancient deity as well as the knowledge of his attributes had to have existed well before the development of the hieroglyphs. Now let us look at the *Corpus Hermeticum*—the writings attributed to Tehuti.

Legend has it that Tehuti was the author of 36,000 books. The Hermetica is comprised of 18 of which 17 are extant. The "mysterious" teachings contained in the *Hermetica* represent a philosophical attempt to raise humanity from a dead level to a living perpendicular. More specifically, its goal, and the goal of all Kemitic mystery teachings, was to raise humanity to the level of *mortal gods* and thereby improve the overall human condition through their god-given power of thought.

The essential teaching of our ancestors was that "*God is Mind.*" And, that both God and humankind create and have their being by and through the agency of thought. Tehuti tells us that "... *in order to know God we must share its identity since only like can truly know like. Mind produces divinity. Through Mind some become god-like, for as Osiris teaches: "Gods are immortal men and men are mortal gods.' Listen, every human heart! Immerse yourself in Mind and recognize the purpose of your birth. Those that bathe themselves in Mind find true knowledge and become complete."*[2]

Our ancestors taught that men are mortal gods because they believed that we are made in the image of the *Neter Neteru* (God of Gods), i.e., the "... *active, [creative] power which produces and creates things in regular recurrence; which bestows new life upon them, and gives back to them their youthful vigor*," and, because we are *living expressions* of the *Divine Essence (spirit), Divine Mind (intellect),* and *Divine Utterance (speech).* They believed that humanity is made in the *image* of God. The words image, imagine, and imagination all derive from the same root, i.e., (L> *imagin*). The Latin word connotes *the power to form mental images of something that is not known to the senses and not existing or perceived in reality.* It follows that when we speak of an image we are, in fact, referring to a *mental construct* created, of course, through the power of thought. The image in which we are made then is not a *physical* one. We do not look like God because God is not a *corporal* being. *God is Mind.* The *image* in which we are created is *mental* and *spiritual.*

Imagine, if you will, the transformative impact of such an idea. God is mind and humanity is made in God's image. We are gods because like God we *think.* We are *mortal* gods because unlike God we die.

At first glance this notion of men as gods may be difficult for the modern Judeo-Christian, Islamic influenced mind to accept. But, it should not be so. Even the Bible proclaims, *"Ye are gods."* The Psalmist first mentions it and Jesus, a devout Jew, later confirms it. Of course, most biblical adherents, including clergymen, do not mention this hard to explain proclamation—most ignore it entirely. It is even more difficult to explain when it is realized that the words are attributed to God who should know if men are, in fact, gods.

Our ancestors, on the other hand, believed that because we are created in the mental and spiritual image of the Neter Neteru (God of Gods), we are inherently capable of creating anything we can think of, in reality and in real time, by utilization of the combined power of Divine Mind and Divine Utterance. Their words are still as true today as when they were first spoken thousands of years ago.

Before we examine the profound legacy bequeathed to us by the *Ancient Ones* whose intention, by doing so, was to insure our continued survival and prosperity, we will digress briefly to correct a popular misconception.

Many people in the African American community and elsewhere have been misled to believe that our ancestors were *polytheists*, i.e., persons who worship or believe in more than one god. The belief is *unfounded*.

I am compelled to disabuse our people of this notion not because I find the idea of polytheism necessarily objectionable, after all it is just one of many speculations about the nature of the divine. I wish to do so because the next section introduces the concept of the *Neter Neteru* and we wish to insure that the reader fully understands the meaning of the term.

THE *NETER NETERU* (THE GOD OF GODS)

Most Egyptologists translate the Kemitic phrase *Neter Neteru* as *God of Gods*. The translation leaves much to be desired. First, it implies that the ancient Kemitic word *ntr* has the same meaning as the English word god. It does not. The second implication is that our ancestors believed in the existence of many gods. We will address the second implication first.

TOTAL BLACK EMPOWERMENT

In the *Hermetica* Tehuti addresses the question succinctly. He states: "Do you think there are many Gods? That's absurd—God is one.... If that seems incredi- ble, just consider yourself. You see, speak, hear, touch, taste, walk, think and breathe. It is not a different you who does these various things, but one being who does them all."

Based upon this statement alone we can say, categorically, that our ancestors did not believe in a multiplicity of *gods* and were, therefore, not polytheists. They were, however, *scientific realists* in their approach to the understanding of deity. They concluded, after millennia of careful observation that there is a *singular source* of all that exists. They also concluded that this singular source was itself a *creative power* that could not have been created, must have always existed and could not cease to exist. That such a power was beyond human comprehension seemed obvious. As a result this power was understood as forever hidden from human comprehension and therefore *unknowable*. But they also believed that this creative force could be perceived mentally and by observation of the world around us. Since the creative power is the *cause* of all things a glimpse of it could be seen by observation of its *effects*. These observable, measurable effects they saw as *attributes, expressions* or *manifestations* of the creative power and called them *neters (ntru)*.

Neters are best understood as the natural, active, creative powers *manifested* in this world by the *Creative Source* whose true name is unknown. In fact, *neters* are best understood as *nature*

The *neters* were seen as *attributes* of the *Creative Source* that are manifested and visible in the material world. There were, for example, *neters* of fire and air, water and earth. Everything that exists has a *neter* that governs it and by which it is known. When we know the attributes of each *neter* we know what they are and how to control them. Additionally, every individual human being is a *neter* in his or her own right. Tehuti was the *neter* of divine intelligence, *Khepri* was the *neter* of regeneration. I am the *neter* of Johnnie Cordero. You are the *neter* of you. The Supreme God, whose name is unknown, is the *Neter Neteru*, the *Neter of Neters*.

Not surprisingly the Latin word *natura* and its derivative the English word nature are both derived from the Kemite word *ntr*. The American Heritage Dictionary defines *nature* as "the material world and its phenomena; *the forces that produce and control such phenomena: the laws of nature.* [Latin < natura.] Exactly how our ancestors understood the neteru.

As fate would have it, it appears that the concept of monotheism is also of Kemitic origin. This should not be seen as approval of the concept on the part of our ancestors. The pharaoh who gave the world monotheism, is also the only pharaoh to *depart* from our ancient teachings. His experiment in monotheism was an utter failure that marked a period of national deterioration, stagnation and decline that took centuries to recover from. Our ancestors forbade us to even speak the name of the degenerate pharaoh who unleashed the scourge of monotheism on the land of Kemit. They refer to him as *the one whose name must never be spoken.*

Our ancestors knew that the concept of monotheism would lead to the concept of the so-called *One True God*. Belief in One True God makes it possible to denigrate and eventually exclude the gods of other people. After all if your god is the *One True God* all other gods must be *false*. Interestingly, an author, scholar and professor of physics who recently published a book on the history of ideas was asked, "what is the single *worst* idea in history?" he replied, monotheism—*the idea of the one true god.*

11

THE CHARACTERISTICS OF OUR MENTAL IMAGE

The sole, single *Creative Force*, called *Neter Neteru* by our ancestors, in its purest essential form, cannot, according to them, be directly comprehended by the finite human mind. We can, however, glimpse the shadow of its substance.

Our ancestors tell us in clear and unambiguous words that "... *God is Mind*...." and, that "... *if it is possible to talk of the substance of God, then Mind is the very divine substance.*" Their words, repeated over and over again, are straight- forward and adamant, "... *Mind is not separate from God it emanates from God like light from the sun.*" They leave no room for confusion when they state that "... *All things are thoughts which the Creator thinks. Mind cannot be enclosed, because everything exists within Mind.*"[1]

This is, indeed, a powerful idea. God is Mind, Intelligence and Thought. We are made in the image of God. All we need do is connect the ideas. God is Mind—The Divine Mind God is Mind. Three words that eloquently express an idea that transformed people who lived in a near brutish state of nature into the preeminent civilization of the time. When these words are properly understood they possess the power to create positive, constructive change that is not only transformative but transcendental as well.

The phrase *God is Mind* vividly encapsulates an idea of the existence of a power so formidable that it can, by merely *thinking of it*, elevate the power of our minds exponentially. It was this idea, the first *transcendentalism*, which gave the *idea* of civilization and then the *fact* of it to the world. The idea that the words contain is so profound that it literally changed the course of human thinking and history.

Tehuti, the preeminent voice of our ancestors, counsels us that:

"Mind cannot be enclosed, because *everything exists within Mind. Nothing is so quick and powerful*. Just look at your own experience. Imagine yourself in any foreign land, and *quick as your intention* you will be there! Think of the ocean—and there you are. You have not moved as things move, but you have traveled, nevertheless. Fly up to the heavens—you won't need wings! *Nothing can obstruct you*—not the burning heat of the sun, or the swirling planets. Pass on the limits of creation. Do you want to break out beyond the boundaries of the Cosmos? For your mind even that is possible. *Can you sense what power you possess?.... Try and understand that God is Mind.*"[2]

CAN YOU SENSE THE POWER YOU POSSES?

Here Tehuti speaks to us of the inherent *power* that each of us possesses. This power is not wealth or weapons; it is not based on who our relatives are or who we know. The power of which he speaks is the *power of the mind*. It is the *power of the intellect*. With this *power*, he tells us, nothing can confine (imprison) or obstruct (hinder from action) us. Nothing is beyond our reach if we will but *understand* that *God is Mind*, and that we are made in the *mental image* of God.

TOTAL BLACK EMPOWERMENT

Tehuti tells us that everything exists in the mind. The mind is the *seat of intelligence*. Intelligence is the power to learn, to understand, to reason, and to apply knowledge in order to manipulate one's environment.

Mind is alive and full of power. Nothing can stop your thoughts and therefore nothing can bind your power to use your minds or the power of your mind. In short, *our minds are our foremost power.*

Tehuti also tells us that the mind is the *soul of God*. The soul is the animating force that gives life to living things. *Think about it.* All living things have souls. God is alive. God too has a soul. Even God, is animated by some power. God is animated by mind. God's soul is mental. God is spirit and *the spirit of God is mind.*

Now you can understand why Tehuti tells us that nothing is *impossible for mind*. We are also told that "*Mind prevails over everything—over law and even fate.*" Mind is the *intelligence* that created and continues to create all that lives and exists—in perpetuity. Mind, he tells us can even control fate. Think about it.

Fate is the power that controls events. The implication is clear—we can control events with our minds—simple yet profound.

We, on the other hand, are living expressions of that necessarily *Divine Mind*. As human beings our intellectual capacity is *unlimited*. The limits of the mind have never been successfully calculated. We do not know of a single human being who has reached the limit of his capacity to store information or to think for that matter. It has been said that we only use one tenth of our brains, but that is, at best, only a guess. No one knows what the brain's capacity is. Not being able to calculate our mental capacity we can accurately say that it is apparently unlimited.

If this is true of the mind of human being's what can we conjecture about the mind of God? According to our ancestral beliefs we are, in fact, a living part of God's *Di-*

vine Mind and in this case the whole must be exponentially greater than the sum of the parts.

Let us be clear here. The Mind is the *seat of intelligence*. We cannot even think of mind without in some way thinking of intelligence. Intelligence is the *product* of *thought*. All that exists is the product of the God's creative *thinking*. All that exists originates in and is forever contained within the Mind of God. The *power* of God's Mind is *infinite*.

If we follow this chain of thought, of connected ideas, we are forced to arrive at a most powerful idea. The image that we are made in is a mental image—the image of the Mind and Soul of God. Through this divine relationship we possess power so great that nothing can obstruct us and nothing is impossible for us, when we cultivate God's creative, innovative power—the power of thought.

GOD CREATES BY THOUGHT

We need only focus our attention on what we do when we think to obtain a glimpse of the power of *Divine thought*.

We know that we are capable of anything in thought. Do not make the mistake of trivializing this concept. It does not mean that we are merely capable of visualizing all manner of things in our minds. That would be far too obvious. The embedded meaning is far more profound. When we consider that everything in this world, without exception, that has been created by the hand of man is the *product of thought*, we begin to glimpse the true message imparted by our ancestors.

Think about it. From the digging stick, to the *shaduf*, to the stealth bomber, from the paper clip to the latest global positioning satellite, all of these things have one thing in common—they began with a *thought*. In a very real sense the history of the world is the *history of ideas*. It is always the *prevailing idea* that directs and controls human activity. The course of human events has always been dictated by a dominant idea. This gives new meaning to the saying that *nothing can stop an idea whose time has finally come.* Put another way, *there is no force greater than the powerful idea.*

If we follow this concept to its logical conclusion we learn that nothing is impossible for mind and that our human minds, though not as powerful as the *Mind of God*, are nonetheless *sufficiently powerful* to develop strategies and tactics to insure our survival and prosperity no matter what the nature of the obstacles with which we are confronted.

ALL THOUGHTS HAVE THEIR ORIGIN IN THE MIND OF GOD

Careful. This one is so simple that many people miss the true meaning. Our ancestors believed that there is a repository of ideas that is (1) otherworldly and (2) that can be accessed by the properly trained human mind. They further believed that this repository of ideas contains two distinct types of information/ knowledge.

First, it contains every thought/idea and all of the knowledge/information recorded in human memories since man became sapient. When it is understood that these thoughts/ideas were believed to be *pure energy* and that they could not be destroyed we appreciate how advanced their thinking was.

We now know that thoughts are *energy*. Thoughts are *electromagnetic impulses*. We also know that energy cannot be *destroyed*. Our ancestors believed that every thought that any living being has ever had, as well as all of the infinite array of thoughts, on all subjects, that anyone could possibly have now or in the future is both recorded and accessible.

TOTAL BLACK EMPOWERMENT

In a real sense, they believed that the *Mind of God* is not only the repository of thoughts but also of *potentiality*. All that can possibly exist, that is, all that can possibly come into existence, already exists as *potential reality* in the *Mind of God*.

In short, the *Mind of God* is the infinite realm of that which can be. *If we can think it, it can be manifested in reality*. Moreover, by searching this record we can find information that no one else has ever thought of, hence, the *original thought*.

Second, It was believed that this vast, unlimited repository of ideas was readily accessible to anyone who was willing to be trained to utilize it. It is much like any other quest for knowledge. If we are in need of knowledge we are greatly assisted in our quest for it if we know *where to look for it*. Our chances of finding it, how- ever, are immeasurably improved if we also know *how to access* the information.

A computer database containing all the information in the world is of little value if we are not computer literate. Our ancestors believed that access to this treasure trove of information was available by one method only. As simplistic as it may sound that one method was, you guessed it, by *thinking*—more precisely by the *control* of *thought*. But, thinking was, for them, a *divine act*. They understood thinking to be the equivalent of communion with God. Thinking was the act of partaking of the *Divine Substance*. When it is remembered that they believed that the "... *mind is the very divine substance*," the act of thinking takes on new meaning.

To think is to partake of the *substance* of God. Profound thought indeed. Every time we exercise our minds we are in some way infusing our very being with the *substance of God*. To our ancestors *rapture* was an everyday event. *Epiphany* was the rule and not the exception. If this divine act could be *controlled* we would have realized the power to not only become one with God but to become gods in our own right. For *the act of thinking is, in reality, the act of creation.* To be creative—to be a creator is the hallmark of God. *We only lack control of our thinking.* To this end our ancestors taught what they referred to as the *Ten Virtues.*

THE TEN VIRTUES AND THE CONTROL OF THOUGHT

The word virtue is now said to mean moral excellence and chastity especially in woman. But the word has a curious etymology. It derives from the Latin *virtus* meaning *man* or the *male function*. The obsolete rendering is force or power as in the power to accomplish. It is by this meaning that we best understand the underlying purpose of the Ten Virtues.

The first of the *Ten Virtues* was, predictably, the *control of thought*. It is no coincidence that the root of the word virtue means *force* or the *power to accomplish*. The *Ten Virtues* were actually strengths or powers that were to be cultivated in order for our people to excel. They were the most important goals because if properly applied they would assure our *mastery of thought*.

First we *control our thinking*, then and only then, can we *control our actions*. In the long trek from savagery to society, from society to civilization, we were absolutely required to control the *beast within us* (known to our ancestors as the *lower Ka*). It was and remains mandatory that the savage impulses that in a state of nature make survival possible be recognized and controlled. In short, *uncontrolled thinking is the quintessential mark of the beast.* The beast in us must be controlled in order for control of our actions to ensue. For this reason civilization cannot take root, unless and until, the beast within us is successfully brought under control.

What we see here is a legacy that teaches the paramount importance of the control of our actions by and through the control of our thinking. *Controlled thinking is rigorous, precise, orderly, productive and planned. Controlled thinking is creative thinking—creative thinking is the thinking of God.*

If we follow this idea to its logical conclusion we arrive at the real import of being made in the image of God. Since, as our ancestors put it, "... *god who is energy and power....*" is also invisible, God "... may only be seen with thoughts—which are themselves invisible."

In short, we are only capable of seeing and knowing God by *thinking*. When we think we do so as the image of God and *in* the *likeness* of God. To the extent that our thinking rises nearer the level of the sublime we more fully and completely live up to the image in which we are created. It is, therefore, the *level of our thinking—the quality of our thought,* through which we express our *God-ness.* God perpetually creates. "All things are thoughts which the Creator thinks."

The distressing thing about it is that this rule, more accurately, this universal law, operates positively and negatively simultaneously. Everything positive exists in the Mind of God but everything negative exists there as well.

Another potentially distressing fact is that everything in creation is *connected.* The existence of one reality creates another. Each cause has an effect and each effect must have a cause. But, each cause has multiple effects that give rise to multiple causes.

We can see from this that slipshod, haphazard thinking can create unanticipated and potentially dangerous ideas and even more dangerous results. The birth of one idea simultaneously engenders other related and often diametrically opposed ideas, the consequences of which may not always be foreseen. Just to name one example. Einstein's

General Theory of Relativity gave rise, in time, to the idea that became the atomic bomb—a fact that he regretted until his death.

12

HOW THINKING BECOMES CREATIVE

We have talked about the creative power of thought. But, how does thinking become *creative*? How does the creative Idea become the creative action? How does what we see in our imagination become manifested in the world of reality? Let us pursue these questions with the thinking of our ancestors.

DIVINE UTTERANCE: THE VOICE OF GOD

According to the teaching of our ancient ancestors there is *Divine Mind* and *Divine Utterance*. The *Divine Mind* was the *thought process* by which God brought things into existence. God begins the creative *process* with the creative *thought*. The act of creation, however, occurs by *Divine Utterance*. In short, God spoke i.e., *uttered the Word*, and the world came into existence.

Tehuti instructs us that "Speech is an image of Mind and Mind is an image of God." And, that "Speech alone cannot convey Truth but the power of Mind is extraordinary, and when it has been led by speech to things [thought] through thoroughly, it can find the peace of true beliefs."

"Primal mind," he continues, "is the parent of the word, just as, in your own experience, your human mind gives birth to speech. They cannot be divided, one from the other, for life is the union of Mind and Word. God's Word is the creative idea—the supreme limitless power which nurtures and provides for all things that through it are created."[1]

We will return to the concepts of *Divine Mind* and *Divine Utterance* later in our discussion. For the moment contemplate *Tehuti's* words:

"Immerse yourself in Mind and recognize the purpose of your birth. Those that bathe themselves in Mind find true knowledge and become complete. Of all the beings that have soul only human beings, elevated by this gift of Mind, may attain knowledge of God. Belief grows from contemplation, and disbelief from lack of thought. Only if grasped by thought, in this way, will my teachings be understood."

SACRED SCIENCE AND WESTERN CIVILIZATION

Think about it. It was this philosophy, this Sacred Science that led to the development of art, chemistry, mathematics, physics, metallurgy, irrigation, religion, theology, medicine, astronomy, astrology, geometry, stone architecture, effective government administration, and the division of labor.

Our Sacred Science provided the foundation for what would later become western thinking and civilization. It was this most sacred of sciences that educated and inspired virtually all of the ancient Greek philosophers.

Our ancestral teachings provided the fundamental teaching of the Masonic Order, the Rosicrucians, the Knights Templar and also fueled the French Revolution.

It was the departure from the teachings of Kemitic Sacred Science that spawned the Dark Ages (c. 476–1000

C.E.) and a return to them that ushered in the Renaissance of the modern age.

In more recent times, Sacred Science inspired the likes of Michael Angelo, Da Vinci, Kepler, Copernicus and Isaac Newton among others. Clearly, the great minds of the last two thousand years have been influenced by the philosophy of our ancient ancestors. Even recent luminaries such as the late Albert Einstein and Steven Hawkings have referred to their researches as an attempt to understand the Mind of God.

Literally tens of thousands of volumes on various aspects of Kemitic culture have been written over the last two centuries and scores of new titles are pub- lished on the subject annually. Entire libraries are dedicated to this one subject.

Unfortunately, because of the relentless historic efforts to demonize the Kemites, discredit their culture and disguise the fact that they were Africans, relatively few African Americans, themselves descendants of and rightful heirs to the intellectual wealth of the greatest civilization in history, recognize the intrinsic value of the culture that everyone else in the world seems to be obsessed with.

This then is the quintessential message contained in the Hermetica. It comes down to us, still pristine and powerful, despite more than two millennia of concerted efforts by the Christian church and some national governments to deprive us of our most important and powerful birthright. God is Mind.

RECAPITULATION

Based upon the information contained in the *Hermetica* we can conclude that the concept of mind has its first appearance in history among the sacred writings of our Kemite ancestors. In our sacred texts it had the meaning of spirit, soul, blood and breath. This amorphous substance called mind was located or manifested in our hearts not in our brains. The brain is merely a device that tabulates our thoughts and ideas. *The heart is the seat of intelligence.*

We have also learned that according to our ancient ancestors like the Creator we are endowed with a mind that is divine in origin and which gives us the likeness and image of God. We are only able to know God, to commune with God in thought. *Thinking is, therefore, a divine act.* To think is to create as God creates. But, thinking can give rise to disastrous results given that every cause has an effect—every action an equal and opposite reaction. Thought must, therefore, be controlled. But, the control of thought cannot be imposed by outside forces. The individual thinker through rigorous training in how to think, not what to think, must accomplish this important task.

To impose control from outside is brainwash and indoctrination. The human mind separates us from the animals by enabling us to create in the fashion of the Creator. The greatest blessing is the gift of mind. By it *we are able to change our circumstances* by the mere formulation of an appropriate idea. Our ancestors developed thinking concepts that were utilized by them to create civilization out of the vestiges of savagery. Our ancestors properly recognized the human mind as divine because it comes from and partakes of the *Mind of God*. By our link to the Mind of God, by our creation in the mental and spiritual image of God we are mortal gods.

DO YOU KNOW THE POWER YOU POSSESS?

PART III
POWER

13

UNDERSTANDING POWER

INTRODUCTION

This section is about power. It is intended to raise the discussion of power in the African American community to the level it rightly deserves when its centrality to our collective problems is considered.

A central premise of the this *mind power primer* is that as a people we are and have been for the entire period of our sojourn in America a *power deficient political group*. It has been our power deficiency that has enabled others to continually thwart our efforts to gain a piece of the American pie proportionate to our numbers in the population.

Our lack of collective power has stifled our development as first class citizens because in America only groups that are perceived to have the ability to act powerfully in the political arena are granted first class status. This is true whether the group is generally liked or not. Frankly, it is our consistent state of power deficiency more than any other single factor that has prevented our advancement.

The reason for our unfortunate state of affairs may lie in the fact that we have yet to define power, as it exists in the real world. Let us begin then by defining the term.

TOTAL BLACK EMPOWERMENT

POWER DEFINED

Unfortunately, we often discuss matters of importance without success because we fail to define, in advance, the terms we employ. We assume that we are discussing the same thing when, in fact, we are not. I have one definition of a key term in mind while you have another. It seems obvious that under such circumstances it is virtually impossible to come to a meeting of the minds. This is why the greatest single obstacle to effective communication is the failure to define the terms we use. Nothing can be more frustrating, and counterproductive than the inability to communicate effectively.

The title of the book you are now reading is *Total Black Empowerment Through The Creation of Powerful Minds®*. The key word in the title is *empowerment*. Empowerment is, obviously, the state of being *empowered*. To *empower* is to provide power to individuals or groups. But what is power?

People who have little or no understanding of what it is use the word power repeatedly. We speak of power with a familiarity that seems to indicate an intimate, pre-existing relationship with it. But, our inability to effect meaningful, substantive change in our life circumstances and the life circumstances of those to whom we owe the duty of protection and care, belies and makes a mockery of any claim that we may have to the existence of such a relationship.

This is not to say that we do not instinctively recognize and respond to the presence of power. We even respond to power that we only imagine exists. The mere vocalization of the word power creates a sensory experience in us. When someone who we believe to be powerful speaks we are immediately attentive. The fact that the person may actually say nothing of importance does not seem to matter.

We thrive on the lives and escapades of the powerful. We live vicariously on the exploits of the rich and powerful. We dream about having power and fuel those dreams through tabloids and soap operas. This is because we know, instinctively, that power is a driving force in the world.

Power is seductive, enticing and attractive. We are drawn to it like a moth to the dancing flame. But, what is this thing that is so mesmerizing yet elusive? Most of us could not define the term if we were paid to do so. If we think real hard about it most of us would come up with the definition that was drummed into us in elementary school. Power, they told us, is the *ability to do work*. We never questioned it. How could we? We were never taught *Critical Thinking*. As a result, we never discovered that the definition is inaccurate and intentionally misleading.

Power is the ability to do work. *Think about that statement.* It implies that if you are able to do work, and by that fact alone, you are *powerful*. If the definition is carried to its logical conclusion we would have to conclude that African Americans are the most powerful people in this country. Why? Because no other people have worked harder, and longer, under worse conditions and without compensation than we have.

We have worked from "c'aint see to c'aint see" and we continue to work from dawn to dusk doing the most laborious, tedious and backbreaking work. Yes, we have the ability to do work, and contrary to popular misconception, we do work, harder and longer than anybody else. But, it would be the height of foolishness and intellectually dishonest to say that we have attained anything that remotely resembles power as a result of our demonstrated *ability to do work*.

The President of the United States is said to be the most powerful man in the world. Does his power derive from his ability to do work—or does it come from his ability to get work done? Is his tremendous power the result of how many ditches he can dig—or the result of his ability to direct the Army Corps of Engineers to build virtually anything he wants, any time he wants?

The President's power does not lie in how much or how well he can do work. Power is much more than the ability to do work.

Power is both a physical substance and powerful idea. Power is energy and thought—process and principle—reality and potential.

POWER AS A PHYSICAL SUBSTANCE

Power is a substance because it can be gauged, quantified, measured, directed, controlled, generated and manipulated. When we consider power as physical substance we necessarily implicate the laws of physics.

The science of physics, including quantum, atomic and nuclear physics, recognizes that energy and matter are essentially the same. Power and energy are, phys- icists tell us, virtually synonymous terms.

In the world of physics power is broadly defined as *force, strength* and *energy* depending on the way it functions at any given time. *Force* and strength are, respectively, *applied* and *stored* power. Force is any kind of push or pull. It is the *application of power. Strength* is the innate capacity of a person or thing to *resist* and *endure*. Strength is the power of *opposition* or *resistance*.

Energy/power is the key to all activity on Earth and in the Universe. It is recognized as the basis of life because it is the core that links all things in the Universe. All things, animate and inanimate, are *expressions* or *manifestations* of power. *Energy is, in effect, the power of life.*

Power is a composite of force, strength and energy. It is force when it is exerted. Power is strength when it causes persons or things to resist or endure. It is energy when it is creative and life giving. It follows that you cannot be forceful, strong or energetic without power. You cannot be assertive, creative or resistant without power, and without power you will not endure. In reality, you cannot even live without power, at least, in the form of energy.

We may logically conclude from this that we cannot assert the force of our collective will to be creative in pursuit of self-determined goals and objectives, or be resistant to or successfully oppose those who would control us, or stand in the way of our progress, without power.

POWER AS A POWERFUL IDEA

Power is also a powerful idea. Power is an idea, concept, notion that is inherently powerful. Power is a monumental idea. It is so vibrant, so energetic and forceful that it has the tendency to invigorate, rejuvenate and resuscitate those who understand the idea and apply its principles. It is for this reason that power has been intentionally given a negative connotation.

We speak of *power hungry people* as crazed villains who will stop at nothing in pursuit of power. We proclaim that *power corrupts and absolute power corrupts absolutely*. We believe, because we have been *taught* to believe, that power is something that is to be avoided like some loathsome disease lest we become diseased and corrupted by it.

It is also for this reason that those who have power are the first to deny that they have it. It is not that they believe the popular tripe that it is in some way negative, or that they are in some way diseased or corrupted by it. Powerful peo- ple only want you to think that power is negative so that you will not pursue it. They know that power will serve any master, without consideration of race, creed or intent.

The proof of this fact, as if proof were needed, is that there is not a single powerful person on the planet who would trade places with a powerless person or even teach the powerless person how to acquire power.

Those who hold power want you to see power in a negative light so that you will never develop a *mind-set* that will direct you to *acquire* and *control* power. The more you believe that power is negative and to be avoided the better it is for them.

It is also for this reason that those who control power not only deny it, but, also conceal it in ingenious ways. If you think power is a negative, corrupting commodity and everyone who has it denies having it and you cannot pinpoint the location where it exists, you many, after a time, conclude that it does not even exist.

Power is *demonized, concealed* and *denied* because even the *idea of power* is, in many ways, as potent as power itself.

People who understand power increase their power by simple possession of that understanding. But, the idea of power alone will not make you powerful, it will, however, make you aware of its existence and create in you, a mind-set that will direct you toward the need to acquire and control power for the survival and prosperity of yourselves and those to whom you owe the duty of protection and care.

Power is manifested in many different ways. Each manifestation represents another aspect or attribute of power. When viewed as a whole these aspects enable us to arrive at an accurate and useful definition of power.

At one level power may be observed in the ways it is created or acquired. Power may be acquired through *violence, wealth* and *knowledge. Violence creates power. Money will beget power.* And, there is always the ancient maxim that *knowledge is power.*

Few people will question the fact that violence and power go hand in hand. The United States of America is universally recognized as the most powerful nation on the planet as well as the most powerful nation that has ever existed. Is it any wonder that it is also the most violent nation in history? Is it any wonder that the creator of the *Gatling* gun and the atomic bomb, the leading manufacturer of chemical and biological weapons in the world is also the most powerful nation on Earth? *Violence creates power.*

Wealth also creates power because you can buy anything from allegiance to violence with it. You can buy nearly anyone, if the price is right, from a prostitute (male or female) to a sitting president.

Let us not overlook the connection between violence and wealth. Violence is often used to gain wealth as well as to protect it. Wealth has always been used to prosecute violence. War cannot be waged without capital. A single smart bomb costs a million dollars. There is a triangular, *symbiotic relationship* between violence, wealth and power.

Knowledge also *creates* power. It does so by enabling you to understand what power is and by such understanding further enables you to *acquire* and *utilize* power in the most suitable and productive way.

Knowledge can be used to create power. I know that many people think that knowledge *is* power, and the popular saying is, admittedly, appealing. It is, however, incomplete and thereby inherently misleading.

If it is true that knowledge *is* power it must necessarily follow that those who have knowledge are, by that fact alone, *powerful.* In 1997 nearly 90% of African Americans between the ages of 25 and 29 had completed high school or the equivalent. At the same time 13.7% of African Americans in that category had completed four or more years of college. Clearly, African Americans have amassed knowledge. It would, however be inaccurate to say that we have also amassed power. Are we powerful because we are knowledgeable?

The time honored phrase that knowledge is power is

inherently misleading because it does not accurately state the proposition it implies. It implies that knowledge and power are synonymous terms—they are not.

Knowledge is simply what has been recognized by and sometimes understood by the mind. The mere acquisition of knowledge no more guarantees the acquisition of power than reading the autobiography of Michael Jordan guarantees you an illustrious career in the NBA.

Knowledge is not itself power. Knowledge and power are not the same things. However, accurate, useful knowledge that is understood, timely and efficiently applied, can create power. By accurate we mean, knowledge that is minutely exact, precise, and free from error or mistake. By useful we mean, knowledge that has practical utility—knowledge that can be used to our advantage. When we speak of timeliness we are referring to knowledge that can be of assistance, benefit or service to us when it is needed, that is now, in real time.

Of course, all of the accurate, useful and timely knowledge in the world is of little value or *practical utility* if it is not *efficiently applied*. By efficient application we mean knowledge applied in a way that produces the desired result with a minimum of effort, expense or waste. *Efficient application of knowledge is the key to transforming it into a powerful resource.* Let us look at a few examples.

The Sun is 93 million miles distant from the Earth. Is this knowledge? Yes. Is it accurate? Yes. But, is it useful? Maybe, if you are about to embark on a journey into outer space. Such knowledge is useless for the average person.

George Washington Carver found more than 100 uses for the peanut. Is this knowledge? Yes. Is it accurate? Yes. But, is it useful? Maybe if you are writing a biography of Carver. The usefulness of this piece of information to the average person is, however, nil.

In each of these examples we do not have to even think about efficient application because there is no desired result. Such knowledge is not power. There is little likelihood that under any circumstances such knowledge could be transformed into power.

The misconception that knowledge is itself power should not lead us to ignore the possibility that *intelligence*, as distinct from knowledge is power.

Intelligence, in its most basic meaning, is the *ability* to learn or understand from *experience*. It is the ability to respond quickly and successfully to a new situ-ation. It is also the ability to use the faculty of reason in solving problems and directing conduct.

Intelligence is *ability*—ability is a form of *power*. Knowledge, on the other hand, is a thing. Intelligence is innate. Knowledge is acquired. *Intelligence is power.* Knowledge is not.

These then are some of the aspects or attributes of power. But, how should power be understood in its fundamental, real life, everyday application? More importantly, how should we view power as that term is used in the context of the *Total Black Empowerment?*

Let us examine real power, kinetic power, power in action, power as it exists in the real world. We will now talk about the power that determines destinies, that transforms slaves into kings and queens and tyrants into beggars.

Real power, in its most basic sense, is a two-pronged, double sided *ability*. It is the ability to take action you deem appropriate, when you deem it appropriate, despite resistance from others. The flip side of the coin of power is the ability to prevent others from taking action they deem appropriate when you deem it inappropriate.

Power is a force that is simultaneously proactive and reactive, initiatory and resistant. It is the ability to *activate* and *prohibit*—at will.

To *activate* is to make active—to take someone from a passive state to a state of action. To take someone from a state of lethargy, contemplation or repose, to wakefulness, movement, progress and advancement. *To animate that which was formally inanimate.*

To *prohibit* is to prevent someone from doing or accomplishing something. *To stem the tide, to retard the growth.* It is the ability to effectively stop some action from occurring, despite resistance from others. This aspect of power is perhaps the most important and the least understood.

In every facet of life, from every point of observation and analysis, survival and *prosperity* are impossible unless and until you can *effectively* and *consistently activate* and *prohibit*.

You cannot survive and prosper, individually or collectively, unless you are able to take *effective affirmative action* when you deem it necessary. And, you can- not survive or prosper, individually or collectively, unless and until you can *stop others from taking action that you oppose*. When you can do neither your very survival/prosperity, your continued existence is in the hands of others who may or may not be favorably disposed to your continued existence or advancement. This is why the acquisition of power requires consistent group effort.

POWER AS A GROUP DYNAMIC

Power may also be described as a *group dynamic* that is something that is generated by *collective thought and action*. This *manifestation of collective power* comes into existence when individuals *decide* to act in harmony to accomplish collective goals and objectives.

Decision-making is a *mental* or *thought* process. Thoughts, in turn, are *energy*. Thinking, then, can be accurately defined as an *energy* or *power process*. Collective decisions and collective action generate the power of the *group dynamic*

It should not be surprising that groups tend to be more

effective than individuals when it comes to decision-making and problem solving. Studies indicate that people working together in groups outperform individuals by a large margin.

The reasons for this fact are numerous. Perhaps the most important is the fact that because there will be more minds of varying degrees of sophistication in the group mix someone is likely to identify the idea that is the best suited to solve the problem. Although these findings may seem contrary to our experience in dealing with group decision-making, in the long run group decisions are more accurate then individual decisions.

THE POWER PROCESS

The power process refers to the continuing forward movement of power, in stages of development, from generation, by thought and action, to accomplishment of its natu ral or contemplated goal or end. This power process is a verifiable group dynamic that is participated in and contributed to by all people. The fact that most of us are unaware of it does diminish its reality.

Without knowing it we generate awesome power by this process that is routinely used against us. As a result we are the unsuspecting creators of enormous, perhaps unlimited, amounts of power that benefits every one but us. This unfor- tunate circumstance is the result of the masterful manipulation of, the *Law of Power Units, and our collective* ignorance of it.

THE LAW OF POWER UNITS

The Law of Power Units holds that when power units are combined the resulting power output increases exponentially so that the whole becomes greater than the sum of its parts. Each of us is an energetic, self-contained power unit that generates power as a natural function of its existence.

As any third grader knows, one times one will always be one. We cannot, alone, multiply our power or ourselves. In order to multiply we must combine with another *power unit*. Then, and only then, does the *multiplication* of power become possible.

According to the *Law of Power Units*, when two or more power units combine the increase in power is *exponential*. Two power units existing separate and apart amount to the force of one power unit each. When the two power units combine the increase in power is exponential because the *power base* is *squared*. In this way combined power units create more power then they could alone.

THE POWER OF THE PEOPLE

Before the advent of civilization human beings would have noted that their ability to secure food and to protect themselves from attack was greatly increased when they joined together and acted as a group. Without knowing it they were applying the *Law of Power Units*.

Eventually, some individual realized that if he/she could, by whatever means, convince the other members of the group to permit him or her to act as *leader of the group* then he/she would be able to control and manipulate the combined power of the group. What the leader wanted to be was the *controller of the power* of the group because the combined power of the group is exponentially greater than the sum of the power of the individual power units. As a result the leader became not only the controller of the power but also the controller of the *excess* power.

Excess power is that which accumulates when power units are combined. Of course, it is the excess power that enables the leader, or *power controller*, to be more powerful than the group. Thus was born the first so-called omnipotent ruler.

In the modern world we may have taken on the trappings of civilization but the underlying *Law of Power Units* is still applied in the same way and with the same result. The power of the ruler still comes from his ability to convince the other members of the group to permit him to control and manipulate the combined power of the group *and* the excess power derived from it. The power that he wields is still generated by the individual power units. It follows that each power unit contributes, at least tacitly, to the power that is wielded by the ruler. Put another way, the power of the ruler is nothing more or less than the often referred to, but little understood, *power of the people*.

The power we generate is used against us to control us, so that it is entirely accurate to say that we are not powerless but rather that our useable power has been appropri- ated by others and has been used against us thereby preventing us from using it ourselves.

As you can see, power is clearly a group dynamic. We are generators of enor- mous, perhaps unlimited, amounts of power. Unfortunately, all too often the benefit of our power is not only denied us, it is also used against us. We are denied use of our potential power for many reasons and by many methods, but the primary reason is because of our ignorance of its existence.

We view ourselves as powerless (which is not the same thing as *being* powerless) because we have not been successful in securing the benefits of power pro- portionate to our numbers in the population. This conclusion is a direct result of our failure to understand power and our failure to utilize *Critical Thinking techniques*.

By way of analogy, what we have done is to conclude from the fact that the car will not start, and the lights will not come on, that the car's battery is dead and that it has no power. Upon careful analysis, that is, by checking under the hood, we find that the battery, the source of the power, is not dead after all. In fact, the battery is fully charged. The problem is that the battery cable is *disconnected. The power is there, in ample measure, its just not getting to where it is needed.*

In the everyday world most of things that we consider to be beneficial are con- trolled and determined by a power that results from the effective manipulation of law of power units. That power is *political.*

POLITICAL POWER

The power that is routinely used against us by our enemies is primarily *political power.*[1] *Political power* is best understood as the ability to *enact* and to *interdict*. To *enact* is to transform the collective will of our people into substantive, affirmative laws that we deem necessary and appropriate to our interests, regardless of resistance. To *interdict* means to prevent others from establishing laws inimical to our collective interests as we determine those interests.

Put another way, political power is the ability to take unilateral action, in the face of the existence of actual or potential resistant force and to succeed in doing so and the corresponding ability to prohibit, thwart, undermine, deter and stop unilateral action by others, in the face of actual or potential resistant force, and succeed in doing so.

Political power is a formidable force. It is a controlling factor in almost everything we do. This enormous, seemingly unlimited power cannot be understood, harnessed and manipulated to our advantage, however, unless and until we understand *politics* and *political organization.*

POLITICS

Politics is popularly defined as the science of government. This accepted definition is incomplete and therefore, misleading. It should be obvious that politics and power are in some way closely related. It follows that any definition of poli- tics that does not include power as its most essential ingredient is, by that fact alone, incomplete and *intentionally* misleading.

As every politician knows, government cannot exist without power. *Political power is the fuel upon which government runs.* It is the lifeblood of government and the object of every politician's quest for political office.

Politics is more accurately defined as the acquisition, utilization, distribution and control of power in the governance of human affairs. To be precise, politics is the science of the application of power in the political arena.

When we speak of powerlessness, particularly as it relates to African Americans, we are really talking about the *lack of political power*. This is unavoidably true because people are recognized as powerful or powerless based on the relative amount of *political power* they control.

In the absence of power we are incapable of *taking action* that benefits us, or of *stopping action* that is detrimental to our collective interests. In both cases, we are incapable of overcoming the *resistant force* of the political power of others.

Political power determines *who* gets *what* and *when* and in this way it is the *exclusive distributor* of government *prerogative* and *largesse*. The measure of politi- cal power is the extent to which others are *forced* to recognize your *authority* and *sovereignty*.

Authority is the power to *give commands, enforce obedience* and to *take unilateral action. Sovereignty is supreme and independent political authority.* Neither authority nor sovereignty can exist in the absence of power. No people can logcally consider themselves empowered until they have both authority and sovereignty. No people can be said to be powerful unless and until they control *real* political power. *In the final analysis it is political power that overcomes resistance.*

Political power, like power generally, is a *group dynamic* and it is, perhaps, the best proof of the existence of the *Law of Power Units*. This is because political power cannot be generated *individually*. Political power absolutely requires group action in order to exist. Political power cannot exist in the absence of *political organization*.

POLITICAL ORGANIZATION

Political organization is a *relationship*. It is a relationship that is created when power units are combined. It is, therefore, a relationship that operates according to the *Law of Power Units*.

A relationship is an affinity, a causal connection that gives birth to a separate and distinct entity that has a life of its own. The reality of this fact is clearly demonstrated in what happens when a man and woman come together. At first, there is woman and man. Thereafter, something comes into existence that they can only describe as the relationship. No matter what the man and woman anticipated or planned, once the relationship exists it takes on a separate existence that seldom resembles what they expected and which seems to have a mind of its own.

In the case of political organization, the relationship is formed through the combination of power units that, in turn, creates a *group power field* which functions as a *power base*. The *group power field* is not the power units themselves. It is the result of the *relationship* between the units. It is much like the *magnetic field* that is created when electricity is passed through coils of copper wire. The *power base* is the foundation from which the political organization derives its life sustaining energy.

The political organization then, is what comes into existence when power units combine to accomplish a political objective. When power units, having a common objective, join together in political organization they multiply their energy and the combined power that results will, invariably, exceed the total of the individual power units by a measurable, predictable, and exponential rate of increase.

In addition, this combination of power units further *intensifies* the enhanced power by giving it *direction* and *focus*, much like sunlight focused through a magnifying glass. Put another way, *political power comes into existence when power units, having adopted a specific political objective, join in a political organization (power relationship) that, in turn, creates a group power field that functions as a power base from which to multiply, focus and direct their combined political power for the accomplishment of their objectives.*

Clearly, the most important component of Empowerment is the political power component. Political pundits, past and present, have argued that *economic* empowerment is primary. While it is certainly true that economic empowerment is important, even vital, the argument remains as misguided today as it was when Booker T. Washington advocated it more than a century ago.

Political power is primary simply because *true economic empowerment is only possible when true political power exists.* It is also true because, contrary to popular belief, economic *power* cannot even be contemplated without capital. In fact, you cannot define economic power without capital. Political power, on the other hand, requires the joining of *minds*.

We have previously noted that political power determines who gets what and when because it is the exclusive distributor of government prerogative and largesse.

This country was built, and its great fortunes were made, essentially because programs and policies were put in place that made it possible for certain *politically favored* groups to succeed. The same programs and policies also prohibited other groups from competition and by so doing doomed those *politically disfavored* groups to lives of marginal economic opportunity and development.

The reason that the politically favored succeed while others of arguably equal intelligence, ingenuity and determination fail is that the politically disfavored lack the *unbridled* and for the most part *unchallenged* political power of the politically favored.

THE POWER PRINCIPLE

Political power is a *principle* as well as a process. By principle we mean a *scientific law that explains a natural action*.

Simply stated the power principle holds that those who have power shall prosper, that is become more powerful, and those who do not have power shall serve those who do. This is a fundamental, universal law that has been proven, confirmed and reconfirmed over time and is abundantly recorded in history. It has been proven to be a natural action that produces a specific effect. This is true because of two specific properties of all power, political and otherwise.

The first property of power is its *neutrality. Power will serve any master and any cause.* It does not care whether you are Black or White, rich or poor, Democrat or Republican, Muslim, Christian, Jew or Pagan for that matter. Because power is neutral its affect is determined by its use. *The negative use of power will result in negative consequences—positive use will bring about positive results.*

The second property of power its *tendency to expand*. Power has the innate tendency to increase in size, bulk or volume. As a result power rewards those who control it with ever increasing amounts of it and it does so without remorse or compassion.

When the two properties of power are understood the old saying that the rich get richer and the poor get poorer takes on new, scientific meaning. The rich get richer because, as we have seen, wealth is a form of power. Wealth expands so that those who have it are constantly increasing their store of it.

Our analysis of power is not complete. There is another dimension of power. That must be understood before *Total Black Empowerment through the creation of powerful minds®* can be realized. The final dimension of power is one that perhaps you have already anticipated; it is the *Spiritual Dimension of Power*.

14

THE SPIRITUAL DIMENSION OF POWER

INTRODUCTION

From this point forward much of what you read may be new and unsettling. It will be *initially* unsettling because you will be required to *engage your mind* in an unavoidable confrontation with your preexisting belief system. This is not done to make the reader uncomfortable, but rather, to force her to use the *Critical Thinking techniques* that have been outlined in previous chapters.

This section is a *mental exercise* that will subject your deep-seated beliefs and belief systems to critical analysis and by so doing *eliminate* that which is *unfounded* while simultaneously *accentuating* what is *real*.

Please remember that it is not my intention to offend the reader's religious sensibilities. It is equally true, however, that if I altered my course to avoid all offense I would also effectively *undermine* the very premise upon which *Critical Thinking* and *Total Black Empowerment* are based.

I would remind you to recall the commitment you made earlier in this *mind power primer* to accept the ideas presented here with an *open mind* subject to your own exacting, critical analysis.

The achievement of Total Black Empowerment

through the Creation of Powerful Minds® absolutely requires that Critical Thinking precede and lay the foundation for the cultural/political chain reaction that will propel us to power proportionality within one generation. Until we cultivate open minds that are free from prejudice and bias and open to new ideas these vital, all-important goals will forever elude us. Let us begin, as always by defining our key term.

SPIRITUAL POWER DEFINED

Spiritual Power is the greatest power in the universe. Spiritual Power is the source from which all power flows. Spiritual Power is a fundamental property of all things. Spiritual Power is the Power of God.

We have said that *power is energy* when it is *creative and life giving*. We have also said that *spirit is energy* precisely because it too is *creative* and *life giving*. Unfortunately, the scientific search for empirical evidence of the existence of the spirit, or soul if you prefer, has been virtually non-existent because in order to search for it scientists would first have to develop a theory that *postulates* its existence.

Since the Ancient Greeks concluded that in order to be *scientific* science must be free from spiritual influence no self-respecting scientist, who values his standing in the academic community, is willing to associate his or her name with a the- ory that postulates the existence of the soul or spirit or the experimentation necessary to confirm or deny it. The result is that there have been no mainstream studies of *spirit, spiritual power* or *spirit as energy*.

Ironically, scientists have studied another form of energy that exhibits the *properties and activity of spiritual power*. This exhaustively studied form of energy is one that literally *dominates* the modern world, is responsible for much of its so-called progress and without which modern civilization would come to a grinding, unceremonious halt. Let us examine this pervasive energy/power to see how its unquestionable existence can provide not only insight into the existence of spiritual power but the characteristics of spiritual power as well.

SPIRITUAL POWER AND ELECTRICITY CONTRASTED

Of course, the form of power/energy I have been alluding to is *electricity (or electrical charge)* and although scientists have identified certain characteristics of it, they still do not know precisely why it exists, what it is or where it comes from.

Scientists do know that electricity is a fundamental property of all matter and that the essential nature of all matter is electrical. They also know that there are two kinds of electricity—positive and negative. Positive electricity has a less than normal complement of electrons while negative electricity has an excess complement of electrons.

Electrons, protons and *neutrons* comprise the basic components of matter and along with other particles they comprise the *atom. Atoms, in turn,* are the basic building blocks of life.

When electrons are passed through a *conductor* their *movement* is called electricity. Simultaneously, the movement through the conductor creates a *magnetic field*. The magnetic field is a *physical force field made of energy*. This energetic force field in turn has the natural ability to infuse with its power some of the things it comes into contact with. This field of force consists of *lines of force* that are *attrac- tive* and *repellant that run from north to south. The strength of the force between the north and south poles can be precisely calculated.* As electricity moves the force field it creates moves through space at the speed of light.

The scientific community has recognized the mysterious relationship between electricity and magnetism for centuries. The recognition of a connection between electricity and spirit has been less than forthcoming. In fact, it is astonishing that no one seems to have investigated such an obvious connection.

Like electricity spirit is believed to permeate all things and to be the essential nature of all things. Spirit too can be positive or negative and because it has both extremes it may be seen as polar as well. When active and in motion spirit creates a *physical force field* that we call the *group field* that can be likened to the magnetic field of electricity.

Interestingly, scientists have now verified that the heart, the home of the spirit according to our ancestors, generates an electromagnetic energy field that is five thousand times more powerful than that generated by the brain, that not only exists before the brain is formed, but, also that can be detected by a magnetometer from ten feet away. It spreads outward and infuses with its power all things that it comes in contact with.

Just as electricity has always existed only waiting for the idea that turned it to use as a boon to humanity, spirit lay dormant as a power to be tapped. Just as electricity has been tapped as a source of power that transformed the world, so spirit, as the first and most important dimension of power can also be tapped to transform our people and ultimately everything we come in contact with.

THE POWER OF THE SPIRIT

Spirit animates all living things. More accurately, that which we *call* spirit *seems* to animate all living things. Certainly living things are animated. Clearly, there must be a *cause* for the animation. It should not be surprising then that the word spirit has been variously defined as the *breath of life*, the *vital force*, the *life principle* and the di-

vine essence. We may add to these definitions that spirit is apparently also a *creative* force. But, the word spirit also means *mind, will consciousness* and *thought.*

Spirit has, therefore, two integrated, interconnected elements—Divine Essence and Divine Utterance. Spirit is simultaneously that which inspires life and that which *motivates mind, thought and will. In short it is through the spirit that we are alive and conscious. These two integrated, interconnected elements also define spirituality—the state or quality of being spiritual.*

SPIRIT AS DIVINE ESSENCE AND DIVINE UTTERANCE

When we speak of spirit we are talking about both Divine Essence, that is, the source of life and Divine Utterance, which is the articulated power of the mind or thought and the power of the will. Together these two elements comprise spiritual power. We should also note here that when we talk about spiritual power and spirituality we are talking about something very different from religion.

Religion is the belief in divine power while spirituality is the physical, mental and emotional experience of the divine power that religion professes to believe in. This fact explains why recent surveys have indicated that a growing number of people who frown on organized religion, nonetheless consider themselves highly spiritual and see no contradiction in the fact. Religion is not synonymous with spirit. Religion is not a substitute for spirituality.

To be spiritual is to be filled, in body and mind, with spiritual power. Spirit is energy. Energy is another word for power. The power of the mind, on the other hand, is expressed in thought and Divine Utterance, the articulated spirit. The power of the mind is spiritual power focused and directed by and through the intellect. When a group of people are in control of their collective spiritual power they not only have life, existence and survival, but they also have powerful minds suffused with powerful thoughts and driven by the indomitable will to succeed, prosper, to become great and yes, to become powerful.

We have already defined Divine Essence. Let us look more closely at Divine utterance and its components speech, *thought and will.*

DIVINE UTTERANCE: SPEECH

In this section we will discuss not just the ability to speak but also the power of speech, the thought that precedes it, and the will that drives it. These together comprise the second dimension of spiritual power. In our attempt to unravel the mysteries of Divine Utterance we must look briefly at speech and sound.

Speech is a curious phenomenon. It is properly defined as the verbal method by which we transfer thought from one mind to another. Speech is also the characteristic, unique and ubiquitous property of human beings exclusively.

We know nothing historically about the origin of speech. We do not know how or when it first came about. We do know, however, that it is infinitely older than writing and that there is no meaningful difference between modern speech and the speech of our ancient ancestors. Ancient languages are, in fact, as subtle and intricate as those extant today.

The speech phenomenon seems to have gone essentially unchanged from the way it was when it first appeared. This seems to indicate that speech came into existence in a state of perfection. It also means that today's speech is virtually the same as it was at the moment of its unknown origin.

Let us begin by noting the fact that although the origin of speech has not been determined it does not mean that it has no origin. We know that every effect must have a cause and that every effect, in turn, becomes a cause in its own right. It follows that the fact of speech points indisputably to a cause for its existence, whether we can determine the cause or not.

When we consider that speech is one of the two dimensions of spirit, and that spirit can only be otherworldly we are forced to conclude that speech too is otherworldly. The conclusion is quite easy to reach.

We can safely say that there is an animating force that gives life to sentient beings. We do not need scientific proof to say this. All we need do is look at a corpse. It is evident from that alone that the one thing that is missing is the spirit—the Breath of Life. We also know that at the moment of conception, that is, when the infant heart begins to pulsate, a flow of electricity begins that does not subside until death and which did not exist before the heart began to beat. (The human heart begins to beat at 18 to 21 days after conception. In 162 days we become conscious). We can also note here that the beating of the heart results from electrical impulses that trigger contraction and relaxation. The origin of these electrical impulses is unknown.

It is this energy, whose place of origin is unknown, that scientists call electricity and I call spirit. This energetic force must come from somewhere. Just as we cannot discern the place of origin of electricity we cannot locate the place of origin of the spirit. Yet we doubt the existence of spirit and not the existence of electricity.

We also know that electricity exists throughout the universe. From this we can say that electricity exists outside of this world. We can say the same of spirit with the same measure of certainty.

We are forced to conclude that spirit, itself, is of *otherworldly* origin. We can also note that all religions have concluded that creation, or the bringing into existence of the things of this world was accomplished by some *spiritual* or *divine power* through the *agency of speech, i.e., the spoken word.*

Since it is also necessarily true that prior to the moment of creation the world could not have existed the speech/word that created the world had to come from some place other than this world, hence, the use of the term *otherworldly.* The unavoidable implication here is that not only is the power of speech a *creative* power and one of the two dimensions of spirit, it also *emanates* from some place other than this world. Speech is, therefore, a *creative act*—the act and the power is *otherworldly and divine.*

The dictionary tells us that to speak is to *intone* and *invoke.* In the context of our present discussion to speak is to invoke *spiritual power, i.e., the power of God.* And, if God is spirit (it is) then speech is also the *voice of God.*

It cannot be overemphasized here that only human beings are capable of speech. Of the millions of species on the planet only one can speak. The statisti- cal probability of this occurring by *chance* is so astronomical as to be functionally non-existent.

Only human beings have been given the *power of Divine Utterance—the cre- ative words—the words of power.* It is through these words of power that human- kind has been able to create the world in which we live. It is more than coincidence that the only specie on the planet that is capable of speech is also the only specie that has been able to mold nature to its will—at least for a time. But, what is speech?

Speech is a series of connected sounds. Sound is vibration. Vibration is a movement in one direction and then back in the opposite direction. When something vibrates in a medium, such as air, it sets molecules in motion and these, in turn, create waves of vibration that produce the effect upon the ear that we call sound. For those who require a technical definition sound is "... mechanical radiant energy that is transmitted by longitudinal pressure waves in a material medium (as air) and is the objective cause of hearing."

To speak then, is to cause vibration—to set things in motion—to create a back and forth motion. In short, speech is the power to set things in motion—it is literally the power of creation.

To create means to *bring into existence*. When we speak we set vibrations in motion that literally bring a sound or sounds into existence. These sounds, in turn, cause things to happen in much the same fashion that most religions postulate that God *created* on the first day of the world.

We know that when certain substances (spirits of turpentine for example) are subjected to certain sound frequencies the particles of the substances reconfigure themselves into *geometric* patterns. This phenomenon shows that sound is not only creative; it also has the power to create *geometric forms*. It follows that speech, words, sound can have an effect on matter—it can literally *create* or bring material forms into existence.

Our dictionary definition of sound tells us that *sound is the objective cause of hearing*. More precisely, it may be argued that hearing is the *effect* and sound is the *cause*. Certainly, there would be no need for ears if sound did not exist.

Hearing is the most *direct* of the five senses. Whether asleep or awake we are always *alert* to sound. It has even been said that the entire human body is a sound sensitive organ, in effect, it is one big ear. Is it possible that sound is the cause of the entire body. *God spoke. Think about it.*

We can also note that the nature of the sound we hear as well as the words cre- ated by the vibration causes us to respond in certain ways. *Sound, being stimulus, creates responsive action*. Parents, particularly mothers, are well aware of this fact.

A mother can be so sound asleep that you have to

knock her out of the bed to awaken her. But, let the baby in another room make the slightest sound and mother is wide-awake and in motion instantly.

How about the difference in sounds. You may hear a child crying and know that it is nothing serious. But, you can also hear another type of crying that will cause you to drop everything and go running immediately. It's a sound that says danger and every parent knows it few, however, can explain it.

We first experience speech and its power as infants. It is a fact that the first thing we recognized about our parents (usually our mothers) is the sound of her voice. It is amazing that infants recognize their mother's voice from all others. Mother's voice has the power to calm and soothe when nothing else will. Witness the eternal frustration of virtually all fathers who have tried everything they can to soothe an infant only to have mother do it with the mere sound of her voice.

As we grow older father's word becomes law. Mother's often tell the story of their eternal frustration at the fact that they will yell until they are hoarse without apparent affect while father will utter a single word and he is obeyed. Not coinci- dently, fathers have referred to this power as putting the *fear of God* into a child. They might more properly call it the *fear of the voice of God*. As you can see the characterization may be more accurate than they suspect.

Speech then is not only a power, it is also a *vehicle* by which we can *command* and *direct* action. Depending on the meaning of the words spoken and the iden- tity of the speaker (that is how much power he or she is believed to have) the words can literally cause things to happen. Speech is a powerful medium. We could anticipate that this vehicle, more than any other, is nearly universally proclaimed to have been the method by which God created the world and everything in it.

TOTAL BLACK EMPOWERMENT

Let us not forget that creation was accomplished, we are told, by the use of *divine words* spoken by the Creator that began as a *thought in the Mind of God—the Divine Mind*. In effect, the divine words caused things to *grow* (every living thing grows) from an *idea* to a tangible *reality*. For this reason it is accurate in this context to refer to thoughts as *Seed-Ideas such that when we speak we simultaneously broadcast seeds in the form of ideas.*

THOUGHTS AS SEED-IDEAS

Speech is preceded and motivated by thought. It is safe to say that you cannot speak without *thinking* first. Thought always *precedes* speech, and because thought creates speech, speech is impossible without thought. In saying this we concede the existence of persons who after we have heard their words we conclude that they could not have possibly thought about them before they spoke. They did think, they just did not think well.

Thought is the power to conceive and create ideas. An idea is a *mental construct*—something created by and existing in the mind as an item of knowledge. Thought precedes speech because speech is the *articulation* of necessarily pre-existing ideas.

When we speak we create the existence of our ideas in the minds of others. We transfer, more accurately transplant our thoughts, *as if by heka*, to the minds of others and create in their minds a chain of ideas that can change the course of their lives and cause them to take action that was, inconceivable to them prior to the *transformation of their thinking by the introduction of our new ideas.*

As you can see a thought is a *seed/idea* that we *transplant to, and implant in, the minds of others by the power of speech.* A powerful seed/idea can also take root in our own minds without our being aware of it. As when a new thought is generated by an idea we have previously heard but not initially understood.

Thought, just like radio and television is, in effect, the manipulation of electrical impulses. In fact, the connection between thought and electrical impulse is also evident when you consider that we do not become *conscious*, that is become aware of the world around us, until 162 days after our first heartbeat which is simultaneous with the arrival of our first electrical impulse.

We should add in passing that even the word thought comes from Tehuti (Greek *Thoth*) the African Kemitic *Lord of Thought*. Again, *all roads lead to Kemit*.

I will now briefly examine the connection between spirit and will to illuminate another aspect of spiritual power.

WILL

The will is essentially a form of power. More precisely it is a combination of power and action. In fact, will and power are so closely related as to be virtually inseparable. This is because Will is ineffective without power to affect its intentions, and Power is random and ineffective without will to give it *direction* and *focus*. Will is the determination of all living things to reproduce and thereby survive.

The will is also the *character* of the mind. It is that which gives the mind its shape and texture. Some have minds with the shape and texture of mush while others closely approximate steel.

The will is part of the spirit. It works together with the intellect to create reason. It balances thought with emotion to create action. The will is the *power of self-determination*. It is a potent, driving force of life. It is that which makes purposeful activity possible. It is itself a stimulus that seems to originate action based on thought. The will functions as the sheer determination to overcome obstacles in the path of existence. When will is understood as *self-determination* its importance to survival and spiritual power becomes evident. The will is also the determination to attain prosperity, which is *the level above survival.*

The will under girds thought—thought creates seed/ideas—speech articulates those ideas and gives them life as *Divine Utterance. Divine Utterance is the creative act that is the Word and the Voice of God.* Without the benefit of a strong will self-determination is virtually impossible and survival is, at best, serendipitous.

THE HISTORICAL IMPERATIVE FOR THE UTILIZATION OF SPIRITUAL POWER

No people on Earth, now or in the past, have become powerful without an *indigenous concept of spirituality*. By concept of spirituality we mean an understanding of their relationship to some spiritual power and its relationship to the world.

Moreover, no people have come to power without their own unique, time-honored speculations about spiritual power. The reason for this is more easily discovered than you might imagine.

We have seen that power permeates all things in the universe. Nothing can be created and nothing can exist without power. When this power is resident in human beings we refer to it as *spirit.*

Spirit is a power. But, it is not just any power. It is the power that creates and sustains life. It is the vital force, the *life force*, the strength and energy of existence. Spirit is the *active, creative power* that many of us understand and refer to as *God,* or the *Creator.*

TWO MIND TRANSFORMING QUESTIONS

It has been said that a properly stated question reveals its own answer. This statement holds implicitly that we answer our most important questions by first finding the ap-propriate question that, in due course, leads us to the an-swer we seek. It has also been said that all we need do is *connect*. Find the synergies and we will find the answers. *Ask questions. Make connections.*

I will here posit two questions that will lead you to make the connections and find the answer that will be truly transformative. Here are the questions, study them well.

- If God is the *active power* in our lives why are we *power deficient*?

- If the presence of God is manifested by the presence of *active power*, why are we unable to protect and defend our basic civil and human rights?

Let us begin to answer these mind transforming questions by acknowledging that the very *concept of God* is meaningless if it is not aligned with the *concept of power*. Think about it.

Even God cannot fulfill its universally recognized roles of *Creator* and *Sus tainer* of the Universe unless it is, at very least, *powerful*. God must be full of power simply because without power God is just—not God.

No people have ever paid homage to a weak God. No one worships a God who they believe to be *powerless*. No one boasts of his allegiance to a God who can do *nothing*. God must, at very least, be *believed* to have enough power to protect and defend worshippers from the hostile forces of the world or It would not be a *logical* object of veneration.

Religion too is dependent on power. Religion is universally defined as the belief in a *supernatural power,* but *power* nonetheless. To the extent that religion serves to bring humanity closer to the *realization* of God it simultaneously serves to bring humanity to the *realization of spiritual power.* In our pious genuflections, devoted prayers, mysterious rituals and other acts of adoration we seek favor with *spiritual power,* by flattery.

In our attempt to understand the *true nature of power* we have discovered a truly *provocative, powerful* and even *revolutionary* idea. No matter how we call it, in the final analysis, we cannot escape the fact that *God is the Supreme Power from which all power flows.*

GOD IS POWER

If you accept the foregoing, you should not be surprised to learn that the oldest extant word for that which we now refer to as God is an African *Kemitic* word that not only means *force, strength and might,* but also the *active power that produces and creates things in regular recurrence and that gives life and restores youthful vigor.*[1]

This means that at the first appearance of a recorded concept of God in human history, God was conceived as an *active power.* The implications of this fact are profound when understood in the context of *Total Black Empowerment.* What this logically implies is that according to the *original African concept of God,* that is, according to our ancient ancestors, we cannot understand God unless and until we also understand *power.* In short, *to understand power is to know God.*

If it is true that *God is power* (it is) we would logically expect to find the *components of power* to be embraced by the concept of God. Let us see if this is true.

TOTAL BLACK EMPOWERMENT

Power, as we have seen, is a composite of *force, strength and energy*. Power is *force* when it is *exerted*, *strength* when it causes things to *resist* or *endure*, and *energy* when it is *creative* and *life giving*. When these composite aspects of power are compared to the ascribed attributes of God the fit is, in a word, *divine*.

Think about it. Virtually all religions agree that God, or at least their particular God, is *forceful, strong, energetic* and *creative*. All religions believe in and propagate an efficacious *God of Power*. It follows that if God were not believed to have such power prayer would be an *illogical* exercise in futility. We pray to God because we *believe* that God is predisposed to grant prayers and that God has the *power* with which to grant prayers.

Moreover, all religions agree that perhaps the primary characteristic of God is *creative power*. Without the *power to create* animate as well as inanimate things God would be ineffective and could not *logically* be worthy of reverence or belief. Without creative power God could not possibly be *The Creator* and there could be no *creation*.

All religions also agree that it is God's power to animate things that gives rise to the *universal laws of motion*. God is, therefore, the *power* behind both *creation* and *movement*. And, of course, independent movement is one of the key indicators of the presence of life.

God is not only power, It is *kinetic* power as well. God is dynamic power that tends toward *constant change*. It is axiomatic that all religions must necessarily agree that God is *alive* and *active* in human affairs.

God is also universally proclaimed to be the moving force in all things. God and power are functionally synonymous concepts. Each embodies the attributes of the other. To define power, then, is to define God. To understand power is to understand God.

When these facts are pursued with an *open mind*, the conclusion reached is a truly powerful and revolutionary idea. *God is power. God is spiritual power. Spiritual power is the source of all power.*

This powerful, revolutionary idea speaks volumes regarding the circumstances in which African Americans find themselves. This idea also provides profound insight into the strategies and tactics we must employ if we are to survive and prosper in the 21st century.

We are compelled here to ask ourselves a most important set of questions the answers to which will enable us to jettison the concepts that impede our ability to tap into the wealth of spiritual power bequeathed to us by our ancestors.

The first question is simple and straightforward. If *God is active power* does it not follow that *power* must be *actively* present among us for us to have formal *evidence* of the *presence* of God in our lives? Think about it.

The second question is equally straightforward, but perhaps, more difficult to contemplate. If the presence of God is manifested by the presence of *active power,* why is it that African Americans, the descendants of the most *powerful, creative, spiritual, innovative and energetic* people in the history of the world, have been, for centuries, without *sufficient power* to enable us to *protect* and *defend* our basic human rights? The answer is as straightforward as the question.

Those who appear to have insufficient power to protect and defend their basic human rights and to claim their fair share of the world's resources simply do not understand that *God is power. God is spiritual power. Spiritual power is the source of all power.*

It is this basic but profound misunderstanding, this failure to apprehend the single most powerful idea of them all, which dooms us to permanent second-class citizenship, not only in the United States, but in the world of nations as well.

An analogy seems appropriate here. Slave master

and slave pray to the same God. The slave master, in his sumptuous mansion nestled on the four thousand acres of his cotton plantation, prays in his private chapel to his powerful God. He prays for the *continued productivity* of his slaves because they are the real source of his and his family's wealth and prosperity. He prays that God will make his slaves work harder to produce more, that they will multiply and increase their numbers every nine months. He also prays that they will remain *docile* and *ignorant* and will continue to *willingly accept* their dejected lot in life. Perhaps above all he fer- vently prays that his human property will *never rise up in rebellion against him*.

At the same time, down on the lower forty, the slave and his family are on their ragged knees, on the beaten Earth floor of their broken down slave quarters. They too pray to God. In fact, *they pray to the same God as the slave master*. The slave family prays with a fervent desperation and sincerity that the master will never know. The slave prays for his *freedom*. He prays that God will make a way for him and his family to be free from the misery, degradation, humiliation and abject poverty.

When freedom does not come to the slave, whose prayer has been answered? Can the slave say that God has answered his prayer? Can the slave master? If freedom does not come to the slave and the *power of control* remains with the slave master it becomes difficult to persuasively argue that the power that is God is not on the side of the slave master because he is undeniably the one with *superior* power.

Freedom, as this example shows, is truly the liberation from slavery or restraint or from the power of another. Put another way, *freedom is the power not to be a slave or second-class citizen for that matter*.

Those who are without freedom are without sufficient power, and those who are without sufficient power cannot be free. If God is Power (It is) and freedom is also a form of power (it is) it necessarily follows that those who have no power have no freedom and therefore have no God or a weak God, which amounts to the same thing.

Let us not forget here that the slave master and the slave are praying to the *same* God. The answer to both of their prayers calls for *power*. As we have seen, power is *neutral*. *Power will serve any master*. We have also seen that power is expansive. Power rewards those who have it with ever increasing amounts of it.

In short, the slave master's prayer will be forever answered by *natural operation of the power principle*. The slave, on the other hand, will forever remain a slave, unless and until, his own power *increases sufficiently* to overcome the power of the slave master or the slave master's power *decreases sufficiently*.

Of course, there were always slaves, then and now, who argue that God has a plan, or that God's time is not man's time or that when slavery was abolished it was the answer to the slave's prayer. There are even those who will argue that God *waited* until the slave was *ready* for freedom. The foregoing arguments represent no more than feeble excuses that are the characteristic, predictable result of the abnormal separation of related thoughts, ideas and emotions that we have described as *dissociation*.

Can we *logically* argue that God *withholds* the power to be free from the slave to fulfill some *divine plan*? That would be the same as arguing that God's plan is for us to be mocked by our prayers and to be cursed in spite of them.

Conversely, such an argument must mean that to be violent, insensitive and brutal is to curry God's favor. As seen through the eyes of the slave, God gives power to those who are the least worthy of it.

God is power. The power of God is spiritual power. Like all power spiritual power will serve any master—provided he or she knows how to *invoke* it. The reasons for this fact bear repeating. *Power is neutral. Power is neither good nor* bad. *Power will serve any master. Power is expansive. Power attracts more power. Power continuously increases its volume to those who control it.* We must accept the fact that power is neither good nor bad—it just *is*.

We must also accept the fact that although spiritual power is the first and greatest power in the universe. It is, nonetheless, a power. Like all power, the same universal laws that govern all power govern spiritual power.

There is one other dimension of *Spiritual Power* that we must account for and without which our understanding of *Spiritual Power* would be less than accurate because it would be incomplete. We have intentionally avoided this aspect of *Spiritual Power* until now. We have done so because it is an aspect that we have been taught not to associate with *Spiritual Power*. In fact, it is an aspect that we have been led to believe, because of our *uncritical acceptance* of a European belief system, cannot possibly be associated with *Spiritual Power*. We have been taught that, directly or indirectly, it is impossible because spirit is pure, while this aspect is, at best, dirty and polluted.

As you will come to understand, European belief systems to the contrary notwithstanding, our ancient ancestors never accepted such a belief. In fact, they would have seen such a belief as patently ridiculous. If you have not figured it out by now we are talking about sex. More precisely, we are talking about the *procreative or sexual dimension of Spiritual Power*.

THE PROCREATIVE DIMENSION OF SPIRITUAL POWER

We have discussed that *Spiritual Power* is, among other things, *creative*. We have seen that that dimension of creativity is manifested as *Divine Utterance*. It is by the *spoken word* that God creates. But, we must not forget, the creative dimension necessarily includes *procreation*. God *creates*, human beings and other living creatures, *procreate. The act of bringing new life into the world is procreation.*

In order to accomplish this wondrous feat of *procreation*, the spirit, as a *creative power*, is endowed with sexual, pro-creative ability that makes possible its creative activity. When we fully understand this we are forced to recognize that sex too is a *power*. It is a creative power that is an inseparable part of the *Divine, creative act*. Of course, the creative *act* is popularly known as sex.

Sex is the act of procreation. It is the *method* by which we are enabled to bring new life into existence. It is the facility by which we come closest to manifesting our most potent, visible *resemblance to God. God creates. Human beings procreate after the fashion of God, that is, miraculously, and mysteriously.*

Each time we engage in the sex act we *reaffirm* both the existence of God and establish the proof of the *existence* of the divine act of creation. We *believe* that God creates. We *know* that man and woman, together, *procreate*.

The spiritual foundation of sex is also demonstrated by the act of sex *without* regard to procreation. When man and woman join in sexual activity what they are doing, beside the obvious, is *joining their energies*. They are commingling, collectivizing their powers, their *pro-creative powers. Spirit is energy. Energy is power. Power is God.* To illustrate the point let us look at a quote from the *Sacred Science* of our ancestors. *Tehuti* speaks:

"... the master of generation [God], bestowed on humankind the *sacrament of reproduction*—full of affection and joy, gladness and yearning, and all that heavenly love that is his Being. I would have to explain the nature of this compelling *sacred bond* that binds a man and woman together, were it not that each one of us, if we explore our innermost feelings, can experience it for ourselves. *Contemplate that supreme moment, when each sex infuses it-*

self with the other. One giving forth and the other eagerly embracing. At that moment, through the *intermingling of the two natures*, the female acquires male vigour, and the male is relaxed in female languor. This *sweet sacramental act we celebrate* is shared in secret, because if performed openly before impure eyes, the ignorant may mock and the *divine power manifesting in both* sexes will shy away."[2]

Sex to our ancestors was a *sweet sacramental act*. In other words, sex was *sacred*. They celebrated it. This is because sex is so wonderful, so enjoyable that the act of procreation that inevitably follows is functionally unimportant. The *supreme moment* (orgasm) when the *two natures intermingle* is so enjoyable that we will do it, over and over again, without instruction, prodding or any other inducement. It is a basic fact of human nature that the more we enjoy something, the more we do it.

You will also note that there is no mention of marriage. Our ancestors did not, for political reasons, denigrate marriage; they just had sense enough to know that the sexual drive is so powerful that it could only be controlled by the mind. That is by a mind-set that celebrated it as a *divine, spiritual* act. Our ancestors *celebrated* sex.

The soundness of this point of view is to be seen in the results of the debasement of sex. If it is true that sex is a component of *Spiritual* Power (it is) debasement of it debases spirit and deprives us of the full use of the *power of the spirit*. A people who hold a jaundiced view of this creative power fail to properly avail themselves of it and, therefore deprive themselves of the creativity associated with it. *What is debased in thought eventually becomes debased in deed.*

All we need do is look at the world around us. Is sex held up as sacred? Is it ele- vated and set apart as a spiritual and divine act? Or is it debased to the level of the common so that it is made to appear unholy, venal and corrupt?

TOTAL BLACK EMPOWERMENT

Look around you. The connection between the teenage pregnancy rate, chil- dren being born out of wedlock, the irresponsibility of young fathers, is all inex- tricably linked to the debased, non-spiritual view of sex advanced by a culture that sees sex as a tool of commercialism.

As a dimension of *Spiritual Power*, sexuality is itself a *power*. Like any power sexuality can be manipulated to negative or positive advantage. By recklessly advertising it like deodorant or tooth paste, by using it to sell cars and household appliances its *attractive power* and appeal has been increased exponentially and to negative effect.

In societies where sex was celebrated as a spiritual, divine act it had no lurid, prurient attraction. In societies where sex it is debased it has become problematic. When sex is sacred it becomes a blessing and not a curse. If the sex act is sacred that which is produced by it must also be sacred. Our ancestors did not lament the birth of children. *They rejoiced in the arrival of new life.* They often saw children as the reincarnation of some beloved ancestor. They were blessed to have a familiar spirit with them again.

We overlook the *procreative dimension of Spiritual power at our own peril*. The greatest evidence of the existence of the power that is God and the greatest demonstration of our kinship with that creative power is in the act of procreation.

If our true desire is to know God then we must *understand* and *accept* all dimensions of *spiritual power*. We must understand that *spiritual power is the power of the spirit*.

RECAPITULATION

Spiritual Power is the greatest power in the universe. *Spiritual Power* is the source from which all power flows. *Spiritual Power* may be accurately described as the *Power of God* because *God is Power*.

Spiritual Power, like electricity, is a *fundamental prop-*

erty of all things. *Spiritual Power* creates, by its *movement*, a physical power (field) that is simultaneously *attractive* and *repellant*, and that can be tapped to *transform* all that it comes into contact with.

Spiritual Power has two dimensions—Divine Essence and Divine Utterance. Divine Essence is the life force. Divine Utterance is the creative act. It is through these two dimensions that we are alive and conscious.

Divine Essence gives us the power to exist like God. Divine Utterance gives us the power to create like God.

15

WHO ARE OUR ANCESTORS?

Before we begin the discussion of the mechanics of spiritual power we are required to satisfactorily determine who our ancient ancestors are. This next step in our intellectual journey is a necessary one because in order to effectively utilize spiritual power we must understand it as our ancestors understood it. And, as you will see in order to utilize spiritual power we must know who our ancestors are.

We will begin by asking and answering three pivotal questions: (1) who are our ancient ancestors; (2) what is our Authentic Ancestral Culture; and, (3) is there an authentic ancestral culture that we may collectively call our own that will enable us to begin to reclaim our rightful place on the world stage.

We must take this step before proceeding to the mechanics of spiritual power because, as you will see, the effective utilization of spiritual power is dependent on our link to our ancestral bloodline.

Our problem in utilizing spiritual power is further complicated by the fact that we have been taught to ignore our duty to our ancestors. Specifically, we have ignored them in our misguided attempt to be accepted by our former slave masters. In so doing we have not only disregarded them but we have acted as if they never existed and taught our children to do likewise thereby perpetuating the cycle of ancestral neglect. Our present condition is partially the result of a detrimental mind-set that is the outcome of centuries of indoctrination. Unfortunately, this mind-set has been reinforced by persons who we hold above reproach and whose love for us is beyond question.

PARENTAL INDOCTRINATION: YOU ONLY HURT THE ONE YOU LOVE

Our parents, whose love for their children is, as a general rule, unconditional, have unwittingly assisted our enemies in the establishment of the detrimental mind-set that has kept many of us in mental slavery until the present day.

Our parents helped to perpetuate the *American Dream/Deception* and the counterpro- ductive strategy of *peaceful suffering* as the only legitimate strategies available to us.

This is not to imply that our parents are to be faulted for the decisions they made. We know that *they did the best they could with what they had*. In fact, they did more with nothing than we are doing with all of our so-called advantages. Our parents gave us what they *believed* in the sincere belief that their beliefs and belief systems would enable us to survive in a racist, hostile world. We have *survived*. Our survival is directly attributable to their noble and blameless efforts.

It is also true, however, that we are now adults. We can no longer rely on childhood fables to instruct us in the technology of survival in the real world.

As children many of us believed in Santa Claus. We believed in *him* because our parents told us that he existed and we believed *them*. Now that we are adults we know that there is no Santa Claus, no Mrs. Claus, no elves and no flying reindeer. We do not fault our parents for providing us with undeniably false informa- tion. We do not fault them because we know that they did so out of the goodness of their hearts. We did, however, discard the falsehood when it was discovered. In fact, many of us have continued to perpetuate that falsehood by teaching it to our own children, even though just like our parents we know that the tale is not true. In the same way we can no longer rely on what we were taught as children without first subjecting it to rigorous scrutiny and analysis by the process of *Critical Thinking*. Nor can we, like our parents, continue to perpetuate beliefs that we know to be based on falsehood—to do so is no more than rank intellectual dishonesty.

One of the reasons that we persist in the counterproductive dissemination of inaccurate information is because we have been indoctrinated to do so. Admit- tedly the indoctrination has continued so long that we have collectively forgotten how and why it occurred. Perhaps an analogy will refresh our memories. Let me share with you the *Story of Grandma's Notes*.

THE STORY OF GRANDMA'S NOTES

Suppose someone who you love dearly, your grandmother for example, spent her entire adult life providing for you and protecting you. It was her to whom you turned when the world seemed to close in on you. No matter what the problem *she always had the answer*. Even when you thought she was meddling, even when you refused to accept her advice in the end she was *always right*.

Let us also assume that just before she departed this life she entrusted to you a book of notes, let's call them *Grandma's notes*. These notes, handwritten and passed down from generation to generation were not just any old notes. They were precious writings kept by her mother and her mother's mother for generations. As her mother had done before her, Grandma religiously added notes of her knowledge and experience to this cherished record over

TOTAL BLACK EMPOWERMENT

the course of her long life. These cherished notes contained the *secrets of survival,* gleaned from generation upon generation of hard earned experience. They contained everything from how to raise children, how to plant crops, build houses, serve God, load a shotgun and how to know an enemy. These notes contained the wisdom of all of your ancestors who had gone before you. These ancestors did not know you *personally,* but they knew you were coming. They knew that if their descendants only *survived* you would one day be born.

They prepared these precious notes against the day when you would need to know how to survive in this world. They prepared them to insure that their fam- ily's bloodline would survive *and* prosper for eternity. These notes were their gift of immortality to you.

Grandma entrusted her notes to you, on her deathbed, with the following words: "I raised you child. I did the best I could. But, I never told you that when times were hard and I didn't know whether we would make it another day I turned to these notes and every time, without fail they helped me make a way for us. I am about to become one with the force that is the Creator. I am giving this book to you. Please take care of it, add to it from your life experiences, record what works for you and guard it with your life. We only came this far because of it. As long as it is with us to guide us we will survive and prosper." With those words she passed on to the other side.

After Grandma departed this life someone came along with whom you shared the knowledge of the existence of Grandma's notes. The person told you that the book was mumbo jumbo, voodoo, and rank superstition. As if that were not enough the person demanded that you destroy the book, forget about it and never mention it again. In the place of your Grandma's notes the person gave you her grandma's notes and told you that hers were the only true, authentic and worthwhile notes.

TOTAL BLACK EMPOWERMENT

What would you do? Is there any power in the world that could constrain you from taking that person's head? Even if you did not believe the information the notes contained they were still written by the hand of a person whom you loved and whose memory you cherish dearly. What would you do? *Think about it.*

This is exactly what has happened to African Americans. The people who enslaved us have told us that what our ancestors believed is *superstition*. As if all religion is not superstition. They have caused us to believe that what their ancestors believed is the *only true belief.*

We cannot be blamed for accepting their beliefs in the days when we were sep- arated from our kin, our homeland and everything that we knew. It is not our fault that we were forbidden on pain of death to believe in or serve our ancestral Gods.

We cannot be held responsible for pursuing our *survival* above all else. In the days when we were forced to abandon our ancestral ways we did it *temporarily,* until we could do better, and never, never in earnest. It was a game we played—the *survival game.* We knew that bye and bye we would be free and would be able to return to our cherished ancestral ways. *That day has come. Think about it.*

We are no longer constrained, on pain of death, to renounce our ancestors and their beliefs. *The day they prayed for has come.* But we, their descendants, remain mentally enslaved to the beliefs of their and our enemies.

Contrary to popular but mistaken belief our ancestors developed and recorded a corpus of knowledge for us that is, in effect, the *technology of our survival and prosperity.* This information is the equivalent of Grandma's Notes.

This corpus of knowledge is comprised of *problem solving techniques* recorded by our ancient ancestor's that are timeless enough to effectively assist us in solving our present problems. Without these invaluable notes we are forced to rely on the counterproductive techniques of those who clearly do not wish us to achieve power proportionality. This only seems logical. How can we possibly believe that they will provide us with the key to the mental shackles that they have forged? They know that when our minds are infused with *powerful ideas* the day of reckoning is not far off.

We might also ask who better to advise us than our ancestors? They formu- lated techniques, strategies and a *technology of survival* that was specifically designed to insure that their descendants would continue to survive and prosper for eternity. In the absence of our familiarity with such *powerful knowledge* we will be doomed to continue the futile, counterproductive tactics we have come to rely on to solve our problems. In short, our present course will doom us to continue to utilize the tools imposed upon us by our historic enemies.

We will now attempt to answer the three pivotal questions stated at the beginning of this section. Who are our ancient ancestors? What is our Authentic Ancestral Culture? And, is there an Authentic Ancestral Culture that we may usefully call our own?

We are African Americans, that is, Americans who recognize that their fore- bears were born on the African continent. Some of us are descendant of American slaves as well. We agree, virtually unanimously, that we are of African descent. We are therefore, connected by blood to the people of the African continent. *We are a product of their history, thought and collective consciousness.*

We are displaced Africans. We are confused, decultured victims of centuries of unrelenting, intense psychological warfare, launched by our enemies and aimed at obliterating our connection to and identification with our ancestral homeland and its culture. This has not been done to enable us to assimilate. The dominant culture in the United States has no place for us and never will. It has been done to insure that we remain, for as long as possible, a battered, listing, wind tossed, rud- derless ship of state without direction or destination. Despite this we are still and will forever remain an *African people*. Our ancestral beginnings, our cultural base, can only be found in *Africa*—the land of our ancestral birth.

In order to determine what our authentic Ancestral Culture is we must begin by understanding what culture is. When we understand culture we will know what we are looking for and why it is so important that we find it. Let us begin with a precise definition of culture.

CULTURE DEFINED

Culture is a ubiquitous phenomenon. Its impact and influence are, in a word, pervasive. Few areas of life are untouched by culture, directly or indirectly. Its ramifications are often so subtle that the connection between it and virtually every aspect of our lives and fortunes is frequently overlooked.

Culture forms an all-embracing web that is sometime so finely spun as to be all but invisible. Like the web of the spider its strength is indeed remarkable. Because of this, the importance of culture is widely neglected or woefully misun- derstood. This fatal misapprehension carries with it the unmistakable portent of the lingering, debilitating bondage of mind and body of those who fail to per- ceive its importance. On the road to civilization and national identity, *culture is everything*.

Culture is, first and foremost, the *technology of survival*. It is a developed and evolved technology that consists of all the tools used by the group, including everything from farm implements like the digging stick and plow, to implements of war like the shield, assagai and drum. This *technology of group survival* also consists of intangible tools such as words, values and ideas. As such culture comprises actions, thoughts, emotions and all communication skills deemed appropriate by the group and which serve to distinguish the group and their behavior from that of others.

Culture is also the *system* by which a society provides its members with the things they need to survive and as such implicates political considerations arising from the evolution of government that is a necessary development in the transition from society to civilization.

Culture is the *vehicle* by which a people are enabled to keep in constant con- tact with their ancient ancestors and drink from the cup of their collective wis- dom. It is culture that permits them to see the world through the seasoned eyes of their ancestors while tapping into the unlimited power of those who have gone before.

Culture is that which answers the core set of fundamental questions whose answers determine the survival and prosperity of the group. The questions are universal. It is the answers that distinguish one people from another.

Culture begins as a loosely defined set of group behaviors that represent the folkways of the ancients that provide resistance to sudden change and a sense of order. It is these *folkways* that sustain a people through the generational vicissi- tudes of life in an increasingly hostile world. It provides that same type of stability to a group of people that instinct provides to the lower animals.

Culture develops through a variant of natural selection whereby methods that have proven to the effective in dealing with the problems of life and survival are informally codified by the group and earmarked as necessary components of survival.

Culture is, therefore, a *systematic technology of survival* comprised of the domi- nant ideas, knowledge and sentiments that permit solitary individuals to survive and prosper as a group. These *group ideas* consist in notions about everything from agriculture to weaponry, to the roles of men, women and children. They determine what shall be the diet staple and who shall marry whom, and who, if anyone shall lead. These rules, based on collective experience, are specific to the group and exist across the spectrum of race and geography.

When in the course of time this set of ancient, shared prescriptions become linked to the wisdom of those who have gone before (ancestors) they become *ancestral*.

Culture is specific and peculiar to the group of people by whom it is devel- oped. The effectiveness of a particular culture, that is its power to affect the survival and prosperity objectives of the group, is identified to, and compatible with, the historical will and spirit of the group exclusively.

This then is culture. With this definition is place we can now answer our second question, that is, *what is the authentic ancestral culture of the African American?*

16

WHAT IS OUR AUTHENTIC ANCESTRAL CULTURE?

I begin by stating categorically and without fear of contradiction that *our ances- tors were Africans*. The implication of this statement is that our *Authentic Ances- tral Culture* is that of the African people.

We anticipate the argument that we have been too long removed, anony- mously, from our homeland to be able to determine from what tribe or clan we descended. And that without such knowledge we are hopelessly incapable of arriving at an acceptable conclusion regarding our *Authentic Ancestral Culture*. We note at the outset that such argument, no matter how presented, is spurious and therefore unacceptable. It is as treacherous as it is inaccurate. It is fundamen- tally flawed because it mistakes individual *tribal custom* for African culture.

The diversity of the African people is well known even if somewhat exaggerated. But the multiplicity of African tribal groupings is, in any event, immaterial. Tribal numerousness is irrelevant when the objective of the analysis is the determination of the *core teachings* that comprise the authentic, foundational cultural beliefs underlying all African custom.

Prior to the unfortunate arrival of the Arabs and Europeans, Africans adhered to a core set of beliefs that comprised their culture. This set of beliefs (belief system) can be found among virtually all tribal groups, and forms, in turn, the core of our Authentic Ancestral Culture. The origin of these beliefs may be ascertained with precision.

It is conceded that the importance of a culture is its stabilizing and cohesive effect on a specific group of people for whom it was designed. It is also conceded that the group cannot become empowered without stability and cohesion. These concessions render the purpose of the search self-evident. They also compel another concession.

In our search we must look for the authentic African culture that has attained the *highest degree of success* in the accomplishment of the goals of culture. These are survival, prosperity, stability, cohesion, longevity and civilization. It seems too obvious to mention that it would serve no useful purpose to emulate any African culture that had not attained the highest degree of success in this regard.

What we are referring to here is form of *natural cultural evolution*. It operates much like biological evolution where organisms develop over time and by natural processes develop variations in their biological makeup that serve to enhance their ability to defend, reproduce and ultimately survive. Inferior adaptations tend to extinction while superior ones are reproduced and benefit the entire specie.

As we have seen culture too is developed as an outgrowth of an evolutionary process. Naturally, the highest state to which a particular culture has evolved would be that which is the most worthy of emulation by virtue of its demonstrated success.

The begged question here is whether there is a culture, African in origin, of ancient beginnings, whose success, gauged by its material and spiritual accomplishments and one that contains the fundamental components of ancient African culture generally, has evolved so far beyond others as to be the epitome of all cultures that partake of the erstwhile fundamental components.

If such a culture may be distinguished it is axiomatic that it, more than any other, must be the superior candidate to accomplish the objectives of culture as applied to the group of African descendants whose cultureless, hence power deficient condition (culture is also a power) among peoples and nations of the world is sought to be remedied.

To sum up, we have found that our ancestors were undoubtedly Africans; that our ancient progenitors subscribed to a *core of fundamental beliefs* that evolved over millennia and which comprised the traditional, indigenous culture that remained pure and consistent from one tribe to the next.

ANCIENT KEMIT: LAND OF OUR AUTHENTIC ANCESTRAL CULTURE

> "... a look toward the Egypt of antiquity is the best way to conceive and build our cultural future."[1]

We must next determine if a superior candidate having all the abovementioned qualifications does, in fact, exist. By this definition there is only one candidate that fulfills all of the criteria. It is found where it flourished for untold millennia among the African Nilotic people known as the Kemites (Greek < Egyptians). These people, an indigenous, black, purely African people, attained a level of civilization through the consistent application of their unique culture that remains unsurpassed in the annals of time.

It should also be noted here that Kemit was an indigenous African culture that acknowledged its ancestral roots were to be found in the bamboo forests of equatorial Africa. Their descent from the Twa people was duly enshrined in their recorded history. The civilization of Ethiopia was perhaps contemporaneous with Kemit. Other examples of refined African culture such as *Kush, Axum, Songhay* or *Timbuktu* are noteworthy and laudable. Their accomplishments are certainly important but remain insubstantial when compared with Kemit. Before there was a Songhay or a Timbuktu there was "Thebes of the Hundred Gates"; before the cathedrals of Europe and the minarets of Mecca there were the towering pyramids of Khufu. The Sphinx, silent watchman over our ancient history and treasures, has stood vigil so long that its date of origin cannot be fixed.

The ancient Kemites were an indigenous black African nation whose ancient civilization is the oldest in the world. Kemit is widely recognized as the birthplace of civilization and the Kemites as the educators of the ancient Greeks. It is by and through this extraordinary group of people, black Africans all, that western civilization has been able to reach its present stature.

Because these people were Africans they are the ancestors of Africans of the Motherland and the Diaspora, which includes African Americans. I anticipate the objection to this line of reasoning that not all Africans were Kemites. This *may* be true but it is irrelevant. In the attempt to find our roots, a necessity made all but impossible by the ancestral disconnect created by the African Slave Trade, we must settle for an authentic ancestral culture of our choosing.

The people of Kemit stated that their ancestors came from the forests at the foothills of the Mountains of the Moon (the Ruwenzori Mountain Range in present day Uganda) in South Central Africa. They stated that these people, their ancestors, traveled down the great River *Hapi* (Greek Nile) and finally settled where the river deposits its rich alluvial soil and creates an agricultural paradise.

This glorious, ancient African culture, once deified became the forerunner, either directly or indirectly, of all the major religions of the world. The teachings of her ancient priests and the example of her system of governance gave Greece its philosophy and Plato his *Republic*. *Pythagoras*,

TOTAL BLACK EMPOWERMENT

after 22 years or more of study was awarded the theorem that made him famous. Hippocrates found his oath there; the Free Masons and the Rosicrucians their secret doctrine; the Jews, Christians and Muslims found their amen and no person can contemplate the Creator without the framework of her spiritual concepts. She is the birthplace of writing and paper, the home of medicine, chemistry and physics. The first armies to conquer the world marched to the beat of her sacred drums under the standards of her African Gods and Goddesses. She was the first superpower in recorded history and the vigilant protector of women and children.

It is posited here, unabashedly, that a collective return to that culture, *modified to suit contemporary standards*, and the cosmic ambience of the new age, will permit a renaissance of our former glory and our ancient birthright as the spiritual and intellectual leaders of the world.

Clearly, an agreed ancestral identity as the initial step in our quest for *Total Black Empowerment through the Creation of Powerful Minds®* is necessary.

The necessity for an agreed ancestral identity derives from the fact that history (our best teacher) informs us that to the extent a people have lost, abandoned or have been forced to depart from their own culture they have, over time, perished completely or ceased to exist as a separate and distinct people within the family of nations. Similarly those who have adopted the cultures of others have almost without exception, remained outcast, disrespected and suspect minorities among the people whose culture they have sheepishly embraced.

History also teaches us that those people who have jealously guarded their culture and consistently adhere to its prescriptions have maintained their identity, self-determination and political power.

Acts of assimilation or acculturation are, therefore, acts of surrender to the collective will and culture of others that demonstrates a dangerous weakness in the collective will of those who do so. Those who abandon the mandate of their ancestors and abdicate their responsibility to avenge the deaths of their ancestors, represent the weak link in the cultural chain that is our connection, our lifeline to the unlimited power of our ancestral past.

It must be remembered, however, that even the damage done by numerous past acts of surrender and weakness are not irreversible. History is replete with examples of people who have re-discovered, revived and resuscitated their ances- tral culture. Each of them has used their ancestral culture as the foundation from which to launch their quest for group identity, collective self-determination and political power. In fact, the groups who have adhered to their authentic ancestral culture have historically exercised political and economic power disproportionate to their numbers.

The primary importance of Authentic Ancestral Culture as the foundation of *Total Black Empowerment Through the Creation of Powerful Minds*® is its ability to *transform* the minds of those who follow its prescriptions.

Since much of what we believe is based on *misinformation* or even *disinforma- tion*, especially regarding the beliefs and practices of our ancient ancestors, it is imperative that we understand not only how they perceived the thinking process and the mind but also what they thought on subjects pertinent to our present dis- cussion. Lest we forget they created the greatest, longest-lived civilization in the history of the world. Clearly, they knew something that apparently we do not.

Until we are able to compare the conclusions reached by our ancestors with those reached by Europeans that we have, for the most part, *uncritically accepted*, we will not be able to determine the validity of the *key revolutionary ideas* set forth in this book.

Again, the solution to our historic, collective power de-

TOTAL BLACK EMPOWERMENT

ficiency lies in our acknowl- edgment of our historic failure to avail ourselves of the powerful tools fashioned by our ancient ancestors and contained in the corpus of knowledge known as Sacred Science. All of our good intentions notwithstanding, we will not be able to understand why we have been intentionally deceived by our erstwhile captors, or why we have fallen for this deception for centuries, unless and until we know what our ancestors actually believed. This is pivotal.

Until we learn to seek out our ancestral beliefs and belief systems we will be disadvantaged by the simple fact that we have, functionally, rejected what our ancestors have painstakingly prepared for us. We cannot judge without accurate knowledge. We must *know* what they believed.

We are a people in search of valiant role models. Our ancestors are our only *reliable* role models. Their history is already written, their beneficial examples carved in stone. *What they stood for stands for eternity. They cannot betray or deny us.* Their value is enhanced when the present condition of our power deficiency is considered. This being said let us now examine the *Mechanics of Spiritual Power*.

17

THE MECHANICS OF SPIRITUAL POWER

In this section we will examine how spiritual power operates and how it may be productively utilized in our quest for *Total Black Empowerment*. We will only scratch the surface. Frankly, there is only so much that we can relate in this text. This is, after all, a *primer*. Before we do, however, we must spend a few moments to dispel popular but incorrect notions about the part played by magic in our ancestral traditions.

HEKA

We live in an age when technological advances are routine. For this reason they are taken for granted. For example, no one gives a second thought to the wondrous, even miraculous event that has occurred when they turn on their radio or television. From some far-flung location we can see and hear, in real time, what someone is doing halfway around the world. We never consider that this feat is accomplished by *invisible waves* transmitted through the air. Nor do we consider that electromagnetic waves that make this medium possible are converted, transmitted and reconverted before they reach our eyes and ears—invisibly and in a matter of seconds. But, we dare not refer to this as *magic. Perish the thought.* This is not magic—this is science, silly boy. After all, magic is the use of *charms, spells, roots, herbs, goober dust, animal excrement, mystical incantations* and the like. Magic is primitive voodoo.

According to European Egyptologists our ancestors, the Ancient Kemites, believed in and used magic to some extent in every thing they did. The implica- tion is that they were just primitives no more than a day or two removed from cannibalism.

Problem is that these were people who gave the world civilization, science, astronomy, geography, architecture, biology, anatomy, chemistry, clocks, calen- dars, writing, books and the list goes on. The Kemites so-called belief in *magic* went hand-in-hand with the development of the sciences. Moreover, these highly intelligent people saw no real difference between science and magic.

Once again the problem is definitional. The word that European Egyptologists translate from the Kemitic tongue to English as magic is *Heka*. As we will see it is a gross mistranslation.

Magic is popularly defined as "... the use of means (as charms and spells) believed to have supernatural power over natural forces." Another definition is "... the art that purports to control or forecast natural events, effects or forces by invoking the supernatural through the use of charms, spells, or rituals."

Heka, on the other hand, is *the power to control natural forces by knowledge of the laws by which they operate.* It is the knowledge of the laws that govern natural things and the ability to manipulate such laws to create a desired effect. It is not charms, spells, incantations or rituals. It is the *knowledge of natural power.*

As an example we may cite the ancient Kemitic tale of the pharaoh (King) who was told of the existence of a great sage and master of *Heka* who could cut off the head of an animal and reattach it and the animal would live. Pharaoh, intrigued by the idea, directed that the sage be brought to him. Upon his arrival the sage assured the king that he could, in fact, sever the head of a goose and reattach it. Before the assembled members of the king's court a goose was brought from the royal kitchen. The sage held the struggling goose by the neck, produced a razor sharp knife, uttered a few unintelligible words and cut the goose's head off. As the sage held the goose's head in one hand the goose ran frantically around the room, blood spewing from its neck, until it dropped dead at the feet of the king. After a few tense moments the sage took the goose's head touched it to its neck and uttered a few more unintelligible words. The goose jumped up, head attached, and waddled out of the room, squawking all the way.

Pharaoh and his audience were astonished. The king inquired how the sage was able to do such a thing. The sage told the king that he was surprised that such an intelligent man who held the future of an entire nation in his hands could be so easily deceived. The king replied that he and the others had seen it with their own eyes. To which the sage replied, you thought you saw me sever the head of the goose. But, you should have known that what you saw was impossible.

Well how then was it done? *Heka* was the sage's one word reply. *I implanted a thought in your minds*. The rest was easy. The moral of the story is that there is no magic—only *Heka*—*the control of natural forces*.

To our ancestors *Heka* was both a *Neter* and a power in its own right. Not surprisingly, the divine words were considered to be a prime example of *Heka*. In other words, the *Neter Neteru* created by *Heka* in the form of divine words. Speech was considered *Heka*. When we speak we transmit our *seed/ideas* to the other minds, invisibly by and through the use of *Heka*. The belief in *Heka* is old as our oldest sacred texts. It appears in the Pyramid texts—the oldest written works in the world.

In the pyramid texts *Heka* is referred as a power and a Neter. It is said to be *in the mouth* and is made active by utterance (speech). It is a power that nothing can withstand. Not surprisingly *Tehuti* was also known as the *Lord of Heka*. He it was who the Creator used to effect creation. *Tehuti* was known as the *tongue of the Creator. Heka is in the mouth*. The Creator originated the idea of creation and his intention was communicated to Tehuti who spoke the divine words that made it happen.[1]

We can see from this that magic is a term that is laden with negative connota- tions. If we understand our ancestral concept of *Heka* we begin to understand why it and not *magic* was central to everything our ancestors did. We can also understand why European Egyptologists translate the word *Heka* as *magic*.

Our Kemitic ancestors changed their world, and by extension the world at large, by their intimate knowledge of *Heka*—the control of natural forces—not by *magic*. We will return to this subject in the next section. Just remember for now that simply because something has modern currency does not mean it is new. Now let us examine the *Mechanics of Spiritual Power*.

First, *Spiritual Power* is the source from which all power is derived. In order to attract and acquire power we must be able to attract *Spiritual Power*. Of course, we must go directly to the source because the shortest distance between two points is always a straight line.

Second, without a spiritual power base our goal of Total Black Empowerment through the Creation of Powerful Minds® will forever elude us.

A powerful mind, as we have seen, begins with an open mind. But, an open mind is not necessarily a powerful one. A powerful mind is one that is full of power- ful thoughts and ideas. A powerful mind is one that exudes power in the process of thinking.

Ideas are, in many ways, like Morse code, in that they are *electrical impulses* that carry messages that are incomprehensible except to those who are familiar with the code. The person who does not understand the code can listen for an eternity and all he or she will hear is a monotonous series of dots and dashes. The person who understands will receive an intelligible message.

Thinking is a process that may also be likened to the movement of electrons through a conductor. In the thinking process ideas are the equivalent of electrons and the human brain is the equivalent of an *idea/thought conductor*. Just as the electrons moving through a conductor create a *physical force field*, so *the movement of thought through the brain creates a physical power field that spreads out, at the speed of light, and attracts much like an electromagnet. A powerful mind will attract other minds and, in turn, infuse them with its powerful ideas.* These powerful ideas are simultaneously *seed-ideas* that are *powerful* in their own right. These seed/ ideas have more or less intrinsic power depending on how close they are to *pure universal ideas.*

PURE UNIVERSAL IDEAS

The concept of purity of ideas is based on *content* and *proximity*. When we speak of *content* we refer to the *actual nature* of the *seed-idea*. We admit that the concept of pure ideas may be viewed as subjective. But, we also recognize that ideas can be objectively positive or negative. For example, universal healthcare is an objectively positive idea. On the other hand, the atomic bomb and Hitler's Final Solution were objectively negative ideas.

When we speak of *proximity* we refer to the *distance* from the point of origin of the seed-idea. As in all electrical activity the signal becomes weaker the further it travels from the source.

It will be profitable here for you to remember that a seed-idea is, first and foremost, a *thought*. Thoughts are energetic (electromagnetic) impulses. Thought is, therefore, a form of *energy*. In the view of our ancestors the point of origin of the seed/idea is the *Cosmic Ocean* and the *Ancestral Stream*.

THE COSMIC OCEAN

Our ancient ancestors have taught us about the process by which energy *emanates* from its point of origin. They refer to an *emanation* as a flowing of energy from a point of origin that results in a *chain of emergence or unfolding* that can be analogized by what happens when a pebble is dropped into a pond.

When a pebble is dropped into a pond it creates a *disturbance*. The distubance results from a *flow* of energy that moves out, in *concentric circles*, from the point of impact. As the waves move further from the center they lessen in intensity.

A *chain of emergence* is what develops as the flow of energy moves through the water. We call these ripples but they are actually *elevations* and *depressions* that unfold in the natural course of the *movement of energy*. It is through a similar *chain of emergence that* pure universal ideation occurs. It explains why and how identical ideas have come to different people at different and far-flung locations at approximately the same time throughout history. These occurrences have been referred to as *vision—the stuff that we are told the people will perish without.*

Our ancient ancestors believed that the point of origin of the seed-idea is the *Cosmic Ocean*. Our ancestors called this cosmic ocean *Nun*.

The Nun is the repository of Pure Universal Ideas. I refer to it as the repository and dispensary of *Divine Inspiration*. Inspiration is here defined as divine guidance or influence exerted directly on the mind.

The *Nun* is *a cosmic* ocean. It is composed not of water, but of *Spiritual Power in its purest form*. This pure spiritual power *emanates* from its center (point of origin) in waveform, *at the speed of light*, causing concentric circles that vibrate and resonate throughout the universe. The cosmic ocean is the *fountain of collective consciousness* from which all humanity may *infuse itself with higher intelligence*. According to our ancestors the *Nun* is also the *location* where we tap into the *Divine Mind*.

The *Divine Mind* is the *consciousness* of God. It is not only the place that we can receive seed-ideas that allow us to know God, but it is also the place where we *get to know what God Knows*.

Some people will find it hard to believe that it is possible to know the *Mind of God* or to know what God knows. Our ancestors took a different view. They believed we are capable of discovering, with the use of the techniques they devel- oped, 64/65 of the knowledge of God. That is 98.4% of what God knows, or all but 1.6% of the knowledge of God is discoverable by human beings.

THE ANCESTRAL STREAM

Within the cosmic ocean move *currents or streams of specific ancestral consciousness*. These *ancestral streams* are currents of inspiration and ideas deposited and accumulated there as a result of the experiences and wisdom of specific, identifiable ancestors. These streams represent a *movement*, a *flow*, of *specific energy* that is within, but separate and distinct from, the cosmic ocean in which they travel.

Each stream has direction and therefore, a *destination*. Each is driven by the collective consciousness of the specific group of ancestors to whom it belongs.

The *Ancestral Stream* is not unlike *ocean, air* and *elec-*

trical currents. An ocean current is a *continuous flow* of water that moves in a *specific direction* and travels *within a larger body* of water. The world's oceans contain numerous currents that although recognized and fairly predictable, still represent a poorly understood phenomenon. Perhaps the best known of these is *El Nino*, the current held responsible for the devastating *El Nino Effect* on global weather patterns.

Air currents operate in the same way as ocean currents and have the additional property of *invisibility*. Both ocean and air currents represent a separate and distinct movement within a larger movement. Both ocean and air currents form the *center* of the larger movement. Both ocean and air currents move in *one direction* and they are both *self-propelled* by a force that is, itself, poorly understood.

We have already noted that the movement of electrons through a conductor is also a *current*; in this case it is known as a *current of electricity*.

The *Ancestral Stream* is best understood as a *combination* of the characteristics of ocean, air and electrical currents. Like the ocean and air currents it is a continuous flow that travels in one direction, faster than the larger body within which it is contained. It is independently propelled and, although invisible, represents a *predictable movement within a movement*. It is perpetual, always moving, always existing.

Like electrical current the Ancestral Stream is a dynamic flow of energy. It is, therefore, an electromotive force, that is created by the movement of energy and its strength is directly proportionate to the strength of the overall movement. Because the overall movement is that of the Cosmic Ocean the strength of the Ancestral Stream is immeasurable.

The Ancestral Stream then, is an emanation, it is a flowing and movement of spe- cific ancestral energy and consciousness that is itself the result of the collective wisdom and experience of our ancestors that travels in and emanates from the Cosmic Ocean. We have not answered the question with which we began this section. How do we tap into the Cosmic Ocean of Consciousness and its attendant Ancestral Streams that together comprise the Divine Mind?

We have previously noted the unreliability of the five senses. We have referred to them as the *Five Thieves* who rob us of an accurate assessment of reality. We will add here yet another evidence of the incompleteness of the five senses.

Our ancient ancestors taught that at least six surfaces must be present for a thing to actually exist. All *tangible* things must have a top, bottom, front, back and two sides. To our ancestors the number six was the number of *material existence*—of the coming into existence of the material world.

In order for anything to exist it must have *six surfaces* (in the case of material existence) or *six elements* in the case of other types of existence. Reality is a form of existence. It too must have six elements, sides, faces, perspectives, points of view. To attain the *understanding of reality* we are absolutely required, therefore, to see reality from all six sides, anything less is *incomplete*.

It follows that in order to truly understand reality we require more than five senses. There must be a sixth sense. The *Sixth Sense* is, therefore, *the sense that completes our understanding of reality* and without which reality will forever be beyond our comprehension. This *Sixth Sense* is often referred to as *intuition*. As we will see, intuition is an imprecise term that lacks breadth and accuracy. Our ancestors knew the *Sixth Sense* as the *Intelligence-of-the-Heart*.

TOTAL BLACK EMPOWERMENT

THE INTELLIGENCE-OF-THE-HEART

Intuition is defined as the direct way of knowing something without the conscious use of reasoning. This popular definition is accurate as far as it goes, but it sounds very much like *instinct*. It could even be argued that intuition and instinct are synonymous terms. Instinct is defined as an innate aspect of behavior that is *unlearned,* that is, *inborn* and *without acquired knowledge.* The only real difference is *semantic.* By virtue of some undefined tradition we refer to intuition in the case of human beings and instinct in the case of the so-called lower animals. The function is essentially the same in both cases.

Instinct is considered innate and peculiar to all specie of animal. It seems to drive certain activities that are characteristic of the specie but are not the result of the past experience of the individual animal.

The caterpillar erupts from its cocoon as a butterfly, takes wing immediately and thereafter reproduces without hesitation having never done or experienced either before. Caterpillars are said to do these things *instinctively.* Similar instincts may be cited for nearly all specie of animal on the planet.

Both instinct and intuition point to a *way of knowing* that is totally divorced from experience and learning but that is also *indispensable* to *life* and *survival.* Both instinct and intuition are accomplished by a *way of knowing,* that demonstrably exists despite our inability to satisfactorily explain it.

In the case of intuition we are talking about the *faculty* by which we receive knowledge/information without the use of rational processes. Faculty and power are synonymous terms. It follows that intuition is a *power.* It is the *power of immediate and direct cognition.*

To our ancestors this power was only a part of the *In-*

telligence-of-the-Heart because in the fullest sense of the term they *envisioned a connective, woven fabric of perception and understanding* that joins individuals to God, to self, to all living things, to the universe *and* the cosmos beyond. The breadth of this *direct knowledge* is only vaguely glimpsed by what is defined as intuition. It is only experienced full-blown by and through the *Intelligence-of-the-Heart*.

The *Intelligence-of the-Heart* is an elusive concept. It resists explanation and defies conventional wisdom. Since it does not derive from the five senses explana- tion of it by them is difficult, if not impossible.

The *Intelligence-of-the-Heart cannot be learned*. It is not something that we can learn because it is not knowledge in the sense of *learnable* information. It is not perception that derives from the five senses. It is not arrived at or deduced from anything. It is not registered in, communicated by or affected through time. It is not finite, stationary or itself quantifiable. It is not located in any place or at any time.

The Intelligence-of-the-Heart is the transforming, transcendent source of all ini- tiative, innovation, creativity, inspiration and will. It is the direct, uninhibited, undiluted voice of God that communicates through and by the heart. Our ancient ancestors could not have selected a better symbol than the heart to illustrate this vital power.

In ancient times the heart was universally recognized as the *seat of all direct human cognition*. Cognition, of course, includes *perception, memory* and *judgment*. The beat and rhythm of life are counted and maintained by the heart. The heart is a device and a function that we do not, at least consciously, control. The mechanism of the heart is fine-tuned and kept functioning repetitively and with a precision that is nothing short of miraculous, for the entire course of our lives without our conscious control. This wondrous timekeeper of life is both the sym- bol and the fact of the *Intelligence-of-the-Heart*.

In short, the Intelligence-of-the-Heart is the power that comes from a reservoir of collective knowledge that forms the collective consciousness that is our natural resource and the source of our greatest power.

We refer to it as the Intelligence-of-the-Heart because it is, strictly speaking, the power that enables us to round out or complete our understanding and assessment of what is real. It is the power by which we know that things are real despite the unreliability of the five senses.

There are, however, two types of intelligence and we must be certain which of the two we are talking about when we speak of the *Intelligence-of-the-Heart*. There is *cerebral* intelligence and *non-empirical* or *a priori* intelligence.

Cerebral intelligence or intellect is based on observation, experience, experimentation and rote learning. It is directly dependent on the five senses. As such it is as reliable or unreliable as the senses upon which it relies. This cerebral intelli- gence lacks depth. It is two-dimensional. Sort of like a stereo system with no bass. *Non-empirical* or *a priori* intelligence is innate. It does not require experience because it is unmistakable and can only be described as *a way of knowing*. It is not what we have *learned* but what we *know*. It is the overwhelming *feeling of certitude* that comes to us *directly* and *without preparation or contemplation*.

Our ancient ancestors concluded that this type of intelligence is derived from the *Cosmic Ocean*, the *Nun*, the same source that controls the beating of our hearts. They believed that this *way of knowing* without preparation of contemplation, this direct knowledge, was *pure reason*. To our ancestors *reason* was the power by which knowledge is obtained. It is through the *power of reason* that we differentiate knowledge, but it is through *pure reason* that we *know*.

Pure reason is the unadulterated form of consciousness that is properly referred to as the consciousness of God. Pure reason is both being conscious of God and the con- sciousness that is God. It is also part of that which we refer to as the Divine Mind or the Mind of God. We should note here that reason, intuition and understand- ing are all synonyms.

The *Intelligence-of-the-Heart* then is the *direct line* to the *Divine Mind*, the *Cosmic Ocean,* and the *Ancestral Stream* that flows within it. In order to *fully understand reali*ty we must drink, liberally and often, from the *Cosmic Ocean.* In order to understand the *specific reality* that is our *destiny* as a people we must *con- struct and maintain a pipeline to our own Ancestral Stream*. This is the only way we will be able to access the *spiritual power* contained within our own *separate* and *distinct ancestral reservoir of spiritual power.*

The *Ancestral Reservoir* contains the *spiritual power* deposited there by our ancestors, in unlimited quantity, for use by succeeding generations of their descendants. The power contained within the *Ancestral Reservoir* is *specialized power created and held in reserve,* for us against the day when we will need it to defend ourselves and our children from increasingly hostile forces bent on our ultimate destruction. Remember, we, and our children are literally the *children of our ancestors*.

Our ancient ancestors, by their existence, caused this *unlimited spiritual power* flow in a *perpetual stream of consciousness* that we might drink from its life-giving cosmic waters in times of peril and *indecision*. In order to tap into or access this source of abundant spiritual power we must adhere to three simple rules:

• BELIEVE IN THE POWER OF OUR ANCESTORS

We must believe in the power of our ancestors to instruct us, through their collective spirits and to intervene on our behalf to focus and direct us in all endeavors to secure our collective survival and prosperity. Without this fundamental belief we cannot begin to tap this unlimited resource.

• CULTIVATE THE POWER OF INVOCATION

We must cultivate our own ability (power) to invoke the unlimited spiritual power contained in the Cosmic Ocean and the Ancestral Stream. Practice makes perfect. We have been so long without practice in the area that we have forgotten how to do it. We call incessantly on the ancestors of others but cringe at the thought of calling on our own. If we believe that Abraham, Isaac and Jacob, Muhammad and other ancestors will assist us why do we disbelieve that our own will?

• INVOKE THE POWER OF OUR ANCESTORS

We must, individually and collectively, invoke the intervention of the spiritual power of our ancestors to focus and direct us to transform the vision of their glorious, unprecedented past reality into our collective present reality.

In short, we will never know if it works unless and until we try it. We must start to call on our ancestors *now*. They will answer but not until we call them. What are we afraid of? Are we afraid that they may answer? Are we afraid that they may disapprove of the course we have taken or of the decisions we have made? They may be *disappointed* in us but their love for us, their willingness to guide and protect us, in spite of our foolishness, is eternal and unbounded. We must *believe, cultivate and invoke*.

- To *believe* is to *mentally accept* something as true or real even though *absolute* certainty may not be present.
- To *cultivate* implies both improvement by care, training and study as well as development and growth.

To *invoke* is to *call on* but the word literally means *in or on voice*. Voice is a vocal utterance that communicates to the mind. In this context invoke is to be understood as *the voice* or *Divine Utterance that communicates with the Mind* of God. The *Mind of God* or *Divine Mind* is, as we have seen, *the repository of Pure Universal Ideas*.

SERVING OUR ANCESTORS

The belief in our ancestors is simply the belief in the perpetual existence of the *residual power* of those who have gone before. This residual power is the energy that remains at the end of the life process. Our ancestors are not only those who have gone before, they are also the source of our blood. Their blood courses through our veins until this day. Recent scientific advances have now proved this concept.

DNA research and researches of the Human Genome Project have concluded that DNA (**D**eoxyribo**n**ucleic **A**cid) is the *innate, natural, universal* method by which *hereditary information* is *transmitted* from each generation to the next. These researches have also concluded that *mitochondrial DNA is such specific information* that it has permitted them to trace all living human beings to a single, Black African mother who lived 150,000 years ago and resided in South Central Africa. Remember that mitochondrial DNA is only transmitted through the female line.

The belief in our ancestors is the belief that they can lend their *knowledge* and *wisdom* to our current efforts to survive and prosper and by so doing fulfill their ancient desire that their descendents would never perish from the Earth. The premise upon which this belief is based is not farfetched. In fact, it is also clearly established by the science of physics.

The science of physics tells us that energy; hence *spiritual power* cannot be destroyed. Energy is simply transformed from one state to another. To believe in the perpetual existence of an indestructible *residual Ancestral Spiritual Power* is not farfetched either if we believe in the physical existence of our ancestors or we know who they are.

ANCESTOR WORSHIP

With few notable exceptions, when the African American thinks of ancestors he/she thinks of the now dreaded term *ancestor worship*. Tucked away in our belief subsystems is a *mental note* that advises us that ancestor worship is *primitive* and *animistic*. It causes us to conjure the thought and picture of naked Africans bowing down to a pile of desiccated bones, speaking a language that we have been told is unsophisticated, barbarian *mumbo jumbo*. Then we promptly get on our knees and call on Abraham, Isaac and Jacob, Moses, Muhammad, Jesus, Mary and Joseph, Paul, Peter and a host of others. Because of our belief subsystems we never realize that every single one of those persons, if they were, in fact, historical beings, is someone's *ancestor*.

Apparently ancestor worship is primitive and to be avoided only when we choose to worship our African ancestors. Worship of the ancestors of others, particularly Europeans and Arabs is acceptable and even required for us.

The term *ancestor worship* is defined as the invocation of the spirits of the dead and is based on the belief that the spirits of the dead continue to dwell in the natural world and that they have *power* to *influence* the fortune and fate of the living. It should be noted here that the term ancestor *worship* is *not* African. The term used by our ancestors was *service*. We did not *worship* our ancestors we *served* them. We cared for them. *We cared for their spirit and their memory.* In any event, the concept of ancestor worship/service is closely related to *animism* another term that the European has taught us is primitive. Next Sunday when you are portioning out the Sunday meal take a separate plate and put some food on it—the same food you are serving everyone else—for your departed relatives. Say or think, this is for you momma, this is for you grandpa—this is to say thank you for your love, your wisdom—come join us. They will come. They will sit with you and partake of the sustenance you have provided. Watch what happens. No ritual is required. Just continue to do what you did when they were alive. Remember the old folks always ate first. Watch what happens. You will see your mind transformed. Answers to the questions that perplex you will come to like magic. But, now you will know that it is not magic but heka.

ANIMISM

Animism is the belief that in every living thing there resides a *power, force or spirit* that governs its existence and that this vital life force or power is separate and distinct from matter. The concept of animism is credited as the *foundation of all religions*. This means that all religion is based on animism because all religions agree that *the spirit of God animates all living things.* You should not be surprised to learn that the concepts of both animism and service to the ancestors had their origin and highest elaboration in Africa, the home of our ancestors.

To worship or serve one's ancestors then is to *invoke* their *power* to *influence* one's fortune and fate. But the invocation must be directed to *your ancestors* in order to be effective. This is because the connection to the ancestors is based on our link to them by the *blood* known as the *Mother Blood*. Blood is, in turn, the *carrier of the vital force or power*. Simply put, you have no *blood connection* to the ancestors of others. As a result your attempts to *invoke* their power will forever be in vain. Their *Mother Blood* is not your *Mother Blood*. It follows that we must know who our ancestors are in order to connect with *our Mother Blood*.

OUR ANCESTORS ARE AFRICANS WE ARE OF AFRICAN DESCENT

We agree, virtually unanimously, that we are of African descent. We do not refer to ourselves as *Asian* Americans or *Arab* Americans or *Italian* Americans for that matter. We refer to ourselves as *African* Americans. We recognize, with few exceptions, that our forebears were brought to these shores, shackled and chained, from the *African* continent. We agree that *Africa is our Motherland*. We are, therefore, connected by *blood* to the people of the African continent.

We are not *Asians* although Africans may be found in Asia and have lived in Asia before the Asians.

We are not *Arabs* although Arabs may have African blood as a result of the constant admixture of their blood with ours during their rapacious control of the African slave trade.

We are not *Hebrews* although the Hebrews may have resided in Africa for a time.

We are certainly not *Europeans* whose entry on the world stage is so recent as to be infantile.

We are African people. More precisely we are displaced Africans. We are confused, conflicted, de-cultured victims of centuries of intense indoctrination aimed at obliterating our awareness of our connection to the unlimited Spiritual Power generated and held in reserve by our ancestors for our use in times of peril and indecision. We are the product of the blood of our ancestors. We are the product of their history and their thought energy. Their collective consciousness is alive, well and flowing in their ever-flowing Ancestral Stream.

We must accept the fact that our ancestors, those who have gone before, were Africans.

We must accept the fact that had we not been violently, ruthlessly and forcibly kidnapped from the nurture and loving care of our ancestors we would have been raised as Africans, and nurtured in African heritage and tradition. We would have been raised to speak an African tongue, to see the world through African eyes. We would have held African philosophical and spiritual beliefs and we would have served an African God of Power.

As Africans we are, and can only be, the descendents of Africans. Let us be sure we clearly, unequivocally understand the true implication of our noble descent. By acknowledging that we are descendents of Africans we simulta- neously acknowledge that we are the descendants of a people who have been rec- ognized, virtually since the beginning of recorded history, as the most *spiritual* people to ever walk this planet. A people who formulated the first, and therefore, the oldest concept of God and who, in so doing, concluded that *God is active, self- existent Spiritual Power.*

Our ancient *African* ancestors were the first to postulate the existence of the soul as a form of *immortal, indestructible energy* that is the *Divine Essence* that resides in each of us.

Our ancient *African* ancestors were the first to develop religious ritual and practice and the first to build towering stone temple structures. These gigantic structures were purposefully built to *attract, focus and distribute the active, self- existent Spiritual Power that is God throughout the land that our people, their descen- dents, might survive*

TOTAL BLACK EMPOWERMENT

and prosper and that we might be forever powerful.

This too is a *powerful idea*. The power of this idea can change the course of human events. It is an idea that will empower those who understand and apply it. This powerful idea holds that:

I can change the course of my life and that of my people by the invocation of the Spiritual Power contained in our own unique, specific Ancestral Stream.

When I do this I tap the residual power that animated, motivated, directed and focused the thought energy and created the seed-ideas of our ancestors, who created civilization and thereby propelled humanity to heights unparalleled until this day.

When I tap into this power I infuse myself with the powerful ideas whose movement through my mind and body creates, in me, a physical, magnetic power field that energizes me by attracting the vital force.

When I tap into this power I simultaneously attract others to me who I energize and who, in turn, energize others. All in exacting accord with the Law of Power Units.

We tap into this power by our individual and collective invocation (by *Divine Utterance*) of the *Mind of God—the Divine Mind*.

There is an ancient saying attributed to our ancient African ancestors that is as old as time itself. It holds that *"to speak of the dead is to make them live again"*.

To bring something back to life is, first and foremost, to bring back its *power*. Our ancestors believed that by speaking of the dead, *by remembering and serving their ancestors and invoking their spirit* we not only bring them back to life but we also bring back their *unlimited spiritual power to assist us and direct us in overcoming the problems that we confront today.* They did not believe the dead ever came back to life physically.

Our ancestors also informed us that to invoke the Power of God we only had to speak the name—literally, *say the word*—and It would immediately respond by revealing itself to us. But, this conception of revelation has been gravely misunderstood. They did not mean that God reveals Itself to you in a vision of itself. They meant that God *becomes one with you and you become one with God.* The effect of this is that *your mind becomes one with the Mind of God. It becomes filled with the energy/power that is the Mind of God.*

Think about it. Your mind becomes the Mind of God. It means that your mind literally begins to *resonate* at or near the vibratory level of the electromagnetic impulse that is the active, creative power that we call God. *Your thoughts become God's thoughts because your thought energy derives from the energy of God.*

By this method we are now able to understand four very important concepts.

First, that prayer that is intended to secure for you any material thing will forever go unanswered because there is no human being or supreme being sitting somewhere waiting to hear and answer your prayers. There is only the active power that produces and creates in regular recurrence.

Second, that reduced to its lowest common denominator all of our prayers and pious entreaties are actually attempts to secure power to deal with the circumstances with which we are confronted—no matter what stripe they may be.

Third, in order to deal with such circumstances we must have an accurate assessment of reality, the power to initiate and prohibit, clear vision and the Power of the Will.

Fourth, prayers are answered through the provision of creative seed/ideas that reside within the Mind of God and are accessible only through the Cosmic Ocean and the appropriate Ancestral Stream.

What greater advantage can one have than to be able to think with the efficiency and unerring power, foresight and intelligence of the Mind of God?

That this Mind is an electromagnetic impulse that cannot deviate from its own universal laws should not trouble us since we receive the overwhelming majority of the information upon which we govern our lives via electromagnetic impulses that we call radio and television.

These concepts are given here in simple form so that the basics will be easily recognized and understood and in accord with the admonition of our ancestors that *complexity is a sign of decadence.*

We invite you now to take a moment to *invoke* the spirits of your ancestors. We suggest that you *begin with the ancestors you know.* Start with those whose memory is still fresh in your mind. Call upon the grandmother who has never been far from your heart and mind though she has departed this Earth plane. Or, the father or brother who guided your youthful steps and came to your aid with words or encouragement when it seemed to you that all the world had crumbled around you. *Call on them. Your call will be answered.* Feel the warmth that enfolds your entire being when the call is answered.

Give your personal Spiritual Power the opportunity to infuse your mind and by so doing forge the link with the *Divine Mind* that will transform you in ways you have never dared to imagine.

After you have done this begin to read again. We will then begin to fill your mind with the *concepts* that are the building blocks of *Total Black Empowerment* so that individually and collectively we will create the *New Mental Attitude* that will cause a *quantum leap* in consciousness that will progressively change the course of your life and the human events they impact.

TOTAL BLACK EMPOWERMENT

RECAPITULATION

We have now seen that in our quest for Total Black Empowerment through the Creation of Powerful Minds®, we begin with Critical Thinking because it is the truth filter and belief controller that when combined with the Intelligence-of-the-Heart enables us to see the world clearly. We then recognize the importance of the seed-ideas and pure reason that are the products of the Divine Mind.

We have seen the importance of both an accurate understanding of power and the knowledge of its acquisition, utilization, control and distribution. Finally, we have learned the importance of the acquisition, through the service of our ances- tors, of *Spiritual Power that is the power source* from which all power emanates. We have seen that this power is accessed from the Cosmic Ocean and our *unique, specific Ancestral Stream* that flows within it.

This *Ancestral Stream* includes the *residual power (the wisdom, knowledge and consciousness)* of our ancient African ancestors that was created by their *physical existence* and the *thought energy* resulting from that existence. We know that energy/power cannot be destroyed. Since spiritual power is also a form of energy we know that it cannot be destroyed.

Our next and final section will examine the universal laws that our ancestors recognized and utilized in understanding the world and fashioning strategies and tactics to maneuver in it. This section will provide a framework for the understanding of the principles that underlay all activity in the Universe. The knowledge of these laws coupled with adherence to their mandates will enable us to overcome the centuries of indoctrination and misinformation that have created the detrimental mind-set that has kept us mired in power deficiency.

PART IV
SACRED SCIENCE

18

WHAT IS SACRED SCIENCE ?

INTRODUCTION

At a time when the mass of humanity remained mired in savagery and ignorance, Kemit, the *Land of the Blacks*, and its high civilization, flourished. Nestled on the banks of the great river *Hapi*, in the heart of Afru-ika, the indigenous African people had already developed writing, several interrelated calendrical systems, stone architecture, chemistry, metallurgy, medicine and all the arts useful and necessary to civilized life.

Millennia before Europe was a Germanic dream or China a Mongol inspiration, the Kemites constructed fifty story pyramids that remain the unsurpassed marvel of architectural achievement. They had plotted the stars, discovered heliocentricity, the Precession of the Equinoxes, atomic theory, and erected massive temples whose axes were perfectly oriented to the circumpolar stars. They formulated answers to the fundamental questions regarding the origin of being and the immortality of the soul. They mapped the geographic boundaries of the Netherworld and reduced to formulas the incantations required to navigate its confines. The basis of their unparalleled achievement was, undeniably, their high, exacting culture. Upon this foundation of the significant contributions of their indigenous African forebears, to whom they gave unstinting recognition, was developed a *science of the sacred* that has been intentionally mischaracterized by European Egyptologists as mere religion. Sacred science was not mere religion. It was the refinement of culture based on the universal laws of nature now known as phys- ics, biology and chemistry. But sacred science was much more than those scientific disciplines. Sacred science embraces the relationship of those disciplines to the divine format and the destiny of humanity.

Sacred science contemplates a purpose for existence and posits a discoverable order in universal and human activities that focuses our attention on a level of vidual and collective responsibility that engenders *Maat* (unerring justice) and *hetep* (perfection peace).

Sacred science was the bedrock of Kemitic civilization and the impetus of her achievement. Through it humanity divorced itself of brutishness and began the long trek toward the evolution of consciousness. It proved to be the seed from which a harmonious, powerful and cultured civilization was born.

In time organized study and application of sacred science became disfavored as a result of the rise of other and foreign cultures which had taken that perfected science, of which the foreigners understood little, and bastardized the teaching into the abnormality of Western civilization and thought.

Through unrelenting and vicious persecution of this science and those who advocated it, and under the pretense of stamping out paganism, the world descended, predictably, into the Dark Ages a period of one thousand years of intellectual darkness from which the world was only extricated upon the resurrec- tion of the same Kemitic science it had viciously attempted to stamp out a thousand years earlier.

TOTAL BLACK EMPOWERMENT

Sacred science fostered the greatest civilization of the ancient world. This fact alone should be sufficient, when properly understood and earnestly applied, to raise the descendants of the discovers of this science to a level of achievement in the modern world that is worthy of its demonstrated potential.

Admittedly, the process of retrieval of the principles of Kemitic culture, as embodied in the teachings of Sacred Science, will not be easy. It will, however, reward the energies of those who succeed far beyond their wildest imaginings.

Sacred Science is the corpus of knowledge and information distilled from the millennia long observation, by our ancestors, of nature in her myriad aspects, human nature in its frailty, and the vital correspondence between the two.

Sacred Science is the *science of organization* from fetal becoming to transfer- ence of seed as well as the concept of organization as applied to all aspects of life. It is the soul of art and the beauty of divine proportion. It is music at the level of divine vibration and literature that focuses spirit and forges will. It is a compilation of the universal and unalterable laws of harmony, number and natural order.

Sacred Science is also the divine formula by which the descendants of the Kemites can attract and focus the active power that is God to energize our individual lives and construct the power base from which to launch a cultural revolution.

We should also consider the connection between knowledge and Sacred Science. The Kemitic word for mankind (*rekhiu*) means the *knowers or those who know*. The word science means *to know*. And something that is sacred is dedi- cated or devoted to an exclusive purpose.

Sacred Science then implies a body of unpolluted or pure knowledge that is set aside for an exclusive purpose. That pur- pose is the attainment and maintenance of civilization in perpetuity. The Kemites apparently recognized the relationship between pure knowledge, survival and prosperity.

When it is further considered that the teaching of Sacred Science had both an overt and a covert purpose that focused on the control of natural forces, it will be understood that the connection between knowledge and power is ancient indeed. In order to apply this scientific knowledge of the sacred to our lives and circum- stances we must reconstruct its fundamental from the debris of our ancestral past. We must begin at the beginning.

THE SCIENCE OF TEHUTI

It has been said that the fundamentals of Sacred Science were developed by the ancient African sage Tehuti in 18,000 B.C.E. Legend holds that he compiled 39,000 books containing the accumulated knowledge of mankind as well as the intelligence and knowledge properly called divine.

Tehuti was an ancient and revered Kemite who by virtue of his laudable accomplishments was deified as the Neter of divine intelligence. He was the per- sonification of intelligence and the husband of Maat the Goddess of righteousness, justice and unerring accuracy. He was known by many titles, each of which memorialized a facet of his multi-faceted character. He was called the *Lord of Writing, Master of Papyrus (paper), Maker of the Palette and Ink Jar,* in recognition of him as inventor of *Medu Neter* (words of god) and writing, arts, astronomy, mathematics and the sciences in general.

Though the agency of his voice he persuaded the people of Kemit to accept the teachings of Sacred Science and was thereafter known as the *Mighty Speaker* and the *Sweet Tongued.* He introduced the precepts that enabled the people to live together in harmony and forge alliances that advanced the common interests of the whole people. For this reason Tehuti was also known as the *Lord of*

TOTAL BLACK EMPOWERMENT

Law, the *Begetter of Law* and the *Maker of Law*. He was also the Chief Judge of the Kemitic Supreme Court.

Tehuti was also recognized as being responsible for the bringing back of, each morning, the light of the sun that had been extinguished the night before. By doing so he became the *Reckoner of Time* and the *Righteous Judge of the Cycles of the Neters*. He kept count of the days and insured that all cycles were carried out according to their time.

During the interminable contests between Heru and his uncle Set, one of Heru's eyes was violently dismembered. The impairment of his vision jeopardized his ability to see clearly or to gain victory. Tehuti reconstructed the eye and returned it to Heru. This act of returning the *Oudjat* or *sound eye* to heru

It was also Tehuti who as Neter of Divine Intelligence first distilled the fundamentals of the science of the sacred that were utilized to establish the high and incomparable civilization of the ancient Kemites. It is for these reasons that Sacred Science was first known as the *Science of Tehuti*.

Modern Egyptologists scoff at the legend and its claimed antiquity. They cannot, however, deny the historical fact of the high civilization and political organization of Kemit. Nor can they deny the repeated references to an ancient and valuable collection of knowledge possessed by her and referred to in the ancient writings of the Greeks, Arabs, Hebrews and others. Moreover, the existence of the Great Pyramid of Khufu remains yet another irrefutable testimonial to the advanced level of their science. That this great architectural feat remains a mystery that cannot be duplicated today, despite several millennia of so-called technological advancement, confirms that modern knowledge is, at best, incomplete.

We are able to infer from these facts that (1) the Kemites attained a high level of civilization and culture; (2) they apparently possessed a corpus of knowledge of ancient origin; (3) they attributed their high civilization that corpus of knowl-edge; (4) the existence of that corpus of knowledge was known to others and attested in ancient records; and (5) the knowledge was originally called the Science of Tehuti and later Sacred Science.

History informs us that the system of government employed by the Kemites was widely extolled as the most efficient, just and admirable by virtually all ancient observers. It is also important to note that this unique form of government continued in unbroken succession, without revolution, for longer than any political structure in the history of the world. This evidently superior form of government was true theocracy and was based on the spiritual, intellectual and philosophical observations derived from the Science of Tehuti.

THE HOUSE OF LIFE

The repository and dispenser of this Sacred Science was the House of Life (*Per Ankh*). This might be expected since the temple that it always adjoined was equipped with astronomical observatories, and the House of Life with vast libraries and a coterie of Servants of the Neter who were specially selected and trained Sacred Science. In Kemit both science and government were sacerdotally administered.

We also know that this science included the *Ritual of the Divine Cult* and that the ritual was modified periodically in accord with the *Precession of the Equinoxes*. In order to fulfill this aspect of this function the temple employed observation of the stars (astronomy) and the interpretation of the effects of the positioning of the stars (astrology) as well as the sciences derived from the observation of the Earth and its relation to numbers and measurement (geometry).

Sacred Science consists of two equally important and inseparable purposes, one was *overt* (unconcealed) and the other *covert* (hidden). We have described the overt purpose above. It deals with the maintenance of universal balance through the performance of the *Ritual of the Divine Cult* and the orderly functioning of the society through superimposition of the order and harmony of the universe as the model of individual achievement and political governance.

The covert purpose of Sacred Science, again promulgated under the auspices of the temple, was the selection and training of individuals in the aspects of the science that dealt with the knowledge of the Neters. This aspect should be under- stood as the knowledge that the Neters possess and is characterized as the ability to control the active power of the forces of nature. In order to do so a corps of enlightened persons, male and female, who would, without fanfare, fear or favor, protect, maintain and transmit the sacred knowledge that formed the golden thread that guaranteed society'sorder and balance in perpetuity. These enlightened ones, called *Sahu*, after rigorous testing designed to insure their selflessness, and thereby their worthiness, were granted the keys to the full knowledge of Sacred Science in the name of and exclusively for the benefit of society as a whole.

The justification for this rather clandestine aspect of the purpose of Sacred Science is based on the fact that the knowledge was considered so dynamic and potentially dangerous that it was transmitted only from *mouth to ear*, and then only to selected, tested and trained persons within the sacred confines of the temple.

This knowledge was considered potentially dangerous because it was *the science of the fundamentals of power in all its myriad manifestations*. The misapplication of such potentially dangerous knowledge results in the release of *decadent energy* like the radioactive energy of nuclear waste. The awesome nature of the knowledge contained in Sacred Science explains why it was kept from the unini- tiated. Yet, it was not secret. It was simply difficult to acquire. All

TOTAL BLACK EMPOWERMENT

who were willing to subject themselves to the rigorous testing, preparation and selfless sacrifice demanded were admitted and *transformed*.

The foregoing information leads us, inexorably, to further conclude that Sacred Science was (1) a body of knowledge distilled from the accumulated knowledge of the world; (2) it was maintained in the promulgated under the auspices of the Temple; (3) its purpose was simultaneously overt and covert; (4) it served two purposes (a) the maintenance of balance and order in the universe and the collective activities of humanity; and (b) to select and train a corps of enlightened persons to maintain and transmit the sacred knowledge to insure balance and order in society inperpetuity.

When it is understood that this sacred science does, in fact, exist, that it was taught only to specially prepared persons and that its faithful application resulted in the creation and maintenance of the greatest longest lived civilization in his- tory it becomes evident that it is worthy of investigation, particularly given the adverse circumstances in which African Americans find themselves today.

When it is further considered that this knowledge represents the exclusive sci- ence of our ancestors and is the embodiment of their unique culture the necessity for serious and urgent investigation is compelling. The fact that this knowledge was the foundation upon which the Kemites, an indigenous black African people and our ancestors, transformed themselves into a the world's first superpower, is viewed through the lens our present state of power deficiency the investigation and application of this sacred science is absolutely *mandatory*.

If the reader will permit, even if only for the sake of argument, that a Sacred Science does exist, that it can be discovered and that it offers at least the possibil- ity of generating the power, plan and leadership we so desperately need to change our collective circumstances for the better and improve the life prospects of our children, further analysis of this science and the culture from which it derived is clearly warranted.

In times of turmoil or foreign domination our people have invariably returned to Sacred Science and its spiritual leadership to inspire, protect and defend them. The importance of this fact consists in the understanding that the foundation of dignity, integrity and power is, and can only be, derived from the steadfast adher- ence by a people to their Authentic Ancestral Culture. With this admonition in mind, let us begin with the First Principles taught by our ancestors through their and our Sacred Science.

FIRST PRINCIPLES

The term first principle is, admittedly, redundant since the word principle also means first. Nevertheless, first principles are basic, predetermined laws or assumptions regarding fundamental circumstances of life and the actions to be taken when such circumstances arise. The most important of these may be broadly categorized as *laws of survival* and their application as the *technology of survival*.

Our ancestors placed great emphasis on *survival*. They believed that if we could only survive we would prosper according to our own definition of prosperity.

This subject is one that most of us would rather not think about. It conjures up unpleasant thoughts because we have become comfortable in our shoe-horned existence and feel that though things can certainly get better they cannot get worse. *Time will tell.*

As our first morsel of food for thought we begin with the imperative nature of our survival.

An imperative is simply a requirement that is both binding and compelling. That which is compelled cannot be ignored or evaded. That which is binding obligates one to act and implies that failure to act will result in some guaranteed adverse consequences. Because of the importance of this foundational element and its relationship to Black Empowerment it must be considered first.

THE SURVIVAL/PROSPERITY IMPERATIVE

The *Survival/Prosperity Imperative* is an absolute requirement of existence that we cannot ignore or evade, and that obligates us to act according to its unalterable dictates. It implies that failure to act accordingly will require one to suffer the most adverse consequences. It is foundational because if we do not understand it, and adhere to its time-honored principles our very existence as a people is gravely imperiled.

GENO-SURVIVAL

The universe, and the existence that we endure in it, is comprised of time, space, energy and life. Each of these concepts has in common the fact that they are forward moving and seemingly teleological. It appears that they have begun at some unknown and perhaps unknowable time in the past and began to move forward, as if commanded to some unknown and perhaps unknowable destination.

What impels this forward motion is best described as the innate tendency of each genus to survive. We call this innate tendency or impulse, *geno-survival,* that is the survival and transmission of specific genetic codes. All species are impelled by this tendency. But, not all species have been successful because of it.

Dinosaurs and Dodo's have become extinct and hundreds of species become extinct each day. Distinct groups of human beings, such as Neanderthals and Tasmanians, have become extinct by their own actions or by the actions of others. When extinction is the result of the actions of the group it may be attributed to a failure of the group's survival technology. When extinction is the result of the actions of others, it is geno-cide.

GENO-CIDE

Geno-cide is the killing of a race or culture. The word was coined in 1943 and comes from the combination of the Greek *genos* meaning race or tribe and the Latin *cide*, which means to kill.

Article II of the United Nations Convention defines genocide as the commission of the following acts with the intent to destroy, in whole or in part, a national, ethnical, racial or religious group by among other things, killing the members of the group or *causing serious mental harm* to the members of the group, imposing measures intended to prevent births within the group, or forcibly transferring children of the group to another group. It should be understood here that genocide can occur without killing if the prohibited acts are part of a policy to destroy the existence of an identifiable group.

Finally, the prevention of births includes the long-term separation of men and women intended to prevent procreation. You will note also that all of the prohibited acts require intent. Intent as we have discussed above may be inferred from a systematic pattern of coordinated acts.

Geno-cide is planned. It is the result of policies developed and systematically implemented for the specific purpose of obliterating a particular race, religion or culture.

Survival is the First Principle of Existence. But it refers to survival of the genus not the individual. The absolute goal of geno-survival is infinite survival also known as immortality. We are not talking about living forever as individuals, which is, at best a fanciful impossibility, we are talking about the continued existence of our people forever, which can only be accomplished by the survival of our children and our children's children, *ad infinitum*. We are talking about the perpetuation of our seed, our bloodline, our lineage, heritage and culture so that they become ever living, never forgotten, and thereby immortal.

GENO-SURVIVAL AFFINITY

The need that motivates survival is what I call the *Geno-Survival Affinity* (GSA). An affinity is something to which you are attracted by some innate/inherent necessity. It is a causal connection between two things. It is inborn and involun- tary. It manifests itself in all of the senses. What naturally tastes, smells, feels, sounds and looks good to you is a result of your personal, inborn affinity. This affinity is survival oriented. The mechanism of its orientation is the gratification of the senses and the mind. In a word it is pleasure, a word that is, oddly enough, synonymous with will. The reason it is oriented to pleasure issimple.

Pleasure attracts we are all drawn to it. When we are naturally attracted to a thing we tend to seek it out. We also tend to memorialize it in song, folklore and myth. We develop techniques and strategies for acquiring it. It should not be surprising then that two of the three things that survival technology is designed to insure are two things that we are most attracted to food and procreation. We are attracted to these things because they increase our physical/psychological plea- sure and because they have *Intrinsic Survival Value* (ISV). Whether we recognize them for their survival value is immaterial since the pleasure we derive from them is what attracts whether we think in terms of survival or not. Survival is the con- tinuation of life or existence in the presence of conditions that threaten to prevent or destroy it.

In human beings this survival technology, this accumulation of memorialized pleasures, is known as culture. *Culture is the technology of survival.* A people with- out culture will not survive and will, over time, become extinct, or fall prey to geno-cide. In order to be effective, this memorialized survival technology must be preserved, and then transmitted, from generation to generation (the word genera- tion itself derives from the root *genus*). For this reason geno-survival is also a group effort. Preserving and transmitting this survival technology is the most important function of culture.

Culture is developed over time by specific groups of people, and is, therefore, group specific. There is no such thing as one size fits all. Culture is the geno-sur- vival gift of the ancestors of specific groups of people. It represents, to the group by whom it is developed, a most important key to survival. *Survival is the cure for extinction.*

SURVIVAL TECHNOLOGY

An adequate survival technology must insure sustenance, protection; and procre- ation. All existing life forms have found and implemented, whether consciously or instinctively (assuming there is a difference) a survival technology that satisfies these three elements. Those who have not have become extinct. Those who have become extinct have done so because they have clung to a survival technology that was, because of changed circumstances, no longer effective or they have developed strategies and tactics that although well intentioned, were ineffective and led, inevitably, to extinction. Others have been the victims of planned geno- cide.

It follows that in the absence of a well-planned, well-executed survival tech- nology, one that takes changed circumstances into consideration geno survival is at best tenuous. This is because survival is motivated by need. Need directs and guides survival. We need only ask what the genus needs, fill the need and you have gone a long way toward geno-survival.

TOTAL BLACK EMPOWERMENT

Survival Technology directs our attention to predators, enemies and diseases. Because survival is an impulse, it is also properly understood as a force. Force and power are, as we have seen, synonymous terms. Survival is a contest of power for all living things. For sapient beings, however, it is also a contest of will the will to survive.

A contest is a fight, a struggle, a conflict in which one power or will competes against another. The struggle may be between individuals, groups or against the elemental power of nature. Either way it is a contest whose prize is continued existence. The recognition of the existence of the survival contest is the first step toward success in the competition. It seems obvious that you cannot successfully compete if you do not even know that a competition is under way.

The second step in the contest of power or will is identification of the oppo- nent. You cannot successfully compete until you know who or what you are com- peting against.

The third step is the understanding and acceptance of the fact that both games and war are contests. The difference in the two, however, is like that between night and day. Games are played for fun. War is played to the death. It is absolutely essential here that we determine which one we are engaged in a game for fun or a war to the death. Survival is a contest, but it is not a game.

GENO-PROSPERITY

If it is true, as we have postulated, that the innate tendency to survive represents a minimum requirement for the continued existence of a genus, we must also rec- ognize that full satisfaction of the minimum requirement has been accomplished by the mere fact that we are here today. It is living proof of our ability to survive. But, having survived is apparently not enough. Why? Because unlike other ani- mals, which apparently survive by instinct alone, humans are sentient, thinking beings whose imagination and creative spirit longs to achieve more than mere survival. In fact, it may be persuasively argued that the survival of human beings unavoidably refers to survival of both body and mind. It follows that the quest for survival is necessary, but is alone insufficient to guarantee success in life for human beings, individually or as a group.

Geno-prosperity is the Second Principle of Existence. To prosper is to become strong, to become powerful. As a people, as a racially homogeneous, culturally distinct group, we African Americans have survived over the last five hundred years under conditions that no other group of people would have successfully endured. Apparently, we are masters of survival. Yet, all we have done is survived.

The *Second Principle of Existence* has been unnoticed or ignored by us because the First Principle of Existence was so demanding. The pressures under which we have had to labor, from "cain't see to cain't see", were so great, so demanding that all our time and energy has been spent in the contest for survival. The old folk used to call it "making do". All of our time and energy, all of our power, has been exhausted "making do". All of our creative, innovative and inventive spirit has been used in a centuries-long war of survival. To our eternal credit we have survived. But, so have countless other species of animal.

The mule is the quintessential beast of burden. It is also one of the dumbest animals on the planet. The mule has also survived even though it cannot reproduce. The so-called dumb animals are also successful at survival. They do it without plan or design on their part. But, they will always remain beasts of burden. We must ask ourselves if what we want for our children and our children's children is for them to merely survive. We must do more than survive or we are no better than the dumbest of the world's animals.

To fulfill our destiny, to reclaim our birthright, to avenge the humiliation and ignoble deaths of millions of our ancestors, we must do more than survive. *We must prosper.*

Survival and prosperity are connected in another way as well. *The rate of survival increases in direct proportion to the level of prosperity attained.* This is why some groups have a higher life expectancy, lower infant mortality rate, better health and general living standards. *We survive to prosper and prosper to survive.*

Understanding the *Survival/Prosperity Imperative* is an essential element of the *New Mental Attitude (NMA)* that creates powerful minds through a revolutionary thinking process that is the key to *Total Black Empowerment.*

Do you want to prosper or merely survive? Have you considered that genocide has been historically considered an acceptable political necessity by certaingroups? Have you considered who these people are and where you and your children are? *Think about it.*

It seems apparent from the foregoing that we must, as a people, begin to *think critically* about how the gift of survival can be turned into abundant prosperity. We must understand that the survival/prosperity imperative absolutely requires our heightened knowledge of not only power but also the *power relationships* that surround and, in many cases, confinues.

Let us clear up one unfortunate discrepancy at the outset. It is said that self preservation is the first law of nature'. Although the statement is appealing, it is superficial and misleading. It is certainly accurate to state that the survival of individuals is required for the specie to survive. This is not the same, however, as say- ing that the survival of the individual is the first law of nature. Since it is axiomatic that procreation, by which survival of the specie is accomplished, is a fundamental requirement for the continued existence of all living things, self preservation cannot be a firstlaw.

Self preservation cannot be a first law because if followed to its logical conclusion it would insure that the specie *not survive* since it is clear that the individual cannot procreate alone. It is also a dangerous proposition because an individual who sees his survival as the first and therefore most important goal necessarily places himself and his preservation before anyone else.

It is posited here and acknowledged by Sacred Science that *survival of the group,* whether the group is family, tribe, clan or nation, not self preservation, is the first law of nature. It is important to note this at the outset of our discussion of First Principles to focus attention on the insidious nature of the current inter- nalization by our people of the European/American preoccupation with individualism.

Clearly a people who are oppressed *en masse* will never find the answer to their collective problems in a strategy that requires them to advance their individual interests over those of the group. We should also consider that our ancestors abhorred competition and we may search for eternity and not find a since example of the concept of individualism among our ancient records.

We should not be surprised to find that our ancestral First Principles focus on survival of the group. They *observed that the key to survival was useful, timely and efficiently applied knowledge.* They focused on three areas specifically. These were self, heritage (culture) and destructive forces.

PRINCIPLE NUMBER ONE: MAN KNOW THYSELF

Civilization is not possible unless and until, humans are raised, by enlightenment from their naturally selfish and counterproductive ways. The advanced state of collective cultural, material, political and social complexity, as well as progress in the arts and sciences, that is the hallmark of civilization is only obtainable by those who have been so enlightened. Thus, advancement toward civilization must begin by raising individual persons from their instinctive, animalistic tendencies. The necessity for each individual to know his or herself is essential to the development of society.

The Kemites believed and taught that knowledge of self was of primary importance because our self is the first thing over which we can exercise the *power of control*. Such knowledge permits us to observe that we have power to control ourselves and compels the following conclusions: (1) we are innately powerful, that is power in the form of a sacred essence, resides in each of us; (2) power itself may be controlled; (3) it is by superior knowledge that power is controlled; (4) self-knowledge is the foundation of all knowledge and the means by which all power may be controlled.

Self knowledge begins with the realization of our innate animalistic tendencies and the need to control them in order to advance toward civilized life for individ- uals and civilization for the people collectively. As a result the mastery of passions is of primary importance. It was also believed that when passions were controlled the energy normally expended in its pursuit could be converted to unlimited power to be used for other and more productive purposes. To that end emphasis was placed on the Ten Virtues that released the self from the Ten Fetters. The first and second of the Ten Virtues were the *control of thought* and the *control of action*, respectively.

CONTROL OF THOUGHT

Control is itself a power. It is the power to direct or regulate. *Discipline is the power of self-control. Control of thought is the power to discipline the mind.* The mind is like a garden whose flowers are matured thoughts. Just as one would cultivate a garden the mind too has to be cultivated.

Thought may also be likened to a *seed* that once planted germinates to bear fruit of its kind. Each seed-thought planted in the garden of the mind will also bear fruit of its kind. Uncultured seed-thoughts are like weeds that grow rapidly and, if left unattended, suffocate the cultivated seed-thoughts in the garden of the mind. Cultivated seed-thought will not grow if it is sown with weeds.

At this level the control of thought is the exclusive power of the individual. It is an internal process that is self contained and operates without the assistance or intervention of others. It is, therefore, individual and exclusive and its impact is internal. When the power of thought is transformed into action it becomes dis- persed and affects the actions ofothers.

CONTROL OF ACTION

The control of action is the second level of control implicated by the First Princi- ple *Know Thyself*. Its importance lies in its potential effect on society. Though it is often said that people act without thinking the fact remains that *human action is alwayspreceded by thought. Thought is the impetus of action.*

The most destructive thoughts are only potentially so. It is when they are acted on that the effect transcends the individual and has societal consequences. It is for this reason that control of action was the second of the Ten Virtues.[1]

Society precedes civilization and is impossible unless people can be enjoined to refrain from activities that impede order and efficiency. Many of our natural inclinations, based as they are on instinctive and animalistic passions, would be destructive of society and prevent entirely the attainment of civilization if acted upon. A person who thinks of committing murder or mayhem threatens society only potentially. If he permits his thought to be manifested in action it is then that society becomes tragically involved.

In the very real sense then, the control of action is the manifestation of the individual's recognition of his or her responsibility to others and to societal order and advancement. In the absence of such control society remains, hopelessly, at the level of the savage.

PRINCIPLE TWO: MAN KNOW THY HERITAGE

Heritage is the combination of birthright and tradition. It is that which belongs to a person by right of birth. But, it is more than material inheritance. As tradi- tion it is a mode of thought and behavior passed down to a people by their forebears and followed by them from generation to generation. It is therefore closely linked to culture.

Knowledge of one's heritage is of tremendous importance to survival for several reasons. To be complete, knowledge of self must include knowledge of one's origins. Not merely in the sense of creation (a question that is, in any event, unanswerable) but of kinship. Heritage is the intimate knowledge of familial relationship magnified through the lens of antiquity. Heritage is, at one and the same time, personal history and the umbilical connectedness that creates belonging and desire for inclusion.

Heritage is also the placement of beings in time and the expression of their obligations and responsibilities in life and society. It is the beacon of pride, nobil ity and dignity. It is the spark of achievement and the fire of collective ambition. It is the burden of the past that is simultaneously the hope of the future. Heritage is the anchor of life and its fixity. Inspiration, goal-orientation and motivation are its perpetual partners.

In the vast universe that imposes the recognition of our comparative small- ness, heritage counters that we are great and powerful precisely because of its magical influence. Heritage is our connectedness to a line of ancestors whose ori- gins are so ancient as to be obscured in the mist of antiquity. It ennobles and strengthens our determination and resolve. We survive because of the inestimable value of their ancient yet timely traditions.

Heritage teaches that it is our obligation to continue those traditions, for whatever the level of their nobility they belong to us. We cannot help but add our contributions to them that the chain of existence will remain unbroken and be strengthened by our having forged new links and joined them to the old.

Heritage and tradition form the chain of culture whose links in time are the individuals of each new generation. To the extent that these individuals are aware of the existence of the chain and their place in it, the chain will continue as the anchor of our stability. Heritage is, therefore, that from which we cannot be separated without adverse and debilitating consequences.

The importance of and reliance upon heritage and tradition by a group of people is evidenced in their use of myth and the so-called practice of ancestor worship. The Kemites were no exception.

MYTH

Societies with strong oral traditions, such as those of the African continent, have always expressed the fundamental realities of life through what has come to be called myth. Because the current usage defines myth as fiction or half-truth the word is misleading as it detracts from the significance of the concept as it was understood by the people who used it.

To the peoples of the world who developed and transmitted the myth over considered it to be the true and unquestionable history of their origins. When myth is seen as fact it is deserving of equality of status with history as a statement of fact.

Myth views reality as a totality. It is not only fact, it is the symbolic expression of the perception of a people based on their unique view of the reality of the world.

The purpose of the myth is to refer a group of homogeneous and interdepen- dent people back to their ancient beginnings. By doing so myth connects people to the reservoir of knowledge from which their current society has evolved and to which they can refer in times of crisis and uncertainty. It is a golden thread of immeasurable strength that binds a group of people together.

Myths are most often stories about individuals who have lived lives that are, in some specific way, exemplary and worthy or remembrance. Myth, therefore, strengthens tradition by documentation of the ancient reality upon which tradition and heritage are based.

Myth is also the story of *symbols*. As such it is a form of *thinking*. The symbolic story relates to a set of ideas about people and events combined to form a symbol system that demonstrates not only history but also a hidden andvaluable truth.

The myth expressed the First Principles of the society by example of the activities of their ancestors. The preeminent mythology (the science of myth) is the Kemitic legend of Asar and Aset. The legend of is extremely ancient origin. It is attested in all periods of Kemitic history as a true account of the lives of historical beings. Asar, known as the *Good King*, and his wife Aset, known as the *Divine Mother* were revered as the original ancestors of all Kemites.

The legend tells of the life and times of the man who civilized Kemit and the world, and of his lovely and compassionate wife who ruled with him *equally*. It is the story of the eternal battle between positive and negative forces and provides encouragement that in the end balance andharmony will always prevail.

The legend clearly fulfills the criteria of the myth. It is a true, historical account of a real person(s) whose life was, in some specific way, exemplary. The legend served to strengthen traditions and apprise the people of the noble heritage in which they allshare.

The legend also relates the basis of a set of ideas through symbols that become part of a *symbol system* that gives meaning to the things of the past and explains their present value and application. Suffice it to say that he Legend of Asar and Aset is the Kemitic myth which served to present First Principles as they relate to heritage.

PRINCIPLE THREE: MAN KNOW THY ENEMY

First Principles are basic, pre-determined laws regarding the fundamental circumstances of life and *the action to be taken when such circumstances arise*. The under-lying concept upon which all First Principles and life itself are predicated is, in a word, *survival*.

If one is diligent in pursuit of self knowledge and heritage the chances of survival are dramatically increased, but survival is still not guaranteed. Survival also requires *security*.

Security implies *safety, protection* and *defense*. Safety is *freedom* from danger; protection is that which shields you from danger; and defense is the power to guard against danger. Interestingly, the word danger derives from and is closely related to the concept of power. The root of the word danger means master and was originally understood as the *power of harm*.

THE POWER OF HARM

The power of harm can decimate or render extinct. It may be of either human or non-human origin. The non-human category of harm includes, but is not limited to, disease, natural disasters and animal predators. The human category is obvi- ous. Both these categories of harm are forces that are destructive of survival and require eternal vigilance. Each is so prevalent as to have required First Principles regarding them. To this end principles were developed regarding animals (their behavior, dangerousness, territory, etc.) as well as natural disaster such as periodic storms and floods. The development of the art of medicine was also an outgrowth of this category of principles.

The human category was less amenable to codification because, unlike the others, it was characterized by *hostility*. In each case, however, the impact of destructive forces could be controlled by some form of adaptation aided by accu- rate knowledge. Human hostility was, however, far more problematic because of its unpredictable nature and because of the element of deceit it invariably involved.

THE ORIGIN OF DECEIT

There are two principle forms of deceit: *utilitarian* and *malicious*. *Utilitarian* deceit is practiced by some animals to gain advantage in the acquisition of food or reproduction and seems to be instinctive. *Malicious* deceit is characteristic of human beingsalone.

Whether in animals or human beings, deceit is a behavior pattern. In humans such behavior may have originated from something as simple as a smile. Facial expressions are the long distance communicators of intention. By the simple act of flexing the muscles of the face we communicate that our intentions are friendly, ferocious, hostile or even indifferent. Each of these facial expressions sends a message that is interpreted by another person who then responds accord- ingly.

The smile is inherently disarming. Perhaps it was the first person who discovered that another person could be caused to drop her guard and could be more easily taken advantage of by flashing a big smile, who was the originator of the human variety of deceit. Following a sufficient number of encounters in which persons were deceived to their material disadvantage, two conclusions would have been virtually compelled: (1) that a smiling person may have altogether unfriendly intentions; and (2) that to judge another's intentions by the presence or absence of a smile was to court danger by uncertainty. The overall conclusion, reached over time, would be that, at best, reliance on facial expressions as an accurate indicator of another's intentions was an exercise in futility. Because of the difficulty of determining, with any degree of certainty, whether a stranger was hostile or not, the concept of the enemy was arrived at.

The connection between hostility and enemies is not only apparent it is lin- guistic and historical. It is more than coincidence that thewords are cognates.

Enemy implies one who is unfriendly or *hostile* to another. In ancient times the word enemy literally meant hostile. The word hostile, on the other hand, means unfriendly, warlike, and characteristic of an *enemy.* Not surprisingly, the word hostile derives from the Latin *hostilis* meaning enemy. When the concepts of enemy and hostility are understood and combined, danger is clearly implied. This danger, which is the power of harm, mandated First Principle to know thy enemy.

KNOWLEDGE OF THE ENEMY

Knowledge of the enemy is subdivided into two aspects: (1) identity; and (2) overall characteristics. The first of these is the simplest because it is categorical. Any one not a member of the ancestral clan was, by that fact alone, an enemy. The method was simple and efficient. If the person was not a member of the clan, smile notwithstanding, defensive measures were immediately taken.

The second aspect required reconnaissance. Information regarding the enemy's number, location, weapons, habits, strength and even courage had to be observed, recorded and transmitted. This information became the basis of the concept of *military preparedness* that is implicit in the ideas of safety, protection and defense.

Defense is the science of protection aimed at the prevention of attack by ene- mies and is comprised of strategy and tactics. Knowledge about one's enemy is, therefore, prerequisite to the development of military strategy. Though essentially defensive, such thinking must include offensive strategies as well.

The Sacred Science of our ancestors focuses on the unchanging laws that undergird the universe. Our ancestors did not believe in chance. They under- stood that chance is but a name for [universal] law not recognized." They also recognized that *Heka* is dependent on the accurate knowledge of natural forces. *Wecannot control what we do not understand.*

To this end our ancestors began their researches with the intention of finding out how natural forces operate so that they might then control them to benefit humankind.

Initiates whose dedication, loyalty and commitment had been rigorously tested conducted this important work of scientific research. The initiates were instructed and guided by sages or *Masters of Wisdom* who insured that the research was governed by spiritual principles. It was through this time-honored method that they developed astronomy, geometry, mathematics, and chemistry.

The seven principles that follow represent the foundation of the Sacred Sci- ence of our ancient ancestors. These principles are actually *universal laws* that are now grudgingly recognized by modern science. We refer to them as universal laws because they apply to everything and everyone all the time *without exception*. Some universal laws are well known others are not.

Newton's law of universal gravitation is a well-known universal law. The seven Hermetic laws are not so well known. Wonder why? We offer these for your con- sideration because

TOTAL BLACK EMPOWERMENT

when properly understood they will provide the working framework for *Total Black Empowerment*. Remember that a powerful mind is an open mind that is filled with and receptive to powerful ideas.

19

THE SEVEN UNIVERSAL LAWS

The Seven Universal Laws[1] are truly powerful ideas from which to accurately understand the world in which we live and perhaps more importantly to under- stand the laws that unlock the secrets of how the world operates and why we have been unable to achieve power proportionality.

It is suggested that you read the laws that follow through once and give them some time to sink in. Then re-read them. Upon your second and subsequent read- ings a whole new world of powerful connections will be revealed to you by the natural law of recombination that will create powerful ideas that will astonish you.

What is presented here is at best a brief synopsis. It is not intended to trivialize our ancient ancestral teachings. Some might even argue that such information should not be presented in this form at all. I believe that those who search ear- nestly for the answers to our centuries-old problems will be benefited and will be inspired to learn more.

1. "ALL IS MIND."

Our ancestors taught that everything exists, first and foremost, in the mind of God. A truly simple yet profound statement that holds the key to the confusion that is the religious state of mind of many African Americans. Let us listen care- fully to the words of our ancestor on this score. Embodied in his words is perhaps the most important, mind-transforming idea that you will ever hear. The next voice that you hear will be that of *Tehuti, Lord of Thought— the Master of Divine Intelligence.*

"Mind cannot be enclosed, because *everything exists within Mind. Nothing is so quick and powerful.* Just look at your own experience. Imagine yourself in any foreign land, and *quick as your intention* you will be there! Think of the ocean and there you are. You have not moved as things move, but you have traveled, nevertheless. Fly up to the heavens you won't need wings! *Nothing can obstruct you*—not the burning heat of the sun, or the swirling planets. Pass on the limits of creation. Do you want to break out beyond the boundaries of the Cosmos? For your mind even that is possible. *Can you sense what power you possess?.... Try and understand that God is Mind."*[2]

All is mind Divine Mind. The first universal law instructs us about the men- tal nature of the universe, the cosmos and all creation. Everything that exists is in the mind of God. Put another way, *nothing exists outside the God's mind.* All thought existed first and only in the mind of God.

It is as if we are all receivers or radio stations that receive their live feed from a central broadcast station. As receivers we can listen to whatever station we want. We can turn off the receiver altogether. Some religions, in their failure to under- stand the teachings that they received from our ancestors or mistakenly believing that they could improve them, interpret this principle as *free will.* It is certainly true that you have *choice* but all of the possible outcomes have been registered. Just remember that *the future is the full spectrum of what can happen. The future is infinite possibility*—but all possibilities are recorded.

When we understand that God is Mind and that we

are made in the *mental image* of God we begin to see that we have at our disposal all of the equipment necessary to change our circumstances over night. This being considered the United Negro College Fund's slogan a mind is a terrible thing to waste" takes on new meaning.

Every invention, every creation from the paper clip to the supersonic transport to the satellites that explore the outer reaches of the universe to the latest vaccine all began as a thought in someone's mind. Everything of human creation is the gift or curse of a thought. It has been said that *the ancestor of every action is a thought*—and so it is.

Why is it so hard to believe that everything else in creation, the trees, the animals the oceans are not also the result of a thought? Is it so hard to believe that we can create as God creates?

2. "AS ABOVE SO BELOW"

This ancient principle directs our attention, by analogy, to the method by which we may solve problems. It provides us with the insight that teaches that we do not necessarily have to go to a place to know about it. This universal law is actu- ally one of *correspondence*. By this we mean it points to the similarities between things.

For example, the science of geometry allows us to plot the distances from one corner of a field to another or from the Earth to Mars. It also teaches that we need not fret over what exists above because it is the same as that which is below. Discover what is below and we can discover what is above without physically going there.

3. "NOTHING RESTS —EVERYTHING VIBRATES"

This is a *restless* world. It is as if things are constantly moving and changing. Our ancestors taught that this too is a universal law. Nothing rests. Everything moves. Everything vibrates. This is important because when properly understood it teaches that *everything is in a constant state of change*. Nothing remains forever. It also points out that everything *vibrates. Vibration is a movement—a back and forth movement*. It tells us that power too moves back and forth. For some of us this is a reason for *hope*. Things cannot remain this way forever we say. That is certainly one way to look at it. But it reminds one of the *gambler's fallacy*.

Gambler's are notorious for saying that my luck has been bad for so long that it has to change. They also interpret a single win after a long series of losses as proof that their luck is changing. The fallacy lies in the fact that there is no guar- antee that the change will come based on the length of a spell of bad luck. Nor is an isolated victory *proof* of imminent or permanent change. We cannot make plans based on the *hope* of change. Nor can we entrust the future of our people to the promise of eventual rewards. If you were offered employment and the terms of your compensation were that you would be paid *eventually* would you take the job? You would no doubt require a date certain for payment. You would certainly not accept employment and *hope* for payment.

The law of vibration alerts us to the existence of constant, unending back and forth movement. Which, of course, indicates constant, unending change. This law gives us assurance based on scientific confidence, not hope based on desire.

4. "EVERYTHING IS DUAL"

We may also refer to this as the law of *polarity*. Our ancestors also referred to it as the *Two Truths*. The law of polarity is truly ubiquitous. It has application in as many areas as the mind can imagine. We will examine only a few. Everything has its opposite. Interestingly, scientists have discovered that a bar magnet (which has positive and negative poles) will maintain the positive/negative polarity when it is cut in half. The polarity will remain no matter how many times the magnet is divided seeming to demonstrate that this polarity is eternal and unavoidable.

In other areas of life we can also see the existence of this law and the utility of the lesson it teaches. In the world of philosophy it applies to what is popularly known as the *problem of evil*. Simply stated the problem of evil arises from the reasonable question asked by critical thinkers since religion of the Judeo-Chris- tian sort has been around.

The question asked is how is it possible that a god of justice and love could create evil or, perhaps more troubling why would an all-powerful god not abolish it? Or if you prefer, how can evil exist if an omnipotent god actually abhors it?

The law or polarity answers the question succinctly. It teaches us that evil exists because good exists. Polarity exists for all things. Everything has its oppo- site. More accurately everything has its *complement*.

When we speak of opposites we generally mean something that *opposes* some- thing else. A complement, on the other hand, is something that *completes or makes up a whole*. If we think of good and evil as *complements* rather than *opposites* the problem of evil becomes less daunting. Evil exists *because* good exists one cannot exist without the other. We can no more have good without evil than we can have upwithout down, darkness without light, life without death.

Our ancestors also embodied this universal law in what they referred as the *Two Truths*. This concept holds, in effect, that there can be no *absolute* truth because every truth is, at best, a half-truth. It follows that when we express any proposition we simultaneously state its complement. Opposites then are merely degrees of the same truth, just as negative and positive poles of the magnet are part of the same magnet that cannotbe separated or divided.

We express this principle when we say that there are *two sides to every story*. The other side of the story is an equal part of it such that the story cannot possibly be true without it. Surprisingly, we fail to realize that universal laws apply to everything, all the time, without exception. Think about that the next time you exclude the other side because it undermines your truth. There can be no light without dark, no good without evil, no right without wrong.

5. "EVERYTHING FLOWS IN AND OUT"

This principle is best understood in conjunction with the principle of polarity. Polarity tells us that everything has its opposite or complementary poles. This law alerts us to the periodic movement between these poles; a swinging back and forth much like that of a pendulum. This is *balancing* (complement also implies balance) or *compensatory* law. The ancients said that *the swing to the left is the measure of the swing to the right*. This law explains everything from the ebb and flow of the tides to rise and fall of conservative and liberal politics. It also speaks volumes about the existence and longevity of injustice and inequality. This law informs us that life and circumstance both have a *rhythm* all their own.

6. "EVERY CAUSE HAS ITS EFFECT"

Chance is a name for a law not recognized." This is really an *anti-chance law*. It alerts us to the all-important notion that nothing happens by chance and that there are no coincidences. Everything has a cause. The importance of this law is that knowing it prohibits us from *logically* concluding that our present circumstances have come about by chance. This notion must lead us to search for *causes* instead of trying to neutralize effects. It informs us that because every cause has its effect it follows that every effect is itself a potential cause. It informs us that all things are linked through their causes and effects. According to this law the cur- rent state of our power deficiency cannot be the result of chance.

We might add here that perhaps more than any other law it is this one that has led to the monumental advances in modern science. It was the search for causes that brought enlightenment to the world. And, it was our ancestors who first recognized it.

7. 'EVERYTHING IS MASCULINE AND FEMININE'

This is perhaps the most instructive of the universal laws recognized by our ancestors. It speaks with particular clarity and importance to African Americans today. The law is simple and straightforward. It observes and implores us to always be mindful that everything is masculine and feminine.

Gender is a vital characteristic of all living things. There is no life, no generation, regeneration or reproduction without gender. This is also a manifestation of the universal law of polarity *everything is dual*.

Where life is concerned the complement of femininity is masculinity. These two represent the poles of biological existence. From plants to humans every spe- cies in existence has its male and female complement. We disregard this fact at our own peril.

If we consider the dominant European culture we find that it is, and has always been, fundamentally *patriarchal*. The European variety of patriarchy, however, has been further characterized by the *exclusion* of females from all areas of political life.

In the Judeo-Christian and Muslim cultures women have been historically relegated to positions closely akin to that of slaves in the antebellum South. Women were by virtue of their sex the property of their husbands, brothers, uncles and males in general. Women were denied the right to vote, to hold public office, to serve on juries or to be employed in government or industry.

The often overlooked aspect of this is that by excluding females a society not only diminishes the value of at least one half of its population it also denies the entire society the benefit of its natural *intellectual* complement. Such a society ignores fully one half of its *collective mind power*.

It is undeniable that men and women are different. We may debate the extent or importance of that difference but we cannot deny that it exists. Clearly, women and men look at the world somewhat differently. Often their views on such subjects as war, abortion and capital punishment are diametrically opposed. They may also view childrearing, nutrition and other basic concepts differently. Can we say that the United States would be the same place if women's views had been considered when important political decisions that affect the entire population were made? Would there have been a Vietnam or an atomic bomb dropped Hiroshima? Would thousands of young lives have been lost in Iraq and Afghani- stan?

This fundamental difference between men and women, a *gender* difference, is not only real it is the complement of the male view. It is not male or female. It is both *male and female*. Together they comprise the whole of the sense impressions that create the *collective reality* in which we live. When a society prohibits the input of half its senses, half of its intellect, it becomes like a person who has lost the sense of hearing or taste or sight. Such a person will undoubtedly compensate for the loss of one sense and will survive. But he or she is still disadvantaged from the standpoint of the ability to perceive the world. It is like having a super computer and disconnecting half of its computingpower.

Perhaps the greatest indication of the importance of

the law of gender is that the continuation of the specie is impossible without it. In order to generate life, to procreate, we must have both sexes. The message here is that all creation, whether biological or intellectual, requires female and male participation. We cannot give birth to new offspring or to new ideas for that matter, without the active participation of both complements of the act of procreation.

The Judeo-Christian religious tradition tells us that *God is a man* and that a *woman* (Eve) brought sin and evil into the world by biting the forbidden apple. If God is *all knowing* and *all wise* and *chooses* to be a man that must say something about which sex is *superior*. After all, God could have been anything he wanted to be. *Think about it.*

African cultures were by and large *matriarchal*. Women were not second-class citizens and contributed fully to every aspect of the life and development of our ancient societies. In fact, when the European first came in contact with our ancestors they noted with *displeasure* the freedom and authority that women possessed. Our ancestral view was fundamentally different than that of the European because we recognized and understood the universal law of gender.

One of the reasons that it came natural to us is our *Sacred Science.* In it the God of creation is recognized as *bisexual and the first created being as a woman*. This is no more than common sense. Human beings are female and male. It is only logical that the creative source would be both female andmale.

Our ancestors believed that the first created being had to be a female. What could be more logical? There are no human beings born of men, *ipso facto*, the first created being had to be a female. As trite as it may seem human birth requires a *womb, always did always will.*

We have presented the *Seven Universal Laws of Sacred Science* briefly and with trepidation because our ancestors intended them to be presented only to the *initi- ated.* Despite this fact I have done so because these ancient ancestral teachings have been so long hidden from their rightful heirs that we have come to relegate them to the category of the unimportant when we think about them at all.

There is another question that I hesitate to mention because of the uncomfortable issues it raises. Unfortunately, we have been so long the dupes of the Euro- pean and his insidious American Deception that we have come to believe that his way is the only way. Perhaps more regrettably we have developed what can only be called a *herd instinct*.

The herd instinct is characterized by the tendency to follow the lead of the rest of the herd without thinking. Even where this instinct predominates there are those among the herd who exercise independent judgment. It is from among this small, important group of independent, critical thinkers that will be found what I call the *Critical Mass* who will form the *vanguard of the new age.*

20

CRITICAL MASS: VANGUARD OF THE NEW AGE

The Critical Mass is the minimum number of enriched persons necessary to sustain a cultural/political chain reaction among African Americans.

The principle underlying critical mass is best understood by analogy. In nuclear physics critical mass is the minimum amount of fissionable material necessary to sustain a nuclear chain reaction. Specifically, it is the minimum amount of uranium or other nuclear fuel (plutonium is another example) needed to create the controlled release of energy in a nuclear power plant or an uncontrolled release of energy in a nuclear bomb.

The theory of nuclear physics is based on atomic theory or atomism. The the- ory of atomism was first developed in ancient Kemit by our ancestors and intro- duced to the Western world by Democritus, a Greek "philosopher" who, of course, studied in Kemit.

According to the Kemitic theory atoms are the basic components of the universe. They are both invisible and indestructible. This theory was introduced to the Greeks by either Democritus or his teacher Leucippus. In any event both of these Greek "philosophers" studied in Kemit and announced their theories after having studied in the land of our ancestors.

According to modern theory, the atom is the smallest unit of an element con- sisting of a dense, central, positively charged nucleus surrounded by a system of negatively charged electrons. The nucleus is held together by the *strong force*. The energy released in an atomic explosion is the strong force contained in the atom. Critical Mass is a necessary prerequisite to the release of energy contained in the atom. Only after critical mass has been achieved can the tremendous energy contained in the atom be released. The method of release is known as *nuclear fission*

Nuclear fission occurs when the atom is *split into two or more fragments*. Interestingly, the concept of fission is taken from a biological process by which one-celled organisms divide into two smaller organisms of equal size that enables the reproduction and growth of biological organisms. In the case of nuclear fission, however, neutrons (particles with no electrical charge) are freed by the splitting of the atom and in turn split other atoms releasing additional neutrons. If the fissionable material used is sufficiently great (has reached critical mass) the result is a *chain reaction*.

The amount of energy released by each individual atom is miniscule. It is the *combined energy* released by millions of atoms that accounts for the tremendous explosion. As the chain reaction gathers momentum it produces greater and greater amounts of energy.

A chain reaction then is any sequence of events each of which results in, or has an effect on, the following events. The domino effect is a chain reaction that con- sists in the toppling of one domino that in turn topples the others in the row no matter how long the row. *Topple the first one and the others will follow suit.*

Nuclear fusion is a second process by which the energy contained in the nucleus of the atom can be released.

In this process the nuclei *join together* to form a new and larger nucleus. The sharing of electrons (positively charged parti- cles) by other atoms surrounding the nucleus causes a chain reaction to occur. When nuclei collide all the particles involved are said to *reorganize* and the nuclear chain reaction is the result.

In *reorganization* the nucleus may absorb one type of particle while rejecting other types. When these nuclei combine some of the mass is converted into energy. This form of energy is referred to as *binding energy*. This energy not only binds the new nucleus together it is also equal to the total amount of mass (matter) that is transformed into energy. Simply put a nuclear chain reaction is the process by which mass (matter) is transformed into energy/power. *The mass to energytransformation cannot occur until Critical Massis achieved.*

Energy is related to mass. *Under certain conditions mass can be transformed into energy.* The rate at which the transformation takes place is fixed. This fixed exchange rate of mass to energy is represented in Einstein's now famous equation $E=MC^2$.

Einstein's *Theory of General Relativity* implies that the exchange rate of mass to energy is a universal law. It also indicates that a small amount of mass may be transformed into a tremendous amount of power. *Critical Mass is a condition precedent to the release of power. Power, therefore, follows Critical Mass at a fixed and predictable rate. When Critical Mass is achieved it will set in motion the explosive release of energy according to the mass-energy exchange rate embodied in Einstein's equation.* But, Critical Mass is more than mere numbers. Critical Mass also requires that the fissionable material be enriched.

In nuclear fission uranium 235 is separated from its twin uranium 238 by a process known as *enrichment* in order to be utilized in nuclear power plants or atomic bombs. Most uranium is only enriched to about three percent. This factor is known as the *concentration*. The higher the concentration of enriched uranium the smaller the amount required to achieve critical mass. The atomic bomb dropped on Hiroshima, Japan, for example, contained only eleven (11) pounds of uranium.

The role critical mass plays in nuclear physics is identical to the role it plays in the quest for Total Black Empowerment.

We have seen that in nuclear physics critical mass is the minimum amount of enriched fissionable material necessary to sustain a nuclear chain reaction. We have also seen that critical mass is a necessary prerequisite to the initiation of a chain reaction. The chain reaction results from release of the energy contained in atoms.

We have also learned that a nuclear chain reaction can be initiated by fusion or fission. Nuclear fission occurs when the atom is split into two or more fragments as a result of neutron bombardment. Neutrons are particles with neither positive nor nega- tive charge.

In *nuclear fusion* nuclei collide, *join together and reorganize* to form a new and larger nucleus. It is the sharing of the *positive charged* particles (electrons) of each of the nuclei that causes the chain reaction. *When nuclei combine mass is converted into energy.* This *binding* energy, as it is called, is always equal to the total amount of mass transformed into energy. As you can now see a nuclear chain reaction is simply the process by which mass is *transformed* into energy. *The mass to energy transformation cannot occur until Critical Mass is achieved.*

In the context of *Total Black Empowerment Critical Mass* is the minimum number of *enriched* persons (male and female) required to initiate a cultural/ political chain reaction that will lead to the release of a *controlled* explosive force.

ENRICHMENT

In this case enrichment is a *process of enlightenment* by

which people of ordinary intelligence, capability and determination are transformed into persons of extraordinary intellect, selfless leadership and transcendent will. This enrichment process is accomplished by *bombardment* with *neutral powerful ideas*. Not surprisingly the number necessary to attain Critical Mass is less than the three percent required in the case of nuclear fission.

The cultural/political chain reaction can be accomplished by *fission* or *fusion*. Fission will require a *split* while fusion requires a *joining*. The fission method is the least attractive for the purpose of *Total Black Empowerment* because it would require a split that would necessarily divide a community that needs *cohesiveness*.

FUSION

Fusion requires a joining together of the Critical Mass to create a greater, more massive *nucleus*. The nucleus is the core around which other parts are grouped. In biology the nucleus is the structure within a living cell that *contains the hereditary information and which controls the metabolism, growth and reproduction of the organism*.

Fusion creates energy/power that serves to melt the individual parts together. Produces less energy than fission but the energy produced by fusion is *controlla- ble* like energy produced in a nuclear power plant.

REORGANIZATION

Nuclei join to form a new and larger nucleus through the sharing of positive ideas. During this process some nuclei are accepted others are rejected based on their level of enrichment. Fusion generates heat. The heat results from the colli- sion of powerful ideas.

BINDING ENERGY

The collision of nuclei and the heat it generates serves to bind the parts together. This *binding energy* is the heat generated by the collision of powerful ideas. The heat also serves to melt these powerful ideas into a master plan.

CHAIN REACTION

This phenomenon results from the collision of powerful ideas. Each collision releases energy and impacts other powerful ideas causing them to release their energy as well. The chain reaction is the explosive force of the idea whose time has finally come. Simply put the chain reaction is the process by which ideas are transformed into power.

When critical mass is understood as the minimum number of enriched persons necessary to sustain a cultural/political chain reaction the result and its potential impact on the course of our collective future is explosive and revolu- tionary. The attainment of critical mass must be, therefore, a most important objective of those whose sincere goal it is to combine their energy, according to the Law of Power Units, with that of others to achieve *Total Black Empowerment*.

We have now properly laid the foundation from which to launch our quest for *Total Black Empowerment Through the Creation of Powerful Minds®*. You now have the tools to enable you to develop a *master plan* that will begin the cultural/political chain reaction that will launch the explosive force that will change the world.

PART V
FOOD FOR THOUGHT

PREFACE TO REVISED EDITION

Much has changed since the first edition of Total Black Empowerment was published in 2007. Perhaps most importantly Barak Obama was elected President of the United States in 2008. While that historic event is certainly worthy of celebration it is the response to it that is most instructive for African Americans and our quest for total empowerment. There are those among us usually but not exclusively younger African Americans who believe that withthe election of President Obama we have entered, at long last, a color blind society where the need for strategies to empower African Americans and other ethnic minorities are unnecessary and even counterproductive.

Those of us who have been around longer and who are, shall we say, more seasoned in such matters, recognize that racism, more properly white supremacy, remains a bed rock, sustaining feature of American culture and politics. Perhaps more importantly, the color blind (some call it post-racial) America theory is more a smoke screen that permits whites to ignore the persistent institutional racism that continues to exist than a harbinger of the New America.

Proof of this fact is not hard to find. For example, by the second year of President Obama's first term and after two years of blatantly obstructionist tactics by the Republican majority in Congress, senate majority leader Mitch McConnell announced that "[t]he single most important thing we [Republicans/white people?] want to achieve is for President Obama to be a one-term president."[1]

Now in the waning months of his historic two term presidency we need take a close look at his actual accomplishments. Certainly President Obama will be recognized by historians as one of the great presidents. His accomplishments are even greater in view of the fact that the Republican strategy was to say no to anything the president proposed.[2] This strategy should remind us of the southern strategy of nullification and interposition[3] championed by Alabama Governor George Wallace and used for years by southern states in a blatant attempt of derail the civil rights movement.

Upon close examination we must admit that President Obama did little to specifically address and/or remedy the unique race specific problems and disadvantages of African Americans resulting from and directly attributable to more than four hundred years of race specific legislation and other governmental and private action.

Let's be specific here. We are not talking about domestic programs like the Affordable Care Act or foreign policy or climate change for that matter. We are talking about the circumstances and conditions that affect African Americans directly and disproportionately. We are talking about mass incarceration and the War on Drugs. We are talking about racial profiling and disproportionate sentences. We are talking about the targeting of African American communities and the destruction of African American families by so-called child protections agencies and the so-called juvenile justice system. We are talking about horrific unemployment and underemployment of African American males. And, yes we are talking about the inequitable distribution of wealth and reparations for past and present government discrimination and conspiracy against the constitutional rights of African Americans.

Unfortunately, but predictably, the presidency of the first African American president has done little to change those circumstances and conditions. As I admonished in the first edition of *Total Black Empowerment* "we have unwittingly become mental slaves to a host of deceptions designed to insure our continued second-class citizenship ... we must control our thinking, if we do not someone else will.

In the first edition of *Total Black Empowerment* we concentrated on the thinking process and critical thinking. Here we concentrate on food for thought - things to think about. These added essays are not to be accepted as true until you have utilized your critical thinking skills to determine both their truth and usefulness.

In the new Part V entitled *Food For Thought* we take a radical look at factors that underlay the problems we are confronted with individually and as a people. We do this in order to better understand how and why such problems exist.

We will begin with what I consider to be the most important civil rights issue of the twenty-first century. It is an issue that we should have been thinking about all along. It is an issue that has been mostly ignored by everyone other than those of us who are directly affected. It is an issue that I am certain would have caused an uproar if not revolution had it happened to the white community. It is the mass incarceration of African American males -- the new slavery. It is an ingenious way to put our young men and increasingly young women under the control of the government. But it is also a blatant attempt to reverse the gains made by African Americans since the days of the civil rights movement. In a way it is as an offense as egregious as slavery and Jim Crow.

While it is certainly true that President Obama has commuted the sentences of more people incarcerated for non-violent drug offenses than any other president and it is also true that the infamous 100:1 cocaine to crack ratio has been reduced to 18:1 for those convicted after the effective date of the Fair Sentencing Act of 2010 there are still thousands of African Americans incarcerated under the crack law and a ratio of 18:1 for the same drug in different forms is still unfair and racially motivated.

Finally, the loss of productivity and earning power of those who have been incarcerated for decades under a law that is now, at long last, judicially recognized as racially discriminatory must be compensated.

It is my fervent hope that these new essays will be effective in beginning a new dialogue among and between African Americans that will foster the creation of a true plan of action based on the reality of our present circumstances. Remember a closed mind cannot receive a new thought. *Hetep.*

TOTAL BLACK EMPOWERMENT

INTRODUCTION

    This section challenges the reader to utilize the skills outlined in the previous sections. Once again this section and in fact this book is not intended to be a plan of action. It is a mind power primer that is intended to develop powerful mindsfueled by powerful ideas.

    The essays in Part V are intended as food for thought. They provide a framework for thinking about issues that I believe are not merely important but are vital to our continued survival and prosperity as American citizens.

    I have written them in an order that will take the reader step by step to a radical understanding of not only the circumstances with which we are confronted today but also to the underlying factors that have created them. I believe that it is these underlying root issues that are the problem. As with any seemingly intractable problem, lasting change can only be made by determining the root cause and removing it so that it will not reemerge next season. As any farmer or gardener will tell you in order to get rid of the weeds that choke your crop and prevent their re-occurrence you must destroy the root. If you do not get all the root what is left will grow into new weeds. In other words unless you get the root all you are doing is guaranteeing the seasonal return of the weed. When we apply this analogy to our struggle it aptly explains why we keep fighting the same battles with each new season.

    The vast number of issues that require our immediate attention are far too numerous and are therefore beyond the scope of this book. I have focused on five areas that will lay the groundwork for radical truly transformative change. I guarantee you that the thinking process you will engage in reading these essays will bring to mind other vital areas of concern to you. And will prepare you mentally to address those as well. As Malcolm X frequently reminded us "of all disciplines history is best suited to reward our study."[4] All I ask you to do is connect. We begin with what I believe to be the greatest civil rights issue since slavery .... the mass incarceration of African Americans.

21

THE MASS INCARCERATION OF AFRICAN AMERICANS

According to the National Association for the Advancement of Colored People (NAACP) Criminal Justice Fact Sheet:[5]

- African Americans now constitute nearly 1 million of the total 2.3 million incarcerated population.
- African Americans are incarcerated at nearly six times the rate of whites.
- Nationwide, African-Americans represent 26% of juvenile arrests, 44% of youth who are detained, 46% of the youth who are judicially waived to criminal court, and 58% of the youth admitted to state prisons.
- About 14 million Whites and 2.6 million African Americans report using an illicit drug. Five times as many Whites are using drugs as African Americans, yet African Americans are sent to prison for drug offenses at 10 times the rate of Whites.
- African Americans represent 12% of the total population of drugusers, but 38% of those arrested for drug offenses, and 59% of those in state prison for a drug offense.
- African Americans serve virtually as much time in prison for a drug offense (58.7 months) as whites do for a violent offense (61.7 months).

- Together, African American and Hispanics comprised 58% of all prisoners in 2008, even though African Americans and Hispanics make up approximately one quarter of the US population.

Clearly, something is going on here. African Americans represent 12% of the general population but nearly 50% of the prison population. It is now conceded that the mass incarceration of African Americans has been and continues to be driven almost exclusively by convictions for drug offenses -- primarily crack cocaine. The primary tool of mass incarceration has been and remains the Anti-Drug Abuse Act of 1986, as amended in 1988.

The complete title of the infamous crack law is itself a cruel joke when its application in the three decades since its passage is considered. The actual title is:

"A bill to strengthen Federal efforts to encourage foreign cooperation in eradicating illicit drug crops and in halting international drug traffic, to improve enforcement of Federal drug laws and enhance interdiction of illicit drug shipments, to provide strong Federal leadership in establishing effective abuse and prevention and education programs, to expand Federal support for drug abuse treatment and rehabilitation efforts, *and for other purposes.*" (Italics added).[6]

AND FOR OTHER PURPOSES

As it turns out the other purposes were targeting of inner city communities; turning drug users into drug traffickers and the mass incarceration of African Americans. But not a word of these was mentioned in the law. We can say this with certainty because although the incarceration of African Americans has sky rocketed the War on Drugs has been a utter failure -- that is if its real purpose was to stop drug abuse. If however, its purpose was the mass incarceration of African Americans it is one of the most successful laws since the Fugitive Slave Act.7

As we mentioned above the law says nothing about the targeting of African Americans or our communities. In short, if the law is neutral on its face how can we be heard to complain that it is unconstitutional? We will let the Supreme Court of the United States answer the question.

HUNTER V. UNDERWOOD[8]

In a case entitled *Hunter v. Underwood*, the Court affirmed the Eleventh Circuit Court of Appeals and held that the statute in question violated the Fourteenth Amendment. The *Hunter* decision is instructive.

In *Hunter*, the Court noted that when Article VIII, 182 of the Alabama Constitution of 1901 was passed its intent was to disenfranchise African Americans. It also found that for that reason the statute violated the Fourteenth Amendment. The statute was neutral on its face and did not mention its true intent. And what, you may ask, was the real intent of the statute? John B. Knox, president of the convention, stated in his opening address: "And what is it that we want to do? Why it is within the limits imposed by the Federal Constitution, to establish white supremacy* in this State."[9]

LEGISLATION INTENDED TO ESTABLISH WHITE SUPREMACY BUT THAT DOES NOT SAY SO IN THE LAW ITSELF

Hunter shows that a state legislature passed a law whose intent it was to disenfranchise African Americans for the purpose of establishing white supremacy. The Alabama legislators were well aware of the limits of the Federal Constitution and therefore drafted the law so that it would be neutral on its face and thereby immune from challenge. Their intent was to disenfranchise by reason of prior conviction for crimes of moral turpitude. The crimes of moral turpitude specifically included crimes that were thought to be commonly committed by African Americans such as vagrancy, living in adultery, and wife beating. Clearly, the law was unconstitutional. The Court found that the purpose of the statute was clear even if it did not appear on the face of the statute itself. Their intent was to disenfranchise by reason of prior conviction for crimes of moral turpitude. The crimes of moral turpitude specifically included crimes that were thought to be commonly committed by African Americans such as vagrancy, living in adultery, and wife beating. Clearly the law is unconstitutional. The Court found that the purpose of the statute was clear even if it did not appear on the face of the statute itself. *The law was on the books and enforced for at least eighty-five years.*

YICK WO V. HOPKINS [10]

There is another Supreme Court case decided nearly a century before Hunter that should be considered here. The case is *Yick Wo v. Hopkins*, decided in 1886. This ancient case still resonates with the circumstances with which we find ourselves confronted today. The facts of *Yick Wo* are simple enough. The City of San Francisco passed an ordinance, neutral on its face, that was subsequently used nearly exclusively against Chinese laundries.

In overturning the ordinance the Supreme Court opined:

"Though the law itself be fair on its face and impartial in appearance, yet, if it is applied and administered by public authority with an evil eye and an unequal hand, so as practically to make unjust and illegal discriminations between persons in similar circumstances, material to their rights, the denial of equal justice is still within the prohibition of the Constitution."

And finally the Court held:

"No reason for it [the ordinance] is shown, and the

conclusion cannot be resisted that no reason for it exists except hostility to the race and nationality to which the petitioners belong, and which, in the eye of the law, is not justified. The discrimination is, therefore, illegal, and the public administration which enforces it is a denial of the equal protection of the laws and a violation of the Fourteenth Amendment of the Constitution. The imprisonment of the petitioners is, therefore, illegal, and they must be discharged." [11]

Before we continue please bear in mind that the legal question of whether the crack law, though facially neutral, violates the Constitution of the United States has never been addressed by the Supreme Court of the United States. This despite the fact that the overwhelming number of persons incarcerated under the statute are African American. There have been numerous opportunities for the Court to do so. Consider also that the Supreme Court picks which cases it will hear. It has not granted *certiorari* in a single case that argued that the crack law violated the Fourteenth or any other amendment to the United States Constitution. One case that I highly recommend that you carefully review is *United States v. Clary*.

UNITED STATES V. CLARY [12]

In *Clary*, the late District Judge Clyde S. Cahill, Jr., the first African American to serve on the court, wrote an exhaustive opinion on the crack issue and found that: "In summary, the Court, after careful consideration, reluctantly concludes that the pertinent sections of 21 U.S.C. § 841 which mandate punishment to be 100 times greater for crack cocaine than for powder cocaine are constitutionally invalid, both generally and as applied in this case. The Court finds that there is no material difference between the chemical properties of crack and powder cocaine, and that they are one and the same drug. The Court further finds that this defendant has been denied equal protection of the laws when the punishment assessed against him is 100 times greater than the punishment assessed for the same violation but involving powder cocaine."

In addition the court found: "... the actions of Congress and the prosecuting officials were influenced and motivated by unconscious racism, causing great harm and injury to black defendants because of their race inasmuch as whites are rarely arrested, prosecuted, or convicted of crack cocaine offenses.[13]

If the passage of the federal crack law of 1986 is analyzed under the standard applied in *Hunter* it is apparent that drafters and sponsors of the bill intended for the law to be applied against African Americans from the outset.

First, the law was intended to severely punish traffickers in crack cocaine. Second, since it was alleged the that crack epidemic was most severe in predominately black and minority inner-city communities the target of the law was intended to be predominately black inner-city communities. That he law was facially neutral is, according to *Hunter*, irrelevant. Moreover, the fact that the legislators may have thought they were doing a service to the African American communityis equally irrelevant.

In Hearings before the Subcommittee on Crime of the Committee of the Judiciary of the House of Representatives[13] we read the following: "Unfortunately, the 1986 Act was expedited through Congress, and its passage left behind a very limited legislative history. Although many individual members delivered floor statements about the Act, Congress dispensed with most of the typical legislative process, including committee hearings and committee analysis of the Acts provisions." at p. 153.

A law that has resulted in the incarceration of thousands of African Americans and that is now the primary reason for one million African Americans being incarcerated today did not even have a committee hearing or analysis prior to passage. "In 1988," the record reflects,

"Congress enacted an amendment to the 1986 Act that made crack cocaine the only drug with a mandatory minimum penalty for a first offense of simple possession."[14] p. 153. This had the effect of turning users into traffickers.

The Congressional Record of the House on p H10260 reports the following remarks of Rep. Shaw (R.Fla.):

"Mr. Shaw: ....there was no racist motivation whatsoever in putting that [100-1 powder cocaine to crack] in the law .... We also found that where it was creating its worst problems were in minority areas because of the cheapness of it. We found this was an area that was being unfairly, unconsciously impacted by cocaine, crack cocaine as it is even today .... it was because of concern for what it was doing in minority neighborhoods, how it was tearing up these neighborhoods, and it has. The gentleman well knows this from his own background [the gentleman is Melvin Watt of NC, an African American]. The problem we have in the inner cities, particularly in minority areas right now, the crime and all of this, is that the drug problem in this country has absolutely torn these neighborhoods apart .... As a matter of fact, it was a question of trying to save the minority neighborhoods from this awful curse that had gone all across this country, and it is not only confined in the minority areas. I will not suggest that. but is seemed that was where it was having its biggest impact and that is where we had to go after the problem and this why we did it."

The Congressman added, at p. 10261

Mr. Shaw:"...I would close by just saying to the gentleman that the inner city neighborhoods the poor minority neighborhoods are the most fragile in the entire country. They are the ones that have to be protected. They are the ones where we have to rid the neighborhoods of the drug dealers." (Bold and italics added).

Here we have an admission from the Congressman who claims to have put the 1988 amendment into the law that he did so to protect inner city minority neighborhoods from drug dealers. But he didn't stop there. It gets better.

Mr. Shaw: "That is the voice of the minorities in the areas that are responsible who want to get their areas up out of poverty, get out of the gutter, get the problems out of their neighborhoods and get the crimes out of the streets so again they can walk their streets and sit on their front porch and they can enjoy life."

Mr. Shaw summoned it all up with the following telling remark: **"It was a question of trying to save minority neighborhoods they were the ones who had to be protected so that's why they were targeted."** (Bold and Italics added).

It should be noted here that this is nothing more than the old antebellum paternalism. We (white folks) know what is best for you people.

Let us not get sidetracked here. Mr. Shaw's argument and similar arguments of others before and since, prove too much. It does not matter that the intent of the legislation was thought to be benevolent. It was still racially motivated. Words such as inner-city, minority, law and order, food stamps and even poverty-stricken are now recognized for what they are -- racial code words. One author notes that the number one racial code word is, you guessed it, is inner-city. [15]

We can logically conclude from this that the federal crack law was racially motivated by virtue of the fact that it was intended to target American's inner (African American) cities. The fact that it was allegedly intended to save those communities is irrelevant even if it is true. The Fourteenth Amendment, let us not forget, passed on July 8, 1868, was passed for the singular purpose of protecting newly freed slaves, thereby legally recognizing them as a protected federal government as well as the states.

We saw in Yick Wo that: "...in the administration of criminal justice no different or higher punishment should be imposed upon one than such as is prescribed to all for like offences. . . . Class legislation, discriminating against some and favoring others, prohibited..."

In the case of cocaine the 100:1 sentencing ratio powder to crack is unjustified and unconstitutional. No matter what they say about how dangerous crack is, it is still identical to powder cocaine. That is to say that both compounds have the same molecular structure.

The Supreme Court of the United States has noted that: *"Chemically, ... there is no difference between the cocaine in coca paste, crack cocaine, and freebase all are cocaine in its base form. On the other hand, cocaine in its base form and in its salt form (i.e., cocaine hydrochloride) are chemically different, though they have the same active ingredient and produce the same physiological and psychotropic effects. The key difference between them is the method by which they generally enter the body; smoking cocaine in its base form whether as coca paste, freebase, or crack cocaine allows the body to absorb the active ingredient quickly, thereby producing a shorter, more intense high than obtained from insufflating cocaine hydrochloride."* (Italics added).[16]

Note the specious distinction and the cowardly attempt to justify it. The active ingredient (what gets you high) is the same in both powder and crack cocaine. The difference, and therefore the only possible justification for the significantly higher penalties is the way it is ingested. The distinction is artificial at best. It is like saying that the penalty for selling tobacco products to minors (a prohibition that all states and the federal government have on the books) should be different for cigarettes and snuff because of the different methods of ingestion. It is the nicotine/tobacco not the method of ingestion. The Fourteenth Amendment argument here is simple and straightforward. The Amendment stands for the proposition that no different or higher punishment shall be imposed..." If the controlled substance is identical how can the punishments be different? Clearly, the crack law violates the Fourteenth Amendment. No matter what the argument the result is always the same. There is a biblical observation that is appropriate here. It posits that the leopard does not change his spots.[17] We should heed it well. In an article appearing in the Harvard Journal of Law and Public Policy[18], Paul J. Larkin, Jr., a research fellow at the ultra conservative Heritage Foundation, vividly illustrates the present tendency of conservative forces in America to justify the mass incarceration of two generations of African Americans on the ground of doing good for the black community. The reasoning is as insidious as it is specious. Mr. Larkin's article is masterful -- in the antebellum sense that is.

Mr. Larkin notes, rightly, the arguments made by critics of the infamous crack law.

"First, law enforcement officials have scrupulously enforced the crack laws against black dealers working in the open-air markets [the so-called open air markets he refers to can only be street corners in our communities] often found in predominantly urban black communities, but law enforcement has not pursued similarly intensive investigations of more discreet powdered cocaine distribution and use in the predominantly white suburbs.

Second, the 100:1 ratio produces a prison population with an exponentially larger number of black than white cocaine trafficking convicts, because the sentences imposed on mostly black defendants convicted for selling crack are far longer than the sentences imposed on mostly white defendants for selling powdered cocaine.

Third, although these aggressive law enforcement efforts take advantage of poor, urban blacks marginalized by society, denied the economic opportunities available to suburban whites, and shunted off into America's urban ghettos, the enforcement efforts do not make a dent in the crack trade. There always will be another dealer willing to step into the shoes of anyone arrested for selling crack because the remote prospect of future long-term imprisonment is not a deterrent to someone with no other option.

The bottom line of the critics arguments, Larkin writes, is that America's "war on drugs has become indistinguishable from a war on blacks. But Mr. Larkin sees it differently. He too knows what is best for the black community. He adds:

"Crack dealers largely sell their wares in urban communities. Given contemporary housing patterns, the residents in those communities, like the dealers themselves, are predominantly black. Residents who are victims of crime will far outnumber those who are perpetrators. Those victims suffer the effects of violence brought on by drug trafficking, and they endure the fear consequent upon living in a community haunted by outlaws. Punishments, even severe ones, may be necessary to protect innocent third parties in the communities where crack trafficking flourishes. By deterring crime and imprisoning offenders, the system reduces the harms that innocent residents suffer and, over time, makes the community a less frightening place. The benefits for residents, particularly those who have nowhere else to go, are immeasurable."

Mr. Larkin's article takes to task the courageous decision of the United States Court for the Sixth Circuit in *United States v. Blewett.* I can understand why.

UNITED STATES V. BLEWSETT[19]

In *Blewsett*, the Sixth Circuit held: "The old crack cocaine statutory minimums are racially discriminatory as the legislative history of the Fair Sentencing Act makes clear, as the Dorsey [*United States v. Dorsey*], case states, and as the Sentencing Commission reports to Congress advise. Perpetuation of such racially discriminatory sentences by federal courts is unconstitutional and therefore the sentencing guidelines must be interpreted to eliminate such a result. Accordingly, the judgment of the district court is reversed and remanded for the re-sentencing of plaintiffs in accordance with this opinion." [20]

The Sixth Circuit, as has no other Circuit Court of Appeals, reached a landmark, albeit long overdue, conclusion.

According to the majority, if a legislature is aware that continued application of a facially race-neutral law has produced a racially discriminatory outcome, *the legislature will be deemed to endorse that discriminatory result if the legislature fails to revise the law.* (italics added).

In other words, even if Congress did not enact the Anti-Drug Abuse Act of 1986 for a racially discriminatory purpose, Congress knew by 2010 that the 1986 law had produced a racially discriminatory outcome. A decision to maintain that disparity by declining to make the Fair Sentencing Act of 2010[21] retroactive would perpetuate exactly the same result that would have occurred if Congress had acted with a racially discriminatory intent twenty four years earlier.

Congress' malign neglect in 2010 therefore must be treated in the same manner as if Congress had acted with a discriminatory purpose in the first instance. Moreover, any court that refuses to apply the 2010 law retroactively would be deemed complicit in Congress's discrimination. "Judges may no more enforce the web of statutes, sentencing guidelines, and court cases that maintain the harsh provisions for those defendants sentenced before the Fair Sentencing Act"[the web indicates an interlocking, interdependent set of statutes that combine to insure mass incarceration. It should also be noted here that the United States Sentencing Guidelines, the Bail Reform Act and the abolition of parole in the federal system were all enacted at the same time and contemporaneous with the crack law] than the bench may enforce racially restrictive real estate covenants like the ones held invalid in *Shelly v. Kraemer*." The only way to avoid a constitutional violation, the Sixth Circuit concluded, was to apply the 2010 statute retroactively.

But a complete and balanced assessment is indispensable to rational policy making (the crack law was passed without any deliberation -- at all) so should it be suspect on that ground alone? The Larkin article does make some valid arguments. But it is cited here mainly because it is an example of the long standing racism in academia particularly

TOTAL BLACK EMPOWERMENT

from those who believe admittedly or not that they stand in *loco parentis* of the black community -- just as they did in 1786, 1886 and 1986.

22

THE WAR ON DRUGS: JUST LIKE SEGREGATION

"Hey, why fret about losing segregation when you can just use the drug war to remove blacks entirely from a city and relocate them to a penitentiary hundreds of miles away, possibly for the rest of their lives? And it's all legal, just like segregation."[22]

"Nothing has contributed more to the systematic mass incarceration of people of color in the United States than the war on drugs."[23]

Let us note at the outset that it is the so-called war on drugs that has been and remains the primary vehicle by which mass incarceration of African Americans has been facilitated. A few facts will set the stage for our further analysis:

For at least two generations[24] the drug laws have successfully facilitated the mass-incarceration of African Americans while doing nothing to stop the availability of illicit drugs in the United States. In short, the war on drugs has been a complete and utter failure unless (here is where critical thinking skills become crucial) its intended purpose was not to control drugs but to control people. Upon careful analysis it is evident that the war on drugs was and remains a highly effective method of social control whose primary target is the African American population.

The Brookings Institution, a non-partisan, non-profit Washington, D.C. think tank, reported that from 1993 to

2009 more than 3 million people were sent to prison for drug violations in the United States more than were sent to prison for violent crimes. During the same period there were more than 30 million arrests for drug violations. the estimated cost to tax payers -- one trillion dollars. [25] That's 30,000,000 million arrests! The African American population of the United States is estimated at 37,685,848. Moreover, if the objective of the war on drugs was to stop drug trafficking, statistics show that it has never worked. The cost of the war on drugs has totaled more than $1 trillion dollars has cost hundreds of thousands of lives and drugs are cheaper, more potent and more available than ever.

In April 2016, an article appeared in *Harper's Magazine*[26] that reported a 1994 interview with John Ehrlichman, a Watergate co-conspirator who was White House Counsel and Chief Domestic Advisor to President Nixon. Though the report was published in 2016 the interview was conducted 22 years earlier.

According to the journalist Dan Baum, he was intent on finding out "[h]ow did the United States entangle[d] itself in a policy of drug prohibition that has yielded so much misery and so few good results?" Mr. Baum reports Mr. Ehrlichmn as saying:

"You want to know what this was really all about? he asked with the bluntness of a man who, after public disgrace and a stretch in federal prison, had little left to protect. The Nixon campaign in 1968, and the Nixon White House after that, had two enemies: the antiwar left and black people. You understand what I'm saying? We knew we couldn't make it illegal to be either against the war or black, but by getting the public to associate the hippies with marijuana and blacks with heroin, and then criminalizing both heavily, we could disrupt those communities. We could arrest their leaders, raid their homes, break up their meetings, and vilify them night after night on the evening news. Did we know we were lying about the drugs? Of course we did."

The conclusion is simple and unavoidable. According to Mr. Ehlichman, who was a first hand witness of the events leading up to President Nixon's War on Drugs, one of the underlying motives was to associate blacks with heroin, and then criminalize it heavily in order to disrupt black communities, arrest their leaders, raid their homes, and break up their meetings. Regardless of the real reason for the war on drugs the result was the mass incarceration of African Americans for the longest periods of time in history.

The real question for the purposes of black empowerment analysis is how did African Americans in a position to stop or at least widely publicize this conspiracy not realize its impact if not its intent in advance? We are still talking about the War on Drugs but now more specifically about the infamous crack law.

THE ANTI-DRUG ABUSE ACT OF 1986 (PUBLIC LAW 99-570)

"... the greatest intentional, sustained offensive against African American development since slavery."

House Resolution 5484 (later Public Law 99-570) was introduced by House Speaker Rep. James Wright of Texas a Democrat on September 8, 1986. It was passed by the House by unanimous consent three days later on September 11, 1986.[27] There were no committee hearings as is customary and therefore no debate. By contrast Nixon's War on Drugs legislation took fifteen months to become law.[28]

Rep. Jim Wright (D. Tex) was never a friend of African American interests. He refused to support the Civil Rights Act of 1964 which required desegregation of public accommodations and established the Equal Employment Opportunity Commission.[29] The Crack Law introduced by Democrats, rushed through Congress under Democratic leadership was signed into law October 27, 1986.

You should remember that the Democrats were the

staunchest proponents of segregation prior to the election of Franklin D. Roosevelt and wrote and implemented most of the infamous Black Codes and other Jim Crow laws.[30]

At the bill signing ceremony for Public Law 99-570 President Ronald Reagan singled out, among others, the following politicians for special mention noting that they had been "real champions" in the battle to get the crack law through Congress: Senator Strom Thurmond of South Carolina and New York Representative Charles Rangel.[31]

Reagan, apparently with a straight face proclaimed that "today marks a major victory in our crusade against drugs -- a victory for safer neighborhoods, a victory for protection of the American family. The American people want their government to get tough and to go on the offensive. And that's exactly what we intend, with more ferocity than ever before." And he meant it.

The truly curious thing here is the alliance of the "real champions" Strom Thurmond and Charles Rangel. Strom Thurmond, the white supremacist, race-baiting, segregationist from South Carolina and Harlem Rep. Charles Rangel successor to Adam Clayton Powell, Jr. Politics make strange bedfellows indeed.

Thurmond amended the bill in the Senate to add the death penalty for certain drug offenses[32] while Rangel amended it in the House to increase law enforcement funding from $100 million to $200 million and to permit the use of funds for non-federal prison construction.[33]

Let's let Mr. Rangel speak for himself. "I really thought that the fear of incarceration would be enough" he said. I was not sophisticated enough to understand the whole country wasn't sophisticated enough to recognize the cost of incarceration is out of proportion to any benefits at all. [34]

So there we have it Mr. Rangel admits, nearly forty years later that he was not Sophisticated enough to understand. What he did not say but is inescapably implied is that he did not *think*. His common sense should have told him that anything that Strom Thurmond was supportive of with regard to black people must be initially viewed with great suspicion and skepticism and thereafter be carefully and critically analyzed.

In fairness to Rep. Rangel we should note that he is a former Assistant United States Attorney whose legal training and experience and the mindset developed by such training and experience would cause him to believe that locking people up could possibly be an answer to the medical problem of drug addiction.

Again in fairness to Rangel and in support of our analysis he was not alone his delusion. The list of congresspersons who also supported the War on Drugs and the infamous crack law specifically reads like a Who's Who of African American Political Leaders at the time.

In 1986 with the notable exception of Reps. John Conyers, Jr., Gus Savage and Alan Wheat every member of the Congressional Black Caucus were co-sponsors of the Anti-Drug Abuse Act.

In 1988, when the law was amended by Rep Clay Shaw, Jr. of (R. Fla) to add the minimum mandatory provisions and the infamous 100:1 powder cocaine crack cocaine ratio every member of the CBC except, again John Conyers, Jr., and then freshman Rep. John R. Lewis voted for the amendment.[35]

The question is how did these seemingly sophisticated, well-educated politicians all representatives of predominately black districts not recognize that such a law had the potential in the hands of racist, white supremacist police departments and prosecutors, to be not only an instrument of mass incarceration but also would launch the greatest, sustained offensive against African American political and economic development since chattel slavery.

This collective mental disorder perhaps better than any other example illustrates both the need for critical thinking and the disastrous consequences of our failure to develop and utilize it. One observer of what I will call the collectivementaldisorderdemonstratedbythe congressional Black Caucus noted naively as follows:

He [Rangel] was effectively playing the role of advocate for a community that was being ravaged by the drug trade.... [h]indsight is always 20/20. [36]

Yet another observer noted more realistically: "His [Rangel's] strong advocacy around the lock-em-up-and-throw-away-the-key approach was instrumental to the devastation of the black family in Harlem, ... [c]ommunities were devastated by that. by lost fathers, by lost income that's no longer in the community. [37] The devastation of the black family was not confined to Harlem - it visited every black community in the United States.[38]

Since Rep, John Conyers, Jr. was one of the four members of Congress who was against the crack law and was not a sponsor of it we will allow him to have the last word. In an interview with *Heart and Soul Magazine*[39] in March of 2008 Conyers, who was then Chairmen of the House Judiciary Committee, was asked the following question:

YRL - *In retrospect, was it in some ways a rush to judgment before all the facts were in and people misinterpreting the impact of powdered coke versus crack cocaine? What kind of thinking should have been done to even address the problem overall?* It has such a strong impact on our communities and families, but it seems like the emphasis was placed on just having really harsh legal remedies. (My italics).

JC - This was initiated by a president of the United States, his Department of Justice, a conservative Republican Congress. There weren't any steps for us to take to avoid it. A law is a law, and many of the earlier court decisions validated it and found the law was perfectly okay. There wasn't any way we could have inoculated ourselves or prevented some of these things from happening. What we're doing now with the Congressional Black Caucus - incredible number from the 13 of us who started it to 43 now with a progressive caucus in the Congress of more than 80 members-we have the power to begin to re-examine the things that we knew were wrong back in the '80s. And that's what we're going to do. *After we get through examining them, we're going to take action to make our system fair and to make sure that justice is available to all.*[40] (My italics).

The interviewer was Yanick Rice Lamb. The heart of her question was "...what kind of thinking should have been done....?". Conyers did not actually answer the question but rather he gave a cogent, but telling *apologia* for the evident lack of thinking on the part of the CBC in 1986.

In fairness to Rep. Conyers he clearly and succinctly states what he and his congressional colleagues were up against -- the president of the United States, the Department of Justice a conservative Republican Congress and the courts who validated the law. So apparently the strategy in response to this was if you can't beat 'em join 'em." After all, there wasn't any way we could have prevented these things that we knew were wrong from happening. So we, (the CBC) co-sponsored and voted for the legislation. Now that we have the power to reexamine we are going to make the system fair. Problem is that we have sacrificed the lives of hundreds of thousands of our young people in the thirty year interim. Now we are ready to reexamine. Spoken like a true politician. Problem is there is something that they could have done. They could have raised hell! Instead they co-sponsoring the bill and voting for it.

The foregoing should not be viewed an indictment of the CBC. But it is an expose' of the counterproductive, inefficient and therefore ineffective mindset that has prevented our attainment of power proportionality in America. Although it may be true that hindsight is always 20/20 leadership by hindsight is both dangerous and counterproductive. Yet many of our leaders have failed to recognize this important fact.

In the Conyers *apologia* we see a tacit but implicit failure to recognize the fundamental principle of any struggle -- never give up! Which brings us to the second essay on food for thought. It's called "We the people"

23

"WE THE PEOPLE"

The Black Lives Matter Movement began in response to the acquittal of George Zimmerman for the killing of African American teenager Travon Martin in Florida in 2013. The underlying impetus was police brutality and the repeated killing of unarmed black men.

A group of brave young men and women tormented by injustice and enraged by the glacial pace of the movement toward equality and justice for African Americans band together and proclaim loudly and disruptively "enough is enough" Black Live Matter! Soon hundreds of these young people and their sympathizers are in the streets *en masse* stopping traffic, marching on city hall calling for transparency or the resignation of this or that chief of police. Sometimes violence erupts -- usually in response to violence. And the news media proclaim the advent of yet another riot.

Déjà vu is the feeling that what is happening now has been experienced before. The French word literally means "already seen".

I applaud the courage and conviction of the young brothers and sisters of the Black Lives Matter movement. But we have seen this before. The same or very similar words were spoken and very similar actions have been taken by the young brothers and sisters of the Student Non-violent Coordinating Committee (SNCC), the Black Panthers and the Deacons for Defense and a host of other lesser known but no less sincere and dedicated young people. All have come to the same end. A moment in the spotlight and they are gone.

The problem is that protest is not now and never will be the answer to our collective problems. *Protest is the tactic of the powerless.* We are power deficient not powerless. Yet we continue to utilize the tactics of the powerless.

The old saying attributed to Albert Einstein is trite but true -- the definition of insanity is doing the same thing over and over again, but expecting different results. Again our failure to think efficiently has condemned us to protests over the things that are actually peripheral. Our attention has been misdirected. How can we really believe that we can effect change by continuing to use the failed tactics and strategies of the past?

We must begin to embrace the notion that our present situation is the result of our failure to develop winning strategies and tactics rather than the superiority or intellectual prowess of the enemy. Again, *it is our thinking*. We must begin by disavowing the counterproductive notion that we cannot win because the forces arrayed against us are too numerous or too powerful. It is clear that whether the problem is racial profiling, stop and frisk, traffic stops, police brutality, and even to an extent mass incarceration they are related to a system of laws that are easily manipulated by law enforcement personnel who desire to do so.

Again to go to the root of the matter the real question and the object of our concern should be why are so many police are necessary in the United States generally and more particularly in the black community. The right question often contains its own answer.

WHY ARE SO MANY POLICE NECESSARY IN THE UNITED STATES?

There are presently 18,000 police departments in the United States with over 800,00 to 1.2 million sworn police officers. By contrast the United States military, all branches, number 1.4 million. Interestingly, the number of police officers in the United States is greater than the standing armies of all but two countries in the world -- China and India. China with an overall population of 1.4 billion has 1.6 million police. India with an overall population of 1.3 billion has 1.6 million police. The population of the United States is 322 million.[41]

WHY ARE SO MANY POLICE NECESSARY IN BLACK COMMUNITIES?

Willie "the Actor" Sutton was bank robber. Mr. Sutton was once asked by a journalist why he robbed banks? His answer was straight forward and obvious. He said he robbed banks because "that is where the money is." The short answer to our lead in question is that is where the arrests are. Note I did not say that is where the criminals are. Every law creates an outlaw. It is the law that makes the act criminal.

The vast majority of crimes committed in this country are committed by white people. This should not be surprising because the majority of people in this country are white. What is surprising is that far more blacks than whites are arrested in the United States.

In Ferguson, Missouri police arrest blacks three times more often than whites. There are 1,600 places in the United States where this disparity is greater -- in some places as high as ten times greater.[42] But how do we account for this dramatic disparity? Might it have something to do with the number of police deployed in black communities? Is it as Michelle Alexander noted:

"[t]he hypersegregation of the black poor in ghetto communities has made the round up easy. Confined to ghetto areas and lacking political power the black poor are convenient targets[?]"[43] The truth is far more sinister and instructive.

Let us begin by noting that the forerunner of the modern day police department was, not surprisingly, the slave patrol. Slave patrols were created to control slave populations. In reality they were created and continue to be maintained to control the behavior of slaves and apparently their descendants.

In an article that should be required reading for all Americans but especially for African Americans the author, Ben Brucato,[44] observed that:

"A main function of the political systems constructed across this history has been to control the Black population, to divide the working class along racial lines and to foster a cross-class alliance among whites. Central to the management and control of non-whites was and remains a criminal justice system that profoundly discriminates against non-whites and especially blacks. This system was devised primarily to administer slavery, then adapted to manage segregation. Today, U.S. police maintains the color line in an officially color-blind polity. *Recent attention to mass incarceration both describes the persistence of white supremacy in this system, and explains it historically with connections even prior to the founding of the nation and rooted in the institution of chattel slavery ....The relationship between the U.S. rate and police hinges on white supremacy, and both work to reproduce this interconnection as an inextricable logic functioning at the core of each institution.* (Italics mine).

Mr. Brucato, concludes that:

"In 1721, the first agency in the U.S. that looked anything like modern police was given its mandate: prevent Black insurrection. This mandate has remained core to U.S. police ever since. Nothing more profoundly explains the persistence in racial outcomes of policing than this genetic moment, as throughout the nearly 300 years since, all reforms to the institution have managed to retain this imperative, when not in directive then certainly in practice. The historical practices of police in fulfilling this mandate have not only shaped contemporary policing, but also established that Black insurrection is to be prevented through constant proximity of police to communities of colour, intensive surveillance, routine harassment and violent terror by agents of the state and white citizens.

Nonetheless, specific political and juridical adaptations have directed these activities. *Since Reconstruction, the line between the symbols 'young Black male' and 'criminal' is difficult to draw. The two categories practically define one another. It is through the surveillance and physical violence of police that the symbolic violence of this identity is made functional, reliable and durable."* (Italics added).

Given the above historical facts it becomes apparent that we are not thinking clearly when we seek to reform a system that is operating precisely as it was intended to. By reforming it do we seek to make it better? Police departments are operating according to their original mandate -- to prevent black insurrection by constant proximity of police to communities of color, intensive surveillance, routine harassment and violent terror. Do we really want to make them better at what they were created to do? Or do we want to remove them from our communities and closely watch them until that is possible?

WHO WILL WATCH THE POLICE IN THE BLACK COMMUNITY?

The ancient Roman poet Juvenal is credited with having asked *quis custodiet ipsos custodies?* The Latin phrase roughly translates who will watch the watchers? Today we might ask who will watch the police? The question is more than rhetorical. It is far too vital to be dismissed as merely semantic. We are in the throes of a nascent revolution. But the revolt is against the people. More and more we see those who are sworn to protect and serve involved in actions that represent the wholesale violation of rights guaranteed and protected by the United States Constitution. We see local police arrayed in military garb, riding military vehicles -- armored troop carriers and tanks rumbling down inner city streets. More and more African Americans are being shot and killed as if it were open season on black males. *Black lives matter*. But they should not only matter to African Americans. All Americans should be concerned. But even if no one else is concerned African Americans must be for it is our survival that is at stake.

The question is begged who do the police protect and whom do they serve? It is often remarked the vast majority of police officers are courageous well- trained, responsible officers who abhor what is happening on their watch. Although I tend to agree that this must be the case I see no real proof of that fact. I have never seen the so-called good officers arresting the so-called bad apples. Not to mention that the mere existence of the well known blue wall of silence that severely undermines any notion that the police will ever be able to police themselves. Why would they if they are doing what they were created to do? But even if it were true that officers are courageous heroes that does not ameliorate the harm done by those who are no more than criminals with badges. Nor does it change the reason for the existence of the overwhelming numbers of police in the inner city neighborhoods. "....Black insurrection is to be prevented through constant proximity of police to communities of colour, intensive surveillance, routine harassment and violent terror by agents of the state..." Of course to protect and serve the black communities the police require guns and assault weapons and armored troop carriers and other armaments, right? Not really.

There are countries whose police do not carry weapons. Among these are Britain, Ireland, Norway, Iceland and New Zealand, officers are unarmed when they are on patrol. Police are only equipped with firearms in special circumstances.[45]

Take Britain for example. In Britain the vast majority of police officers do not carry weapons. The British philosophy is called "Policing by consent". It means basically that the police have the support of the public. The public's consent is based, as is the legitimacy of the police, on the transparency, integrity and accountability of the police.<u>49</u> Our laws are derived from the English Common Law. Unfortunately, we have not seen fit to emulate their approach to policing.

Who else has a greater stake in watching the police than the residents of the black communities? Who else is better positioned? The participants in the Black Lives Matter movement are , whether intentionally or not, the watchers of the police.

Who will watch the police? We the People ... in order to establish justice...." will watch the police! The notion that the people, all people, but particularly the African American people can both watch and control the police in their own communities is not far-fetched. It is deeply rooted in the concepts upon which this nation was founded.

ALL POWER COMES FROM THE PEOPLE ALL POWER BELONGS TO THE PEOPLE

The Founding Fathers intended that the people shall control the government, not the other way around. The government is comprised of all its functionaries whether elected, appointed or civil service -- state or federal. They include everyone from the president to the judges (United States Supreme Court included), legislators, ambassadors, cabinet members and all of their employees. These also include law enforcement, federal and state. Government, its agencies and employees are servants of the people. They serve at the sufferance of the People. It is important that we understand that the Founding Fathers provided certain inalienable rights to the people. These rights cannot be taken away. It is equally important that we understand the reason for the rights.

THE FOUNDING FATHERS DISTRUSTED GOVERNMENT

While recognizing the necessity for government they also recognized the potential for abuse when government becomes powerful and self-interested. In order to prevent government abuse of the ample power granted to it checks and balances were created. The ultimate power, however, was left squarely in the hands of the people. Among the great fears of the Founding Fathers was the fact that the government was, of necessity, granted the power to raise armies. Of course, this power was for the purpose of protecting the people from foreign attack. But a standing army could also be used against the populace. Hence, the right of the people to bear arms. It must be remembered that at that time (1787) there were no police departments.

The first police department in the northern United States was established in Boston in 1838.[46] But the first police department in the South was established in the Carolina colonies 1704 it was a slave patrol.

"Slave patrols had three primary functions: (1) to chase down, apprehend, and return to their owners, runaway slaves; (2) to provide a form of organized terror to deter slave revolts; and, (3) to maintain a form of discipline for slave-workers who were subject to summary justice, outside of the law, if they violated any plantation rules. *Following the Civil War, these vigilante-style organizations evolved in modern Southern police departments primarily as a means of controlling freed slaves who were now laborers working in an agricultural caste system, and enforcing "Jim Crow" segregation laws, designed to deny freed slaves equal rights and access to the political system.*"[47] (Italics added).

An armed group of government employees is, for all intents and purposes, an army. The only difference, which may have given the Founding Fathers pause had they thought about it, is that the police have authority to act against the populace while the military does not. It was because of the very real possibility that the government could turn on the people that they enshrined that fear and its protection in the Constitution of the United States with these words:

"WE THE PEOPLE of the United States, in Order to form a more perfect Union, establish Justice, insure domestic Tranquility, provide for the common defence, promote the general Welfare, and secure the Blessings of Liberty to ourselves and our Posterity, do ordain and establish this Constitution for the United States of America." [48]

It is the people of the United States from whom the limited powers in the constitution flow not the government. In fact, it may be accurately stated that the purpose of the constitution is, among other things, to establish justice. But what happens when the constitution does not or cannot establish justice? The answer is both simple and unavoidable. The power must be recalled by the people and used by them to establish justice. That this notion may seem revolutionary or even subversive by those who lost or never developed a radical mindset is not surprising. But a close historical look at the views of one of the Founding Fathers may be helpful.

Thomas Jefferson is credited with having asked "what country can preserve its liberties if their rulers are not warned from time to time that their people preserve the spirit of resistance? He also noted that "[t]he tree of liberty must be refreshed from time to time with the blood of patriots and tyrants. It is it's natural manure."[49] John Locke said more bluntly, "... the *Community* may be said ... to be *always* the *Supream Power*, but not as considered under any Form of Government, because this Power of the People can never take place till the Government be dissolved."[50]

THE DECLARATION OF INDEPENDENCE

Another document that is often overlooked and which has been relegated to the National Archives but has been deemed to have no legal authority[51] is the Declaration of Independence.

The Declaration of Independence contains these immortal words: "... Governments are instituted among Men, deriving their just Powers from the Consent of the Governed, that whenever any Form of Government becomes destructive of these Ends, it is the Right of the People to alter or to abolish it, and to institute new Government, laying its Foundation on such Principles, and organizing its Powers in such Form, as to them shall seem most likely to effect their Safety and Happiness."

Significantly, the Declaration also states:

"... *But when a long train of abuses and usurpations, pursuing invariably the same Object evinces a design to reduce them under absolute Despotism, it is their right, it is their duty, to throw off such Government, and to provide new Guards for their future security.*"

It cannot at this late date be seriously argued that the African American has not been a victim of a long train of abuses and usurpations. Or that these have been at the collective hands of the federal and state governments and private criminals. Even the acts of private criminals can be attributed to the governments (including their police departments) who aided and abetted them before and after the events. The long train of abuses include, but are not limited to, slavery, black codes, segregation, and institutional racism. More importantly it includes all acts to deprive African Americans of the rights contained in and protected by the United States Constitution.

Many people, some well intentioned some not, will say that these abuses are ancient history and are better forgotten -- after all time heals all wounds. The viewpoint might be worthy of consideration were it not for one fact -- *the abuses have never stopped.*

24

A LONG TRAIN OF ABUSES

We have suffered slavery, lynchings, Black Codes, Jumpin'Jim Crow, segregation, integration and re-segregation at the hands of state and federal governments. These violent and intentional assaults on our dignity, progress and humanity have continued unabated for nearly four centuries. To define these as a long train of abuses is understatement at its best.

Since the beginning of the Obama Administration in 2009 the Department of Justice has launched civil rights investigation of twenty-one police departments resulting in multiple findings of civil rights pattern and practice violations by police departments throughout the United States.[52] Significantly, the police department are all in African American of Hispanic communities. It follows that the long train of targeted abuses continue and are not just ancient history.

FERGUSON MISSOURI AND THE DOJ

As an example we will take a look at one United States Department of Justice Report entitled *Investigation of the Ferguson (Missouri) Police Department*, dated March 4, 2015.[52] Among other findings the DOJ concluded the "Ferguson law enforcement practices violate the law and undermine community trust, especially among African Americans."

The DOJ made the additional significant findings:

A. FERGUSON'S POLICE PRACTICES

"Ferguson's strategy of revenue generation through policing has fostered practices in the two central parts of Ferguson's law enforcement system policing and the courts that are themselves unconstitutional or that contribute to constitutional violations. In both parts of the system, these practices disproportionately harm African Americans. Further, the evidence indicates that this harm to African Americans stems, at least in part, from racial bias , including racial stereotyping. Ultimately, unlawful and harmful practices in policing and in the municipal court system erode police legitimacy and community trust, making policing in Ferguson less fair, and less effective at promoting public safety, and less safe." (Report, p.15).

It should be noted here that in the above passage the Report refers to a strategy that fostered unconstitutional practices. The Report goes on to list some of the unconstitutional police practices the Department of Justice investigators found. They found the Ferguson Police Department engages in a pattern of unconstitutional stops and arrests in violation of the Fourth Amendment and engages in a pattern of excessive force in violation of the Fourth Amendment. Let us take a quick look at the violations that were found.

B. FERGUSON'S MUNICIPAL COURT PRACTICES

"The Ferguson municipal court handles most charges brought by FPD [Ferguson Police Department], and does so not with the primary goal of administering justice or protecting the rights of the accused, but of maximizing revenue. The impact that revenue concerns have on court operations undermines the court s role as a fair and impartial judicial body. Our investigation has uncovered substantial evidence that the court s procedures are constitutionally deficient function to impede a person s ability to challenge or resolve a municipal charge, resulting in unnecessarily prolonged cases and an increased likelihood of running afoul of court requirements. At the same time, the court imposes severe penalties when a defendant fails to meet court requirements, including added fines and fees and arrest warrants that are unnecessary and run counter to public safety. These practices both reflect and reinforce an approach to law enforcement in Ferguson that violates the Constitution and undermines police legitimacy and community trust." (report p. 42).

1. Court Practices Impose Substantial and Unnecessary Barriers to the Challenge or Resolution of Municipal Code Violations.

2. The Court Imposes Unduly Harsh Penalties for Missed Payments or Appearances.

C. Ferguson's Law Enforcement Practices Disproportionately Harm Ferguson's African-American Residents and Are Driven in Part by Racial Bias.

1. Ferguson's Law Enforcement Actions Impose a Disparate Impact on African Americans that Violates Federal Law.

2. Ferguson's Law Enforcement Practices Are Motivated in Part by Discriminatory Intent in Violation of the Fourteenth Amendment and Other Federal Laws.

The DOJ found that a pattern and practice of First and Fourth Amendment violations exist in the Ferguson, Missouri Police Department. The DOJ also found substantial evidence that the Ferguson court's procedures are constitutionally deficient. This is important. It means that the procedures (methods by which the court operates) violate the United States Constitution. In short, the police and courts work together, by design, to violate the Constitutional rights of African Americans. Here the Department of Justice investigators found violations of the Fourteenth Amendment to the United States Constitution as well as other federal laws.

The point of all of this is to show that to a greater or lesser degree the police and the courts have in some cases acted by design, with malice aforethought, in a clear pattern and practice to deprive African Americans of the ability to exercise rights guaranteed and protected by the United States Constitution. That these acts are sufficient to warrant the use of the attendant right of revolt seems clear. It is also clear that the police very often violate the law and the courts aid and abet them in their criminal acts. When these acts are carried out more than once by an enterprise they also violate the Racketeering Influenced and Corrupt Organizations Act (RICO).

RACKETEERING INFLUENCED AND CORRUPT ORGANIZATIONS ACT

The RICO statute provides in pertinent part: "It is unlawful for anyone employed by or associated with any enterprise engaged in, or the activities of which affect, interstate or foreign commerce, to conduct or participate, directly or indirectly, in the conduct of such enterprise's affairs through a pattern of racketeering activity or collection of unlawful debt."[53]

WHAT IS AN ENTERPRISE?

An "enterprise" is defined as including any individual, partnership, corporation, association, or other legal entity, and any union or group of individuals associated in fact although not a legal entity. 18 U.S.C.A. § 1961(4) (West 1984). Clearly, police departments can violate RICO. Please note that the criminal acts necessary for a RICO violation include drug dealing, murder, robbery, obstruction of justice, obstruction of criminal investigations, obstruction of State or local law enforcement, tampering with a witness, victim, or an informant, retaliating against a witness, victim, or an informant. In fact, at least one police department has been found to be a criminal enterprise under RICO.[54]

Apparently, the Ferguson Police Department is not the only one where a pattern and practice of constitutional violations exists. Since 2009, the Civil Rights Division has opened 25 investigations into law enforcement agencies and is currently enforcing 19 agreements, including 14 consent decrees and one post-judgment order.[55] Since the Ferguson investigation the DOJ has made similar findings in Baltimore, Maryland, Chicago, Illinois and Detroit, Michigan.

There are 18,000 police departments in the United States how many others operate under a continuing pattern and practice of constitutional violations of the rights African Americans?

Given the long train of abuses and usurpations spanning centuries and continuing until the present day would African Americans or any people under similar circumstances not be justified in concluding that they are, as John Locke would put, "in a state of war".[56]

According to Locke the right of revolution was a natural right that existed as an bulwark against tyranny by the government. Natural rights are those that derive not from the government or laws but are universal, cannot be taken away and are, therefore, inalienable.

A STATE OF WAR AND THE USE OF FORCE

"In all States and Conditions the true remedy of Force without Authority, is to oppose Force to it. The use of force without Authority, always puts him that uses it into a state of War, as the Aggressor, and renders him liable to be treated accordingly."[57] John Locke's words ring ominously true today.

The use of force without authority creates a state of war and the remedy is to oppose force to it. So why is it that when African Americans respond to the long train of abuses including the use of force without authority it is always reported as a riot? Again, it is critical thinking that is required.

RIOT OR REBELLION?

Is it possible that what we have seen and will see again are not riots but rebellions? The question must be asked: what is the difference between a riot and a rebellion?

Webster's Dictionary defines a riot as a violent disturbance of the peace by a crowd. It lists synonyms as: uproar, commotion, upheaval, disturbance, furor, tumult, melee, scuffle, fracas, fray, brawl, free-for-all; violence, fighting, vandalism, mayhem, turmoil, lawlessness, anarchy, violent protest.

A rebellion on the other hand is defined as open, organized, and armed resistance to one's government or ruler. Apparently armed resistance is not violence. The issue here is that what motivates African Americans who are always termed rioters are the same circumstances, the same long train of abuses that made George Washington and the boys revolutionists -- not rioters. Could it be that George Washington and his fellow revolutionists were white?

Jack Schneider writing in the Huffington Post has authored an in-depth analysis of the riot/rebellion distinction and its historic use that is well worth reading. Mr. Schneider notes:

" This is deeply problematic. Not just because it denies motive and reason to people of color. But also because it precludes us from seriously considering -- and addressing -- the root causes of such events. After all, you don't respond to the concerns of rioters; you pepper spray them.... If we want to put urban unrest behind us, we need to see rebellion for what it is. We must consider the possibility that patriotism comes in all shades."[58]

PATRIOTISM COMES IN ALL COLORS

The point is that if any people on the planet have the right to revolt it is African Americans. The only thing that is really surprising is that African Americans have not launched a full scale rebellion before this.

It is hard for today's Americans to recognize the profound connection between the uprisings in Ferguson, Missouri and other American cities and the United States Constitution. It is even harder for them to understand that these uprisings are as American as apple.

The connection between the recent uprisings and the rights contained in the United States Constitution is overlooked simply because neither the vast majority of Americans, nor the media see the persons involved in these events as related to them in any meaningful way. They see these events as the acts of rioters, looters and thugs. We are seen as people (just barely) who prey on their own already benighted communities. In short, we deserve what we get. On the other hand, they see the police as champions of law and order who daily place their lives on the line to protect and serve. The loss of life, whether during an uprising or a routine traffic stop is mere collateral damage in the quest to maintain law and order.

The same observers who are usually, but not always, white and privileged, are the first to proclaim that the Constitution and laws must be obeyed. They cannot fathom the notion that the events that they have witnessed in Ferguson, Missouri and other places can in any way be related to the wholesale deprivation of the rights of African Americans historically and presently.

More importantly, they cannot or will not see that it is the events leading up to so-called rioting that both cause and legitimize the later violence that they so abhor.

NON-VIOLENCE

"Concerning non-violence: it is criminal to teach a man not to defend himself when he is the constant victim of brutal attacks."
Malcolm X

We are constantly told that violence is never the answer. No matter what atrocities are perpetrated against us we are repeatedly told we must not respond in kind if that means violently. We are told that "An eye for an eye and a tooth for a tooth"[59], what Malcolm X called that "good ole time religion" has no place in our fight for freedom and protection.

The notion that non-violence is an answer to violence is not only itself indefensible it should prompt a critical thinker to ask what is the question? Is the question how do we best perpetuate the continued brutalization of our people and ensure our continued second-class citizenship? Or is the question how do we stop it? The answer to the former question is apparently non-violence. The answer to the latter is vigorous, unrelenting self-defense. What astonishes me is that non-violence has been so successfully advocated as a strategy for so many years.

Dr. King said: "Nonviolence is a powerful and just weapon which cuts without wounding and ennobles the man who wields it. It is a sword that heals." Huh? He also said: "'[Nonviolence] is directed against forces of evil rather than against persons who happen to be doing the evil. It is evil that the nonviolent resister seeks to defeat, not the persons victimized by evil." Huh? He also said: "The non-violent resistor not only avoids external, physical violence, but he avoids internal violence of spirit. He not only refuses to shoot his opponent, but he refuses to hate him. And he stands with understanding, goodwill at all times." Say what?

Finally, Dr. King said: Please be peaceful. We believe in law and order. We are not advocating violence, I want you to love your enemies... for what we are doing is right, what we are doing is just -- and God is with us." [60]

[America] ". . . a civilization which has always glorified violence -- unless the Negro had the gun . . . The country is only concerned about non-violence if it seems that *I'm* going to get violent. It's not worried about non-violence if it's some Alabama sheriff."
James Baldwin

Curiously, no one calls for non-violence on the part of the most violent groups in America. No one calls for non-violence on the part of the police or the military. The argument is always that the police must use violence to protect the public (the Supreme Court has held that the police do not have duty to protect anyone) and of course the military is in the war business of which violence is a fundamental, defining part. Diplomacy notwithstanding, you cannot fight a war non-violently. Again here is where our thinking needs to be upgraded.

We still have not recognized that we are, in fact, at war. We have been at war for the entire time of our unfortunate, forced sojourn in the land and culture of the gun.

This is a violent society born of a violent culture. There are an estimated 265 million guns owned by civilians in the United States and these are owned by 3% of the population.[61] Do the owners of those 265 million weapons including millions of assault weapons intend to use them non-violently? Are they hunters in search of prey to feed their starving families?

In the last quarter of 2016 (October - December)a record 7,665,979 background checks were done for the purchase of guns in the United States. [61a] Americans are arming themselves in record numbers. Have we forgotten about Tulsa Oklahoma, in 1921?

Non-violence is not a strategy it is an accommodation. It is acquiescence in oppression. It is the white flag of surrender and the advance signal of defeat. In this regard it should be remembered that the Dr. Martin Luther King, Jr., who advocated non-violence and Malcolm X (Al Hajj Malik Shabazz) who advocated self-defense both died by violent means. The lesson here is that no matter what the strategy any form of resistance will be met with violence because wars are violent by nature. Our problem is again a thinking problem -- *we are the only ones who do not think we are at war.*

25

GUN!

For the entire time of this country's existence or at least from the 17th century blacks have been prohibited from owning guns. The reason is obvious. Slaves must never be given the ability to revolt. Free blacks must not be allowed to own guns because of the "dangerous example" that a slave could be free. So fearful were slaveholders that it was made unlawful for a black person to own anything that could be used as a weapon which included everything from a cane to a dog.[62]

However, in 1791 the Second Amendment to the United States Constitution was adopted. The Amendment provided that "...the right of the people to keep and bear Arms, shall not be infringed."

The Supreme Court of the United States has finally concluded that the Second Amendment means what it says. The right to bear arms is an individual right that applies to all citizens and is provided for self defense.[63] Despite the holding in *McDonald* criminals (felons) and the mentally ill may still be lawfully prohibited from owning or possessing guns. Of course if it is true that citizenship cannot be forfeited/revoked (except for conviction of treason or attempting by force to overthrow the United States Government or conspiring to do so)[64] and citizens may not be deprived of rights guaranteed by the United States Constitution, it must also be true that the right to bear arms cannot be lawfully taken away.

The National Rifle Association (NRA) is considered by many to be the champion of Second Amendment rights. They have successfully fought for the Second

Amendment right of citizens to bear arms for decades.

Curiously, these Second Amendment purists don't think it applies to all citizens. Violent felons, among others may be denied the right to bear arms. Violent felons should also be denied the vote.[65]

Note too that a felony conviction may be for a non-violent crime and also prohibits the possession of ammunition. Perhaps now you can see the importance of felony convictions. They not only affect voting rights and mass incarceration but also gun rights including carry permits. Note that even so-called open carry states where all citizens may legally carry weapons[66] an African American with a gun is subject to be stopped, harassed and killed.[67]

It is my hope that the reader will notice that the open carry states and stand your ground laws though neutral on their face are already having a discriminatory impact.[68]

EXTRA JUDICIAL EXECUTIONS[69]

The United States Constitution provides that the no person shall be held to answer for an infamous crime without indictment by a grand jury. And, no person may be deprived of life, liberty or property without due process of law.[70] It follows that a law enforcement officer who kills a person for some real or imagined crime has, in effect, as an official arm of the state, taken the person's life without indictment and without due process of law in clear violation of the Fifth Amendment. In fact the officer has performed, as an agent of the state, an extra judicial execution. Why this fact is never mentioned is understandable from the law enforcement community but not from the African American so-called leadership. Can you say execution without indictment or trial?

Every police officer who shoots or kills a civilian should be indicted and tried and not be allowed to resume his/her duties until acquitted. The officer's alleged crime is performing an extra judicial execution, a Fifth Amendment violation. Moreover the process should be handled by a special prosecutor. The notion that an internal investigation by the police department or the local prosecutor will ever result in justice is laughable. That's like having the Mafia determine whether a whack was justified. Let us be clear here, a police officer should be, must be held to a higher standard simply because he/she is an agent of the state. The state cannot be allowed to summarily execute its citizens. To put it in John Locke's words "... *the use of force without authority creates a state of war and the remedy is to oppose force to it.*"

Finally, the oft-cited argument that a police officer is privileged to use lethal force if he/she feels endangered is at once insulting and indefensible.

The criminal law (at the federal and state level) recognizes justification, also known as self-defense. But it is an affirmative defense that must be pleaded and proved beyond a reasonable doubt. Of course in order to use this defense you must be charged. The charge is avoided by the finding (either by an internal police investigation or prosecutor investigation) of what is known as a *good shoot*.

GOOD SHOOT

A good shoot is, in police parlance, a justified homicide. The problem with this concept is that it means an extra judicial execution is justified and not subject to prosecution because a police officer felt threatened and based on that fear executed a civilian. It also means that the actual presence of a threat is not important. It is what the officer reasonably believes. If he believes a twelve year old with a toy gun on a public playground is a threat -- *good shoot*. If a wallet was thought to be gun -- good shoot. If a nicotine dispenser was thought to be a gun -- good shoot. If an armed black man scares me because he looks to me like a monster -- good shoot.

In 2015 police killed at least 102 unarmed black people -- about two per week. Thirty-seven percent of unarmed people killed by police were African American though we are only thirteen percent of the population.[71]

Curiously several states have recently enacted stand your ground laws.[72] These laws provide that there is no duty to retreat before using force (including lethal force) in self-defense if the person reasonably believes doing so will prevent death or great bodily harm. It is this type law that allowed George Zimmerman to be set free after murdering Travon Martin.

So now what we have is a host of states where white folks are carrying guns, can use them if they feel threatened, police can execute African Americans with impunity because they feel threatened and the rest of the population views black males as threatening and dangerous.

FELONY CONVICTION AND CIVIL DEATH

As we have seen in Hunter v. Underwood, and the Nixon Administration's War on Drugs the underlying intent was to criminalize African Americans to insure that we could be vilified and our voices silenced. The tactic was felony conviction.

At English common law a felony was a crime for which the death penalty and civil forfeiture could be imposed. Today felony conviction creates a different kind of death -- civil death.

Long after sentences are served and in some instances for life the felony conviction rears its ugly head in employment, education, housing, and professional licensing even food stamps and public housing can be prohibited. Pardons are virtually impossible. Commuted sentences are all but non-existent. Yet even Robert E. Lee the confederate general was restored by joint Congressional resolution in 1975 retroactive to 1865.[73]

Similarly, in 1978 Congress removed the service ban

from Jefferson Davis, president of so-called Confederate States of America.[74] Just as an interesting aside Davis was never tried for treason though 620,000 Americans were killed during the Civil War.

26

TIME TO TAKE OUR COUNTRY BACK

"A lie, repeated a thousand times, becomes a truth."
Joseph Goebbels, Nazi Minister of Propaganda

Donald Trump is now the 45th President of the United States. That his election makes for a potential sea change in the circumstances of African Americans seems apparent. But I have learned from this election that what seems apparent may not be so. Again, we are hard pressed to utilize critical thinking to make sense of our situation in light of Mr. Trump's election.

First, Donald Trump rose to prominence on the basis of a lie. The lie has come to be known as the birther movement or birtherism.[75] It was actually a thinly disguised attack on the legitimacy of the first African American to hold the office of President of the United States. The attack was launched by a private citizen. It cleverly forced the President of the United States to produce his birth certificate and prove his right to hold office after he had been duly elected. Donald Trump knew the claim was a lie. He maintained that lie for five years after the birth certificate had been produced. This stunt marked the beginning of the Donald Trump for president campaign.

"When they say, " we want our America back"Well, what the...f%#k do they mean? Before the gays had their agenda, Before the slaves were freeBefore that man from Kenya took the presidency"

Jill Sobule

TOTAL BLACK EMPOWERMENT

Second, when Donald Trump officially launched his campaign it was with the slogan "Make America Great Again". But what does that slogan mean? Does it mean America is no longer the most powerful nation on the planet? And if America is not great now when was it great? 1865, 1933, 1945 or prior to the election of the first African American president?

To answer this question we must look at where the concept originated. Remember Trump said "It is time to take back our country *and* make America great again."[76]

It may have been forgotten by some but the slogan *take our country back* was the mantra of the Tea Party as well as other fringe white supremacist organizations including the Ku Klux Klan.

The Tea Party movement began in full force following the election of America's first African American president. They began their string of political successes in 2010 when they secured majorities in both the United States House of Representatives and the Senate. In 2016 they succeeded in securing control of all the organs of the federal government. It could be argued that they have succeeded in their objective. But a closer examination reveals that this is only part of their goal. They are now in a position to accomplish the only thing that the slogan can possibly mean take our country back *in time, i.e., before the election of Barak Obama*. This is necessarily true because any time in the past say the fifties or even the eighties would be a time when income taxes for corporations and the wealthy were higher and government regulation was greater. Then as now white males were in control of the government until the election of President Obama. It follows that take the country back has a dual meaning. *Take it back to the time when white males had exclusive and unchallenged control. And, to a time Barak Obama became president.* Let us be clear here. The only thing that has changed is that an African American -- a black man was elected president of the United States -- twice.

Finally, it means take us back to the time before these things were possible. In this regard we only need look at President Trump's cabinet appointments to date. He has appointed subject to Senate confirmation none other than United States Senator Jeffrey Beauregard Sessions (D. Al).

One must be skeptical of the appointment of a man who the senate rejected as a candidate for a federal judgeship in 1996 based on his demonstrated racism to now become United States Attorney General. We already recognize that the leopard does not change his spots.

More importantly, however, Mr. Sessions has been a staunch opponent of the Voting Rights Act which facilitated the election of Africans Americans. If he becomes Attorney General, which appears certain, he will also have control of the Office of Civil Rights . We can say good bye to pattern and practice investigations that have forced racist police departments throughout the country to stop violating the civil rights of African American communities.

The last stage of the take back our country movement will come in the form or reversal of voting rights gains since 1965 if Jeff Sessions is in charge. We must remember that of all the disciplines we may study history is best suited to reward our research. African American preachers all over the country are calling for calm, non-violence and advising us to give Trump a chance. At the same time white folks are arming themselves in record numbers.

REMEMBER BLACK WALL STREET

On June 1, 1921 an mob of armed whites aided and abetted by the local police and the national guard systematically destroyed an entire black community killing nearly 300 people. The following excerpt is from the Final Report of the Oklahoma Commission to Study The Tulsa Race Riot of 1921:

"As hostile groups gathered and their confrontation worsened, municipal and county authorities failed to take actions to calm or contain the situation. At the eruption of violence, civil officials selected many men, all of them white and some of them participants in that violence, and made those men their agents as deputies.

In that capacity, deputies did not stem the violence but added to it, often through overt acts themselves illegal. Public officials provided fire arms and ammunition to individuals, again all of them white. Units of the Oklahoma National Guard participated in the mass arrests of all or nearly all of Green wood's residents, removed them to other parts of the city, and detained them in holding centers.

Entering the Greenwood district, people stole, damaged or destroyed personal property left be hind in homes and businesses.

People, some of them agents of government, also deliberately burned or otherwise destroyed homes credibly estimated to have numbered 1,256, along with virtually every other structure including churches, schools, businesses, even a hospital and library in the Greenwood district.

Despite duties to preserve order and to protect property, no government at any level offered adequate resistance, if any at all, to what amounted to the destruction of the neighborhood referred to commonly as Little Africa" and politely as the Negro quarter."

Although the exact total can never be determined, credible evidence makes it probable that many people, likely numbering between one and three hundred, were killed during the riot."

Not one of these criminal acts was then or ever has been prosecuted or punished by government at any level, municipal, county, state, or federal.

Even after the restoration of order it was official policy to release a black detainee only upon the application of a white person, and then only if that white per son agreed to accept responsibility for that detainee's subsequent behavior.

As private citizens, many whites in Tulsa and neighboring communities did extend invaluable assistance to the riot's victims, and the relief efforts of the American Red Cross in particular provided a model of human behavior at its best.

Although city and county government bore much of the cost for Red Cross relief, neither contributed substantially to Greenwood's rebuilding; in fact, municipal authorities acted initially to impede rebuilding.

In the end, the restoration of Greenwood after its systematic destruction was left to the victims of that destruction. [77]

The Black Tulsans then and we now have cause to believe that their personal safety, like the defense of themselves and their community, depended on them alone."

The memory of Black Wall Street begs the question: What will we do if they come in the morning? Think about it.

27

CRITICAL THINKING IN THE AGE OF TRUMP

DONALD TRUMP'S NEW DEAL FOR BLACK AMERICA: "WHAT THE HELL DO YOU HAVE TO LOSE?"

"I'm asking today for the honor of your vote, and the privilege to represent you as your President. Here is the promise I make to you: whether you vote for me or not, I will be your greatest champion . . . I work for you and only you."

Dimondale, is a small village in Eaton County, Michigan. The population was 1,234 at the 2010 census. African Americans represent .07% of the population - that's 8 African Americans.

Dimondale is 93 miles from Detroit, Michigan. The population of Detroit is 84.3% African American. Total African American population of Detroit is over 700,000.

Mr. Trump made his offer of a new deal for African Americans in a place where there are no African Americans and just an hour away from the city with the largest African American population in America.

But the content of his new deal for African Americans was even more insulting than where he gave it. Of course, he did speak about Detroit in Dimondale.

President Trump proclaims as his new deal for black America.

- law and order
- urban renewal
- enterprise zones

Of these new deal specifics (if they can be accurately called that)international trade and building infrastructure are ideas that no one can argue with. The problem is that even if they could be put into effect (which is highly unlikely with a conservative Republican House of Representatives intent on reducing deficits and the size of government) they would not directly or immediately inure to the benefit of the African American communities. Except possibly through President Reagan's now debunked trickle down economic theory or some variation of it.

The theory basically holds that lower taxes for the rich will help everybody else. This is one of those ridiculous theories that only the rich and non-critical thinkers could believe. The premise is flawed. Think about it. Giving the wealthy more disposable income by lowering their taxes will cause them to invest in things will create jobs for the poor. Huh?

According to Steven Greenhouse "[b]etween 1979 and 2005, after-tax household income rose 6% for the bottom fifth [of the American population] .... That sounds great until you see what happened for the top fifth -- an 80% increase in income. The top 1% saw their income triple. Instead of trickling down, it appears that prosperity trickled up."[78]

As far as enterprise zones are concerned they have been tried before. They sound good but in practice they do not work at least not for African American communities. Studies indicate that on balance these programs benefit large corporations and not the local communities. One study concluded that "[e]nterprise zones attract workers from far and wide. In most of the enterprise zones we looked at, *the majority of jobs were taken by commuters from outside the enterprise zone."*[79](Italics added).

That being said let us take a closer look at the other new deal programs that President Trump envisions and promises for African Americans -- Law and Order and Urban Renewal.

DIGRESSION ON THE RULE OF LAW

> "When we [Americans] talk about the rule of law, we assume that we're talking about a law that promotes freedom, that promotes justice, that promotes equality."
> U.S. Supreme Court Justice Anthony Kennedy, Interview with ABA President William Neukom (2007)

Before we look at law and order and urban renewal I want to take a moment to look at the so-called Rule of Law. We often hear that in America we are governed by the Rule of law and not the rule of men. It is this distinction we are told that differentiates us from dictatorships and communists. But what is the rule of law?

At best the rule of law is an ideal that has never been and perhaps can never be achieved. At the outset its premise is obviously flawed.

Clearly the law is the product of legislators whose motives may or may not be altruistic. Second, once the law is in place it is enforced by police (who often act arbitrarily), prosecutors who bring charges or not based on there virtually unreviewable notion of right and wrong, and finally judges themselves in many cases appointed by policital hacks (at the federal level for functionally life terms)apply the law using their ample discretion which is itself essentionally unreviewable. It follows that the rule of law is and can only be the rule of men who we conveniently do not refer to as dictators.

The World Justice Project has proposed a working definition of the rule of law that comprises four principles:

TOTAL BLACK EMPOWERMENT

1. A system of self-government in which all persons, including the government, are accountable under the law;

2. A system based on fair, publicized, broadly understood and stable laws;

3. A fair, robust, and accessible legal process in which rights and responsibilities based in law are evenly enforced;

4. Diverse, competent, and independent lawyers and judges.

The world Justice Project has created a Rule of Law Index that rates countries on the basis of a set of 9 criteria to determine the countries compliance with those standards. Among these is the criminal justice category.

The index rates nations on an overall scale of 0 (lowest) to 1(highest). The United States overall rank is 18 of 113 nations.

It is beyond the scope of this work to address the implications of the rule of law in the context of total black empowerment. Suffice it to say that no matter what the system is called it has been and remains an effective social control method that does not, at least for African Americans promote, freedom, justice and equality.

LAW AND ORDER

"I am the law and order candidate."[1]

"But at the same time we have to give power back to the police, because *we have to have law and order*," he said. "*We have to give strength and power back to the police*. You're always going to have bad apples .. [but] the police have to regain some control of this crime wave and killing wave that we have in this country."[2]

" We will police our streets. . . . Safety is a civil right. The problem is not the presence of police but the absence of police."[3]

The phrase law and order is now recognized as a racial code word for controlling blacks. It's use as part of Nixon's Southern Strategy and part of his Law and Order Playbook has been frequently noted.

"As president, Nixon focused intensely on law-and-order themes, subtly tapping into the fears of white Southerners, as well as many white working-class Northerners, who associated the rise in crime with urban riots specifically, and African Americans more generally. Nixon recognized this connection when he privately reviewed one of his campaign's hard-hitting television ads in 1972 about urban crime and remarked, this "hits it right on the nose. *It's all about law and order and the damn Negro-Puerto Rican groups out there.*"[4]

Do not miss the point here. Not only is Mr. Trump as the law and order candidate recycling Nixon's racist law and order playbook, he also advocates and intends to deploy *more police in African American[5] communities*. He advocates more state and federal funding to remove certain elements (gang members, drug dealers, criminal cartels)from our neighborhoods. [6]

> "Hitler massacred 3 million Jews . . . there is
> 3 million drug addicts (in the Philippines),
> there are ... i'd be happy to slaughter them."
> Rodrigo Duterte

As an aside but relevant here is the fact that Philippines President Rodrigo Duterte has stated that Mr. Trump "praised" his approach to his countries drug dealers.[7] and stated that Mr. Trump informed him that he is tackling his country's drug problem the right way.

"He was wishing me success in my campaign against the drug problem. He understood the way we are handling it and he said there is nothing wrong with protecting your country. It was very encouraging in the sense that I suppose that what he wanted to say was that he would be the last to interfere in the affairs of our own country. "[8]

During his campaign Mr. Duterte promised that upon his election he would order police and the military to find and kill drug dealers and users -- "that the funeral parlors will be packed." Since his inaguration on June 30, 2016 his anti-drug policy known as "double barrel" has reportedly taken the lives of nearly 6,108 people -- an average of 1,015[9] killed per month. Mr. Duterte has utilized extra judicial executions of more than six thousand alleged drug dealers and users to accomplish is goal of a drug free Philippines. Mr Duerte has

---

also admitted that during his term as mayor of Davao City he commited extrajudicial murders.[10]

> "If you know of any addicts, go ahead and kill them yourself as getting their parents to do it would be too painful."[11]
> Rodrigo Duterte

President Duterte like Mr. Trump is also a law and order advocate.

The truly curious thing is that Mr. Trump has never tweeted that Duterte's statement was incorrect or expressed disapproval of his barbarous, Draconian tactics.

The official statement from the Trump Transition team was:

"President Rodrigo Roa Duterte of the Philippines offered his congratulatory wishes to President-elect Trump," the readout said. "In their conversation, they noted the long history of friendship and cooperation between the two nations, and agreed that the two governments would continue to work together closely on matters of shared interest and concern."[12]

Mr. Trump has only said the murder of unarmed African American men by police is "troubling". Mr. Trump has never mentioned a word about the numerous Justice Department investigations and findings of pattern and practice violations at police departments thoughout the United States -- always in African American communities. The most recent being the Report of the Investigation of the Chicago Police Department where it was found that the department engages in a pattern and practice of unconstitutional excessive use of force and has done so for decades.

Mr Trump has also believes that the Black Lives Matter movement have in some way instigated the killings of police officers suggested that he will direct the attorney general to investigate the group.[13]

Should we then be reassured by Mr. Trump's nomination of Senator Jeff Sessions of Alabama to be the next Attorney General of the United States?

The Late Mrs. Coretta Scott King perhaps said it best:

"Anyone who has used the power of his office as United States Attorney to intimidate and chill the free exercise of the ballot by citizens should not be elevated to our courts," and that Sessions's conduct in prosecuting civil rights leaders in a voting-fraud case "raises serious questions about his commitment to the protection of the voting rights of all American citizens." She also stated that:

"The irony of Mr. Sessions' nomination is that, if confirmed, he will be given a life tenure for doing with a federal prosecution what the local sheriffs accomplished twenty years ago with clubs and cattle prods," and, "I believe his confirmation would have a devastating effect on not only the judicial system in Alabama, but also on the progress we have made toward fulfilling my husband's dream."[14]

I hasten to add Mr. Sessions was found to be too racist to be a federal judge but apparently according to Mr. Trump he is fit to be the nation's chief law enforcement officer.

Need we mention that as Attorney General Session will be in charge of the Civil Rights Division of the DOJ and perhaps more importantly the enforcement of the Votings Rights Act.

The nuts and bolts of his African American new deal was laid out more specifically in a speech in Charlotte, North Carolina on October 26, 2016. [15]

President Trump proclaimed as his new deal for black America, among other things *law and order, urban renewal,* and *enterprise zones.* In that speech Mr. Trump said he wanted to talk about an issue that was dear to his heart -- the issue of urban renewal and the rebuilding of "our" inner cities.

URBAN RENEWAL

". . . urban renewal, which means moving the Negroes out. It means Negro removal, that is what it means. The federal government is an accomplice to this fact."[16]
James Baldwin

It is both amazing and insulting that Mr. Trump could use the term *urban removal* in 2016 much less cite it as a strategy for rebuilding African American neighborhoods in the future. That it is dear to his heart is not surprising. Mr. Trump comes from a long line of racists. You will remember his family tradition of not renting to African Americans (then designated "c" for colored). In 1973 the DOJ found that the time the trump organization was the largest rntal propeoner in nd em loated

It appears that Mr. Trump is intent upon using urban renewal to rebuild the inner cities.

Urban renewal has been the scourge of African American communities since it began in the 1950's. A brief look at the history of urban will remind of how little regard Mr. Trump has for African Americans. It should also act as a grave warning.

In urban renewal programs of the past properties, in many cases whole neighborhoods taken through eminent domain a legal doctrine that basically says the government can take privately owned property for public use. Once the land was acquired it was then sold to private developers who build everything but affordable housing for low income former residents.

Between 1949 and 1973 thouands of construction projects were initiated on more than two thousand acres of inner

TOTAL BLACK EMPOWERMENT

city land. The result was the destruction of entire African American neighborhoods. More than six hundred thousand buildings were demolished, and more than two million residents were forced to move along with thousands of small businesses. [16]

In New York City alone more than one hundred thousand African American inner city residents were displaced. Clearly, urban renewal is a code word for black or African American removal. Donald Trump wants to bring it back.

In our quest for Total Black Empowerment we must not be fooled or confused. Donald Trump like his predecessors is intent on continuing the subjugation and second class citizenship of African Americans. No matter how much he pretends to embrace the Don Kings, Steve Harveys, Ben Carsons and Kanye Wests he remains the leopard with unchanging spots.

The thing about the leopard and all others predators is that they are creatures of habit and cannot change. The reason that we can control predators who are better than humans in everything but thinking is because we know what they will do and how they will do it and can therefore develop strategies and tactics that nullify their presumed prowess.

A predator will always be a predator. It is their nature and their weakness is that they are incapable of change. President Trump is dangerous and his mindset and the policies that flow from it will prove detrimental to our people. Some of us do not and will not believe that. But time will tell. But those of us who recognize him for what he is will prepare now for the battle that is surely coming. Now more than ever before critical thinking and powerful minds infused with powerful ideas will be needed. listen carefully to President Trump analyze what he says and formulate the strategy to thwart his plans. if you do so you will recognize the following contours of his thinking and his plan.

28

CALL TO ACTION

We hear a great deal about radicalization today. It is as if the word radical is as sinister as those who seek to terrorize innocents and wreak havoc in the world. Of course the truth is far more enlightening.

The word radical comes from the late Latin radicalis "of or having roots" from Latin radix (genitive *radicis*) "root". It indicates only the quest to find the root of things. Here is where critical thinking is important. We have seen the wholesale violation of rights of African Americans for centuries yet we continue to utilize strategies that have proven time and time again to be ineffective and even counterproductive. At this late date we can no longer blame the white man or the system. As the old saying goes fool me once shame on you -- fool me twice shame on me. From the stand point of those who exercise the power of control there is no reason to change the way they do business because we will do no more than protest - peacefully and non-violently. Remember too that random violence is not a strategy and certainly cannot be a tactic. A strategy is simply a plan of action. Random violence cannot be a strategy because by virtue of its randomness it cannot be planned. And because tactics is the science and art of disposing and maneuvering forces in combat random violence cannot be logically seen as a tactic. Clearly, random action can never be either a strategy or tactic. Non violence can be seen as both but it must also be seen as ineffective and counterproductive.

POWER PROPORTIONALITY

We need power proportionate to our numbers in the population. We must, at very least, control the engines of government in our own communities and in states where we represent a significant percentage of the population.

Your task should you choose to accept it is to find and organize the *critical mass. Time is of the essence.*

The states with the largest African American populations are: Mississippi (37.30%); Louisiana (32.4%); Georgia (31.4%); Maryland (30.1%); South Carolina (28.48%); Alabama (26.38%); North Carolina (21.60%); Delaware (20.95%); Virginia (29.91%). Cities with the largest African American populations are: Detroit, MI (84.3%); Jackson, MS (80.1%); Miami Gardens, FL (77.9%); Birmingham, AL (74.0%); Baltimore, MD (65.1%); Memphis, TN (64.1%); New Orleans, LA

CONCLUSION

When you began this intellectual journey you were told that this book is a *mind power primer* that is intended to facilitate the development of a *New Mental Attitude* in African Americans. You were also told that the *New Mental Attitude* would be fueled by powerful ideas that would develop in you the kind of thinking that would produce fundamental change in the way you think. I pointed out at the beginning that our ancestors gave civilization to the world through their intellectual prowess born of critical thinking techniques and reliance on the reservoir of knowledge contained in their *ancestral stream*.

I also noted that our fall from a position of intellectual supremacy was marked by a departure from this ancient, time-honored technique. The unstated purpose of this mind power primer is to develop, among African Americans, a cadre of critical thinkers who, by use of these ancient techniques, will become the *vanguard of the new age*.

In the historical context it is clear that when radical change comes to a society it is never as a result of the concerted efforts of the masses. This is true because the masses are always so involved in the unending pursuit of life's daily necessities that they are prevented from acting decisively as a group. *African Americans are no exception*. It is for this reason that the reliance on a mass grass roots movement among African Americans as the impetus for change is misguided. It is equally true that the hope of a single leader, a black messiah, if you will, is misguided as well.

Charismatic leaders come and go. *They are never a real threat to established power*. This is because as human beings necessarily beset with an array of human frailties they are easily compromised or simply assassinated. Invariably the death of the charismatic leader means the death of the movement. *It is the powerful idea that cannot be stopped.*

History demonstrates that it is always a small group of enlightened persons; we may call them *visionaries*, who sow the powerful *seed/ideas* of social and political change. These visionaries are invariably people of normal intelligence who have become *critical thinkers*. It is they who form the *Critical Mass*. It is the *Critical Mass* that initiates change. Mass action only becomes possible after the *Critical Mass* is formed and active. It is only then that the masses, compelled to choose sides, are forced to take affirmative action.

The long road home begins with our *minds*. Our greatest power comes to us through our contact with the ancestral reservoir of knowledge known as the ancestral stream. Therein lie all of the answers that we seek. We must be critical thinkers who have learned to tap into our own ancestral stream. We will never find the answers we seek unless and until we begin to make peace with our ancestors and call upon them for guidance.

The alternative is to adhere to the inevitable inertia that attends the *herd instinct*. The herd instinct is a need to identify with a group that causes many people to follow leaders or ideas without critical examination; the herd instinct in its worst manifestation can be downright genocidal.

I am confident that this mind power primer will accomplish its intended goal. But, it will only do so if its readers are themselves willing to intellectually challenge what they believe. There are no sacred cows in the pursuit of *Total Black Empowerment*.

We must also understand that Critical thinkers, above all, must *understand* power. We must understand power because God and Power are one. The power we must know is not black power or white power, but pure unadulterated power.

TOTAL BLACK EMPOWERMENT

We must understand what we believe. Our beliefs run the gamut from the merely fantastic to the downright *ridiculous*. A fantastic or ridiculous belief cannot exist if it is at odds with *reality based* core beliefs. This is not to say that we cannot think such things but rather that no such belief can long survive that is opposed to our core beliefs.

Our core beliefs are fundamental to our understanding of the world. These social, political and religious beliefs are interconnected and as such are dependent on each other for validity. Our beliefs must be repeatedly weighed against the reality of the world in which we live. We fail to do so at our own peril.

Donald Trump is now President of the United States. He will not change his spots. Predictably he will attempt with the guidance of Steven "Rasputin" Bannon to roll back the accomplishments that have been made in the realm of civil rights. Remember his chief adviser and his soon to be Attorney General Jeffrey Beauregard Sessions will be in a position to set back civil rights to the 1950's. We must also be concerned with defending ourselves against the growing strength and ferocity of white supremacists emboldened and encouraged by the election of Donald Trump. We must do all of this while advancing our interests in survival and prosperity in the twenty-first century and beyond. This is a hard reality. We must face it as we confront the problem of maintaining the hard won civil rights achievements of the past and advancing our cause going forward, This not the time to retreat -- or become complacent. Forewarned in forearmed.

The goal of Total Black Empowerment is possible only through the creation of powerful minds. Powerful minds are minds infused with powerful ideas. This mind power primer has been developed to assist in the attainment of that goal. Hetep.

DO YOU KNOW THE POWER YOU POSSESS?

NOTES

TOTAL BLACK EMPOWERMENT

PREFACE (xviii-xxix)

1. Woodson, Carter, G., *The Mis-education of the Negro*, (Trenton, New Jersey: African World Press, Inc., 1990).

2. Unless otherwise indicated all dictionary definitions are from *The American Heritage Dictionary of the English Language*, 4th Edition. (New York: Houghton Mifflin Company, 2000).

CHAPTER 1 (32-43)

1. Schwaller de Lubicz, R.A., *Sacred Science*, (New York: inner Traditions, International, Ltd., 1982).

CHAPTER 2 (44-58)

1. Evan, Dylan, *Mind over Matter in Modern Medicine*, (New York: Oxford University Press, 2004).

2. Janis, Irving L. Victims of Groupthink: A psychological study of foreign policy decisions and fiascoes. (Boston: Houghton Mifflin Company, 1972)

CHAPTER 3 (59-77)

1. National Institute of Mental Health, *The Numbers Count: Mental Disorders in America*, 2006.

2. American Psychiatric Association. *Diagnostic and Statistical Manual on Mental Disorders*, 4^{the} Ed. (DSM-IV) (Washington, DC: American Psychiatric Press, 1994)

CHAPTER 4 (78-93)

1. Herodotus (Histories, 2.104.2)

2. Plato's *Phaeton*

TOTAL BLACK EMPOWERMENT

CHAPTER 9 (131-139)

1. Haynes, Julian, *The Origin of Consciousness in the Breakdown of the Bicameral Mind* (Boston: Houghton Mifflin Company 1982)
2. Free, Timothy & Gandy, Peter *Hermetica: The Lost Wisdom of the Pharaohs* (New York: Penguin Putnam, Inc. 1999).

CHAPTER 10 (140-147)

1. Boland, Patrick, *Thoth: The Hermes of Egypt* (Chicago: Ares Publishers, Inc., m 1987).
2. Freke & Gandy, *Lost Wisdom*

CHAPTER 11 (148-156)

1. Freke & Gandy, *Lost Wisdom*
2. Freke, Timothy, Gandy Peter, *Hermetica: The Lost Wisdom of the Pharoahs* (New York: Penguin Putnam, Inc. 1999).

CHAPTER 12 (158-161)

1. Freke & Gandy, *Lost Wisdom*

CHAPTER 13 (162-180)

1. See generally Cross, Theodore, L., *The Black Power Imperative*, Faulkner, 1984

CHAPTER 14 (181-204)

1. Budge, E.A. Wallis, *The Egyptian Book of the Dead* (New York: Dover Publications, 1967)
2. Freke, Timothy, Gandy Peter, *Hermetica: The Lost Wisdom of the Pharoahs* (New York: Penguin Putnam, Inc. 1999).

TOTAL BLACK EMPOWERMENT

CHAPTER 16 (214-220)

1. Diop, Chiekh, Anta, *Civilization or Barbarism* (New York: Lawrence Hill Books, 1991)

CHAPTER 17 (221-244)

1. Boylan, Patrick, *Thoth: The Hermes of Egypt* (Chicago: Ares Publishers, Inc., 198

CHAPTER 18 (245-271)

1. The Ten Virtues were part of the initiatory program of the Kemitic Temple. The remaining eight virtues are (3) a demonstrated and firm purpose; (4) evidence of spirituality; (5) evidence of spiritual calling; (6) evidence of a life's mission; (7) absence of resentment when persecuted; (8) confidence in the power of the teacher; (9)) con- fidence of your owen power to learn; (10) evidence of readiness for initiation. From James, G.M., *Stolen Legacy* 1954.

CHAPTER 19 (272-281)

1. Three Initiates, The Kybalion: A Study of the Hermetic Philosophy of Ancient Egypt and Greece (Chicago: The Yogi Publication society, 1912, 1940).

2. Freke &Gandy, Lost Wisdom of the Pharoahs.

PART V
FOOD FOR THOUGHT

PREFACE TO REVISED EDITION (289-292)

1. Glenn Kessler: *When did McConnell say he wanted to make Obama a 'one-term president'?* www.washingtonpost.com/blogs/fact-checker/post/when-did-mcconnell-say-he-wanted-to-make-obama-a-one-term-president/2012/09/24/79fd5cd8-0696-11e2-afff-

TOTAL BLACK EMPOWERMENT

d6c7f20a83bf_blog.html?utm_term=.dc86347169bdSeptember 25, 2012.

2. Andy Barr, The GOP's no-compromise pledge, http:// www. politico.com/ story/2010/10/ the-gops-no-compromise-pledge-044311 10/28/10

3. "Interposition refers to the right of the states to protect their interests from federal violation deemed by those states to be dangerous or unconstitutional. Nullification is the theory that states can invalidate federal law it considers unconstitutional." *Byron Williams, The Cyclical History of Interposition and Nullification.* 04/30/2010 05:12 am ET | Updated May 25, 2011. http://www.huffingtonpost.com/byron-williams/the-cyclical-history-of-i_b_480070.html

INTRODUCTION (293-294)

4. Speech by Malcom X quoting the Hon. Elijah Muhammad, 1/10/63 http:// www. historyisa weapon.com/defcon1/malcgrass.html

CHAPTER 21 (295-307)

5. http://www.naacp.org/criminal-justice-fact-sheet/

6. Formal Title of the anti drug abuse act

7. The Fugitive Slave Act of 1793 was an Act of the United States Congress to give effect to the Fugitive Slave Clause of the U.S. Constitution (Article 4, Section 2, Clause 3 Note: Superseded by the Thirteenth Amendment) which guaranteed a right of a slaveholder to recover an escaped slave.
    Note too that the Thirteenth Amendment did not free any slaves and more importantly it did not abolish slavery. In fact, slavery is still legal and Constitutional in the United

States for felony conviction. The Amendment reads in pertinent part: "Neither slavery nor involuntary servitude, *except as a punishment for crime whereof the party shall have been duly convicted*, shall exist within the United States, or any place subject to their jurisdiction." [italics added].

8. 471 U.S. 222 (1985)

*White supremacy is at heart a political ideology. It holds that white people are superior and that because of that superiority and the inferiority of other races that it necessarily implies white people should rule over non-white people politically, economically and socially.

9. Official Proceedings of the Constitutional Convention of the State of Alabama, May 21st 1901 to September 3rd, 1901, p. 8 (1940).

10. 118 U.S. 356 (1886), was the first case where the United States Supreme Court ruled that a law that is race-neutral on its face, but is administered in a prejudicial manner, is an infringement of the Equal Protection Clause in the Fourteenth Amendment to the U.S. Constitution.

11. See Chin, Gabriel J. (2008). "Unexplainable on Grounds of Race: Doubts About *Yick Wo*". University of Illinois Law Review. 2008(5): 1359 1392. Where the author argues that *Yick Wo* has nothing to do with race and cannot be applied in the criminal context. Apparently the Sixth Circuit does not agree as it cited *Hopkins* favorably in its decision.

12. United States v. Clary, 846 F. Supp 768 (E.D. Mo. 1994).

13. The decision was reversed by the Court of Appeals for the Eighth Circuit see 34 F.3d 709 (8th Cir. 1994).

14. Cocaine and Federal sentencing policy: hearing before the Subcommittee on of the Committee on the Judiciary, House of Representatives, On Hundredth Congress, First Session, June 29, 1995,

15. Jenee Desmond-Harris lists 8 Sneaky Racial Code Words and Why Politicians Love Them., The Root, 3/15/14. Citing Ian Haney Lopez, Dog Whistle Politics: How Coded Racial Appeals Have Reinvented Racism and Wrecked the Middle Class, Oxford University Press, 2014.

16. *Depierre v. U.S.* 564 US 70 (2011).

17. Jer. 13:23. The full passage reads: "Can an Ethiopian [Cushite] change his skin or a leopard its spots? Neither can you do good who are accustomed to doing evil. NIV

18. Paul J. Larkin, Jr., Crack Cocaine, Congressional Inaction, and Equal Protection, Vol. 37 pp. 242-294.

19. United States v. Blewsett, 719 F.3d 482 (6th Cir. 2013). Gilman Circuit Judge dissenting.

20. Id.

21. Fair Sentencing Act of 2010 (Public Law 111 220 Aug 3, 2010). Under the provisions of the Act no one will automatically receive a sentence reduction.

CHAPTER 22 (308–315)

22. Jacob G. Hornberger, Racism and the Drug War, article, Future Freedom Foundation, March 2013.

23. Michelle Alexander, The New Jim Crow, (2010).

24. The average span of time between the birth of parents and that of their offspring. For African Americans a generation has been fifteen years on average.

25. Jonathan Rothwell, "Drug offenders in American prisons: The critical distinction between stock and flow," (Brookings Institution, 2015) http://www.brookings.edu/blogs/social mobility-emos/posts/2015/11/25-drug-offenders-stock-flowprisons-rothwell.

26. Dan Baum, Legalize it all, Harpers's Magazine, April 2016.

27. https://www.congress.gov/bill/99th-congress/house-II/5484/actions24. *The first 9/11 was apparently the day a legislative bomb was dropped on the African American community by a Congress intent on saving the African American community from itself.

28. Nixon's Special Message to the Congress on Drug Abuse Prevention and Control. *June 17, 197*. http://www.presidency.ucsb.edu/ws/ ?pid=3048

29. Timothy R. Smith, Jim Wright, House Speaker who resigned amid an ethics investigation., dies at 92, Wash Post 5/615. http://www.seattletimes.com/nation-world/jim-wright-house-speaker-forced-out-over-ethics-dies/

30. Fund, Setting the Record Straight on Jim Crow, , National Review 7/22/14. See also, Richard Winser, The Rise and Fall of Jim Crow, 2002 Educational Broadcasting Corp. for purposes of Total Black Empowerment analysis.

31. Excerpt of remarks of President Reagan upon signing Public Law 99-570. October 27, 1986. Reagan Library.

32. S. Amdt 3378, 10/15/86. www.congress.gov/ amend-

ment/99thcongress/senateamendment/ 3378/text?q=%7B" search"%3A%5B"strom+thurmondamendments+to+the+anti+ drug+ abuse+act+1986"%5D%7D

33. Rangel, Amendment 1196, H.R. 5484. ANTI-DRUG ABUSE ACT, 9/11/86. Congress.gov

34. Will Bredderman, Harlem's Lion in Winter—A Requiem for Rangel, Observer news and Politics, 2/16/16 http:// observer.com/2016/02/harlems-lion-in-winter-a-requiem-for-rangel/

35. http://prisontime.org/2013/08/12/timeline-black-support-for-the-war-on-drugs/
36. Will Bredderman, http://observer.com/2016/02/harlems-lion-in-winter-a-requiem-for-rangel/

37 id.

38. id.

39. Conyers discusses Mandatory Minimums with Heart and Soul, March 2008. https://conyers.house.gov/media-center/press-releases/conyers-discusses-mandatory-minimums-heart-and-soul

40. id

CHAPTER 23 (316-326)

41. http://www.politifact.com/punditfact/statements/2016/jul/10/charles-ramsey/how-many-police-departments-are-us/ http://www.therichest.com/rich-list/the-biggest-freeze-the-10-biggest-police-forces-in-the-world/;

42. Brad heath, Racial gap in U.S. arrest rates: 'Staggering disparity', USA Today, 11/19/14 http://www.usatoday. com/

story/news/nation/ 2014/11/18/ferguson-black-arrest-rates/19043207/

43. Alexander, p. 124.

44. Ben Brucato, *Fabricating The Color Line in a White Democracy: From Slave Catchers to Petty Sovereigns."* Theoria: A Journal of Social and Political Theory, 61(141).

45. Rick Noack, 5 countries where most police officers do not carry firearms— and it works well. Washington Post, 7/8/16.

47. *Gary Potter* The History of Policing in the United States, Part 1 http://plsonline.eku.edu/insidelook/history-policing-united-states-part-1

48. Preamble to the United States Constitution.

49. *Extract from Thomas Jefferson to William Stephens Smith Paris Nov. 13, 1787.* http://tjrs.monticello.org/ letter/100

50. John Locke, Second Treatise, §149, 1689

51. *Cotting v. Godard*, 183 U.S. 79 (1901)

CHAPTER 24 (327–336)

52. *Investigation of the Ferguson (Missouri) Police Department,* https://www.justice.gov/sites/default/files/opa/press-releass/attachments/2015/03/04/ferguson_police_department_report.pdf

53. 18 U.S.C.A .§1962© (West1984). RICO was passed by Congress with the declared purpose of seeking to eradicate organized crime in the United States. *Russello v. United States,* 464 U.S. 16, 26-27, 104 S. Ct. 296, 302-303, 78 L. Ed. 2d 17 (1983);*United States v. Turkette,* 452 U.S. 576, 589,

101 S. Ct. 2524, 2532, 69 L. Ed. 2d 246(1981). A violation of Section 1962(c), requires (1) conduct (2) of an enterprise (3) through a pattern (4) of racketeering activity. *Sedima, S.P.R.L. v. Imrex Co.*, 105 S2.2C1t. 3275, 3285, 87 L. Ed. 2d 346 (1985).

54. http://www.nytimes.com/1984/07/01/us/key-west-police-department-called-a-criminal-enterprise.html

55. https://www.justice.gov/opa/pr/justice-department-releases-report-civil-rights-division-s-pattern-and-practice-police-reform

56. John Locke Second Treatise section 155 http://press-pubs.uchicago.edu/founders/documents/a2_1_1s1.html

57. id.

58. Jack Schneider, Ferguson: Riot or Rebellion? Huffington Posthttp://press-pubs.uchicago.edu/founders/documents/a2_1_1s1.html

59. The full passage reads: "But if there is serious injury, you are to take life for life, eye for eye, tooth for tooth, hand for hand, foot for foot, burn for burn, wound for wound, bruise for bruise." Exodus 21:23-24.

60. see generally, mlk quotes

61. **Lois Beckett,** Gun inequality: US study charts rise of hard-core super owners. www.theguardian.com/us-news/2016/sep/19/us-gun-ownership-survey

61a. Source: NICS Firearm Background Checks: November 30, 1998 - January 31, 2017. www.fbi.gov/file-repository/nics_ fire-arm _ checks_ -_month_year.pdf

TOTAL BLACK EMPOWERMENT

CHAPTER 25 (337–341)

62. see generally, Norman L lunger, the Loud Debate about Gun Cun Control.

63. *McDonald v. City of Chicago,* 561 U.S. 742 (2010)

64. § 349(7) of the Immigration and Naturalization Act (INA). No African American has ever been convicted of treason.

65. NRA's Wayne LaPierre Freaks Out About Ex-Felons Voting, Is Fine With Them Carrying Guns, http://www.huffingtonpost.com/entry/nra-felon-voting-rights_us_573f5bd2e4b0613b51a3ead

66. Thirty one states have open carry laws where no permit or license is required. WSJ 8/22/14

67. Eugene Robinson, In America, gun rights are for whites only September 22, 2016. www.washingtonpost.com/opinions/in-america-gun-rights-are-for-whites-only/2016/09/22/3990d370-80f2-11e6-8327-f141a7beb626_story.html?utm_term=.f73e0b4cb5eb

68. "Data indicates that SYG laws introduce bias against black victims and in favor of white defendants. These laws have been shown to have a particularly pernicious effect on minority youth, who are more likely to fall victim to an aggressor's gun in SYG jurisdictions. "Stand Your Ground" Laws: International Human Rights Law Implications, http://lawreview.law.miami.edu/wp-content/uploads/2014/09/Stand-Your-Ground-Laws.pdf

69. Extrajudicial execution is a euphemism for murder. More

specifically, extrajudicial execution is when the state kills someone without due process of law. This can either be by the direct agents of the state (such as the military or police), or indirectly by private citizens whom the state elects not to punish for its actions .... It is often forgotten that one of the longest running campaigns of "extrajudicial executions" was that of lynching in the United States. For half a century, it was commonplace in the southern United States for mobs of whites to hang African Americans for merely breaching the social etiquette of the times. Afterwards, none of the participants would be punished in any way. Sometimes the participants included local government officials, including law enforcement.

70. U.S. Constitution, Amendment V: *No person shall be held to answer for a capital, or otherwise infamous crime, unless on a presentment or indictment of a grand jury,* except in cases arising in the land or naval forces, or in the militia, when in actual service in time of war or public danger; nor shall any person be subject for the same offense to be twice put in jeopardy of life or limb; nor shall be compelled in any criminal case to be a witness against himself, *nor be deprived of life, liberty, or property, without due process of law.* nor shall private property be taken for public use, without just compensation. (italics added).

71. https://mappingpoliceviolence.org/unarmed/ police killing of unarmed black people

72. The states are: Alabama, Alaska, Arizona, Florida, Georgia, Indiana, Kansas, Kentucky, Louisiana, Michigan, Mississippi, Montana, Nevada, New Hampshire, North Carolina, Oklahoma, Pennsylvania, South Carolina, South Dakota, Tennessee, Texas, Utah, West Virginia.

73. General Robert E. Lee's Parole and Citizenship, Spring

2005, Vol. 37, No. 1
https://www.archives.gov/publications/prologue/2005/spring/piece-lee.html

74. The pardon of Jefferson Davis and the 14th Amendment October 17, 2016 by NCC Staff. http://blog. constitution center.org/ 2016/10/the-pardon-of-jefferson-davis-and-the-14th-amendment/

CHAPTER 26 (342–346)

75. Birther: a person who doubts the legitimacy of Barack Obama's presidency because of a conspiracy theory that Obama is not a natural-born US citizen [and thus constitutionally ineligible]. Oxford Living Dictionaries

76. https://www.facebook.com/ DonaldTrump/ videos/10156591076765725/

CHAPTER 27 (347–356)

77. Final Report of the Oklahoma Commission to Study The Tulsa Race Riot of 1921 Compiled by Danney Goble, p. 10-11

CHAPTER 28 (357–358)

78. Steven Greenhouse, The Big Squeeze: Tough times for the American Worker bh th, pp.6-9)

79. Alan H. Peters, Peter S. Fisher State Enterprise Zone Programs: Have They Worked? http://research.upjohn.org/up_press/41/

1. http://www.politico.com/story/2016/07/trump-law-order-candidate-225372

2. https://thinkprogress.org/donald-trump-on-black-lives-matter-we-have-to-give-power-back-to-the-police-6769b42e96fb#.papxa4c2q

3. http://www.realclearpolitics.com/video/2016/10/26/trump_proposes_new_deal_for_black_america_in_charlotte.html

4. http://www.politico.com/magazine/story/2016/07/donald-trump-law-and-order-richard-nixon-crime-race-214066

5. http://www.realclearpolitics.com/video/2016/10/26/trump_proposes_new_deal_for_black_america_in_charlotte.html

6. http://www.cnn.com/2016/12/03/politics/trump-duterte-phone-call/

7. http://www.cbsnews.com/news/duterte-donald-trump-praised-philippines-drug-crackdown/

8. http://www.aljazeera.com/blogs/asia/2016/12/duterte-drug-war-death-toll-6000-161213132427022.html

9. Duterte's drug war: Death toll goes past 6,000 http://www.aljazeera.com/blogs/asia/2016/12/duterte-drug-war-death-toll-6000-161213132427022.html

10. https://www.theguardian.com/world/2016/jul/01/philippines-president-rodrigo-duterte-urges-people-to-kill-drug-addicts

11. Id.

12. Reena Flores, Duterte: Donald Trump praised Philippines drug crackdown *December 3, 2016*, http://www.cbsnews.com/news/duterte-donald-trump-praised-philippines-drug-crackdown/

13. http://www.cnn.com/2016/07/18/politics/donald-trump-black-lives-matter/

14. Wesley Lowery, Read the letter Coretta Scott King wrote opposing Sessions's 1986 federal nomination www.washingtonpost.com/news/powerpost/wp/2017/01/10/read-the-letter-coretta-scott-king-wrote-opposing-sessionss-1986-fede

15. Tim Hains, Trump Proposes "New Deal For Black America" In Charlotte. realclearpolitics.com/video/2016/10/26/trump_proposes_new_deal_for_black_america_in_charlotte.html

16. http://www.encyclopedia.com/history/united-states-and-canada/us-history/urban renewal